Also by Robert Scott

*A Season of Madness**

And Then She Killed Him

The Last Time We Saw Her

Shattered Innocence

Rivers of Blood

Lust to Kill

Driven to Murder

Killer Dad

Dangerous Attraction

Deadfall

Like Father Like Son

Married to Murder

Monster Slayer

Rope Burns

Savage

Unholy Sacrifice

Kill or Be Killed

Most Wanted Killer

Blood Frenzy

e-Book

Available from Pinnacle

KILL THE ONES YOU LOVE

ROBERT SCOTT

PINNACLE BOOKS
Kensington Publishing Corp.
http://www.kensingtonbooks.com

PINNACLE BOOKS are published by

Kensington Publishing Corp.
119 West 40th Street
New York, NY 10018

ISBN-13: 978-0-7860-3152-8
ISBN-10: 0-7860-3152-2
First Kensington Mass Market Edition: November 2013

eISBN-13: 978-0-7860-3153-5
eISBN-10: 0-7860-3153-0
First Kensington Electronic Edition: November 2013

10 9 8 7 6 5 4 3 2 1

Printed in the United States of America

Acknowledgments

I'd like to thank my editor at Kensington Publishing Company, Michaela Hamilton, and my literary agent, Sharlene Martin. I'd also like to thank the staff at the Coos County District Attorney's Office and staff at the *Coquille Valley Sentinel*.

CHAPTER 1

Coos County, Oregon—February 7, 2010

It was Super Bowl Sunday and millions of Americans all around the nation were gathered in front of their television sets. A party atmosphere pervaded in many of those homes, replete with snacks and refreshments. It was no exception at a home in Coquille, Oregon, on that Sunday. Coquille is a town situated along the banks of the Coquille River, in an area of forest and farmland not far from the Oregon coast.

Sixty-two-year-old Robin Anstey and her boyfriend, forty-eight-year-old Robert Kennelly, who generally went by the name "Bob," were at a friend's house for a Super Bowl party. As luck would have it, Robin, Bob and their friend were in for a great game. The New Orleans Saints, which had been terrible for most of their forty-two years in the franchise, were on a red-hot streak now.

They were playing one of the best teams of the past few years—the Indianapolis Colts. The quarterback for Indianapolis, Peyton Manning, was one of the decade's greatest quarterbacks, but now Manning was being challenged by his up-and-coming New Orleans rival, Drew Brees.

Right from the start, it was an exciting and entertaining game, and Robin Anstey should have been riveted by the gridiron showdown, like millions of other football fans were. That was not the case, however. Robin was afraid, and the person she was afraid of was her thirty-three-year-old son, Gabriel.

Gabriel Morris, commonly known as "Gabe," could be friendly, gregarious and charming. He was definitely intelligent and had even been a deputy sheriff for a while up in Idaho. Married to thirty-three-year-old Jessica Morris, they had a cute four-year-old daughter named Kalea. The family appeared to be an advertiser's dream of what a nice young family should look like.

But for the past few months, Gabe had become more and more erratic in his behavior. Gabe's comments to his mother's live-in boyfriend, Bob, were especially caustic. Gabe even began talking back to his mother in an angry and disrespectful tone. To make matters worse, Gabe was having serious financial problems, which only fueled his anger. Robin had originally encouraged Gabe and his family to move to Bandon, Oregon, where she and Bob lived, so he could try and make a clean start. Now she wondered if that had been such a good idea.

Partway through the Super Bowl game, Robin's friend Sam Haroldson (pseudonym) who was hosting the party received a phone call from Gabe, asking to speak to his mother. Sam handed the receiver to Robin, and he could see her becoming more and more upset as the conversation continued. Sam even heard Robin say, "No, we've made plans here! We're going to have to cancel dinner with you. We can have this conversation later!"

When she hung up the phone, Robin turned to Sam and said in a distressed voice that Gabe was being very, very difficult. She added that he was angry a lot and took out his anger on her and Bob. And then Robin added one more chilling sentence: "I'm afraid to go home tonight."

Sam was alarmed by this comment and told Robin, "Stay here tonight. We've just changed the sheets in the guest bedroom."

Robin just shook her head and replied, "No, we have to go home and take care of this."

The Saints went on to win the game in an exciting fashion, but there was now a dark cloud hanging over the household. It was nearly midnight when Robin and Bob said their good-byes and exited the door, getting ready to face whatever task lay before them, as far as Gabe was concerned. After they left, a thought passed through Sam's mind, one that he would express out loud later: "The look on Robin's face—you don't see a mother afraid of her child like that. It's not normal."

Robin Anstey had every right to be afraid. By the evening of Super Bowl Sunday, Gabe was fuming with anger. On a long road trip back toward Bandon, from Southern California, he'd become more agitated as the day went on. He was putting the blame for his string of bad luck on many areas, and one of the areas where he squarely placed fault was on his mom and her boyfriend. The one place, however, where he didn't seem to lay any blame for his various misfortunes was on himself.

CHAPTER 2

Gabe was the product of a broken home. When he was age ten, his mother and his father, Danny Morris, were divorced. And it had been a very messy divorce, with Danny constantly filling Gabe's head with lies about his mom. Danny did everything he could to blacken Robin's name, even saying she was a drug addict, which was not true.

At least this bad-mouthing was mitigated by Gabe's older half brother, Jesse McCoy, Robin's son by a previous marriage. Gabe liked Jesse a lot; and Jesse, in turn, was always a proponent of his mom's good qualities. In time, Gabe began to see things Jesse's way as well, and once again was on good terms with his mother. It seemed that whatever poisonous feelings he might have had toward her was a thing of the past.

By early 2010, however, all of those good feelings about his mom had evaporated. And to make matters worse, Gabe truly disliked his mother's new boyfriend, Bob Kennelly, although Bob didn't deserve Gabe's ire. Bob was a lot younger than Gabe's mom; he was fourteen years her junior. Right from the beginning, Gabe and Bob rubbed each other the wrong way. Gabe thought that Bob didn't treat his mother well, although there was nothing in reality to back that up. Bob thought that Gabe was nothing more than a freeloading, stoned loser. Gabe just sat around the house all day while his wife went out and earned a paycheck.

There had been a lot of water beneath the bridge in Gabe's life by that point, and most of it had been turbulent. Despite being intelligent and resourceful, he had made one bad decision after another. He had also seen one goal after another collapse in failure: dreams of being a jet fighter pilot, detective in a sheriff's office, Alaskan bush pilot. They had all failed. Searching for scapegoats, Gabe literally looked no further than his mom and Bob.

Gabe's delusions about his mom grew until he imagined that she had never understood him and, in essence, had abandoned him as a child. None of that was true, but in Gabe's mind those power-ful images stuck. He began to imagine that his mother was deceitful and relished his misery. It also made him angry that she would not accept the wild claims he now made about himself.

Gabe had always thought of himself as special, but now he truly believed he had special powers—abilities that God had given only to him. He said that he could run through the forest at night blindfolded and hear God's voice and see God's face.

God told him where all of the tree trunks and roots were. Things that applied to lesser mortals no longer applied to him. These fantastic remarks so frightened Robin that she told Gabe he needed psychiatric help. This only made Gabe more angry. He didn't believe he was mentally ill. He believed he was one of God's chosen, and nearly a super-hero by that point.

Whatever blowup Gabe had with his mother and Bob that night was not later recorded. Gabe's actions of the preceding week were, however. He was so upset that he had told Jessica to grab a few items and Kalea, and they took off on an erratic journey up and down the West Coast. It started out in Medford, Oregon; then they bounced north-ward from Portland and Seattle, then back down south to San Diego, California, in a very short space of time. Gabe was searching for friends who would give him money and also would believe in his wild claims. He was also seeking refuge from his thoughts and schemes, which were driving him onward in a manic manner. At the end of the week, he had gathered neither; he was angrier than ever. Someone was going to have to pay, and Gabe was more angry at his mom and Bob than anyone else in the world.

All morning long on February 8, 2010, Gabe Morris hid in bushes and trees and watched the residence where his mom lived. She was living with Bob Kennelly in a beautiful home up on a ridge overlooking the Coquille River Valley. When Gabe saw Robin and Bob leave for the day, he sneaked into the house and made sure that no one else was there. Then he escorted Jessica and Kalea into the home to take a shower and get some rest.

Meanwhile, Gabe paced up and down, stewing about all of his misfortunes. He also scavenged through the house for things of value. One thing he found was a .40-caliber semiautomatic pistol, which belonged to Bob. Gabe stuck the gun in his jacket pocket and pondered his next move. While he pondered what he was going to do, Jessica and Kalea were so tired, they went upstairs and fell asleep on a bed.

Shortly after 8:00 P.M., on February 8, 2010, Robin and Bob arrived home and parked in the driveway. Suspecting nothing amiss, they walked to the front door and entered the living room. They took a few steps into the interior of the house and were met by an astonishing sight. Gabe was on an upstairs balcony, which overlooked the living room. He was primed and ready, with a gun in his hand.

Robin and Bob started running toward the front door just as the semiautomatic pistol erupted with one shot, then another and another. Bob collapsed in the interior of the house, already dying of his wounds. Robin managed to stagger outside onto the front deck. Gabe followed her. As she crawled toward the driveway, Gabe came up alongside her. Then he lowered the barrel of the pistol;

without a word, he sent a bullet into his mother's brain. He gazed down upon what he had done—as if he hadn't just killed his mother, but had dispatched a complete stranger.

In the bedroom, Jessica heard some loud noises coming from the front of the house. She stirred restlessly in bed, until Gabe unexpectedly burst into the room and told her in an agitated voice that they had to leave immediately.

Shaken and confused, Jessica did as she was told, awakened daughter Kalea and made a dash for the door. Jessica and Kalea were in their pajamas and Kalea wasn't wearing any shoes. In fact, even Gabe was not wearing any shoes. Jessica had no idea where they were going or why; but as soon as Gabe hustled her and Kalea out the front door and into Bob's pickup truck, all questions about "why" disappeared. Jessica looked down in amazement at the dead bodies of Robin and Bob.

Gabe started the pickup truck and hurtled down the driveway at breakneck speed. He nearly flipped the vehicle over a couple of times and careened off a steep, wooded bank at one point. Once he reached the highway, Gabe sped off into the blackness of night under the sheltering trees. But before he left the area completely, he had one more task to perform.

CHAPTER 3

It was already a strange story, and it was about to get much stranger. On February 9, 2010, the Coos County District Attorney's Office got a phone call from Fred Eschler, who lived in Coquille. District Attorney R. Paul Frasier personally knew Fred, but Frasier was not in his office at the time, and did not receive the information that day. Fred Eschler conveyed to one of the staff at the DA's office that on the evening of Monday, February 8, he had been contacted at home by a person claiming to be involved in counterterrorism activities with the U.S. government.

Fred did not identify this individual at the time, but he did say that the person had come by his home and asked for help. The reason this person needed help was that supposedly he had been working undercover and had been involved with some recent homicides in the Bandon area. This person claimed that he'd infiltrated a terrorist cell in the area, and had barely escaped with his life. He had killed one of the terrorists; but, unfortunately, two other innocent bystanders in the area had been killed by the terrorist group. Since Fred had known this individual over the years, knew that he had been a law enforcement officer and trusted him, he had helped him by lending him a vehicle, a gun and some other items.

When DA Frasier finally got the news from his staff, he was unaware of anyone being murdered in the Bandon area in the previous week. He had his staff contact Fred Eschler to get more information. Since this might involve the federal government, a DA staff member told Eschler to contact the Federal Bureau of Investigation (FBI) directly. During this phone conversation, Fred told the staff member that he was very concerned about the individual in question, and he had provided that person with a gun and a vehicle. The individual in question had said that he had to get out of the area—not only for his own safety, but that of his family as well.

Meanwhile, unbeknownst to DA Frasier or anyone in his office, ever since February 5, Coos County Sheriff's Office (CCSO) sergeant Dave Hermann had been working on a potential missing person's case involving a female named Jessica Morris. Hermann had received a "concern call" from the Women's Safety & Resource Center in the area. Jessica Morris was a volunteer there and they had not heard from her since very late in January. Jessica was a reliable person, and never before had she acted in this manner. She was also in charge of a fund-raiser, to be held on the day before the Super Bowl, which was supposed to raise money for the center. Jessica had not done this, and nothing had occurred in that regard.

Sergeant Hermann went to the women's center and learned that Jessica worked at Bandon Book-keeping. That was Sergeant Hermann's next stop, where he spoke with Mary Ann Donaldson. Don-aldson told Sergeant Hermann that Jessica had been employed at Bandon Bookkeeping for the previous two months, but the last time she came to work was on January 28. Jessica had mentioned something to the effect that things were not going well in her household, and that their finances were in trouble. After that, Jessica had not returned to work at all, nor had she picked up her last pay-check. Not unlike the people at the Women's Safety & Resource Center, Mary Ann also spoke of Jessica as a reliable person, who had performed her tasks well and was liked by others there.

Donaldson told Sergeant Hermann that Jessica was married to Gabriel Morris, and added that Gabriel's mother was Robin Anstey. In fact, accord-ing to Donaldson, Jessica, Gabriel and their daugh-ter, Kalea, were living with Gabriel's mother in a home off Highway 42 South. Donaldson said that she had once driven Jessica home, when Jessica didn't have a ride, and she was not sure of the exact address on the highway. She did give Ser-geant Hermann some directions and he was finally able to determine that it was at a location on Flower Hill along Highway 42 South.

Sergeant Hermann went out to the house, but no one was home at the time. He did notice some boxed-up items there, as if someone was getting ready to move. Hermann took off and planned to go out to the place in about a week, to check on matters once again.

Looking further into the situation, Sergeant Hermann learned that Jessica's father was a gentleman named William "Bill" Pope, of Blackfoot, Idaho. Hermann had wondered if Jessica might have shown up there in the previous week. Hermann phoned the Popes; during the conversation, Bill Pope told Hermann something very interesting. He said that before Jessica married Gabriel Morris, she had $100,000 in the bank from a settlement she received from a very bad sledding accident in that state. This had happened when Jessica was thirteen years old. Bill said that once Jessica married Gabriel, they went through that money very quickly. He was sure that Gabriel was the reason why. According to Pope, Gabriel always had some grand scheme going, but none had succeeded.

In an irate voice, Bill Pope added that in the not-too-distant past, Gabriel had cheated on Jessica, having an affair with a woman in Pocatello, Idaho. Gabriel and Jessica split up for a short while; but after the affair ended, Jessica took Gabriel back. Plus, Jessica's father said, he was absolutely stunned when the woman in Idaho, with whom Gabriel had been having the affair, called him and said that she wanted to find out where Gabriel was. She said she intended to sue Gabe for using her credit cards without her permission and running up huge balances on those accounts.

Bill told Sergeant Hermann it was he who had told Gabriel and Jessica to return to Coos County, Oregon, because Gabriel was from there. Once they were there, Bill suggested, they should declare bankruptcy and try to get their finances in order while staying in Bandon with Gabe's mom and her boyfriend, Bob. In fact, Bill said that he had given them $7,000 to move to Coos County from Idaho so they could have a fresh start. He had loaned them a small red pickup truck as well. The pickup truck did not run well, but it was better than nothing, since Gabe didn't even have any vehicles anymore. They had been repossessed.

Bill related that the last time he had spoken with Jessica was on February 5, and she was all right at that time. Nothing seemed to be amiss. Then her father added, "I believe Gabriel was nearby and manipulating her conversation with me."

Around the same time that all of this was occurring, a resident in Coquille complained about an abandoned pickup truck in that town. The Coquille Police Department (CPD) sent out an officer to investigate and found the pickup truck parked on the 1000 block of North Dean Street. As it turned out, that was the same block where Fred Eschler lived. When an officer went to check out the vehicle, he learned that the vehicle belonged to Robert Kennelly, who lived between Bandon and Coquille on Highway 42 South. Since this was a Coquille police officer, he had no jurisdiction out on county land, and he didn't know about CCSO sergeant Hermann's journey out to that property a few days before.

Because of the illegally parked vehicle, CCSO deputy Adam Slater was sent out there to tell Bob that he needed to move his pickup truck from the street in Coquille. What Slater found, however, was beyond his wildest expectations. He found the bodies of two dead adults—one within the house and another just outside the front door.

More and more officers began arriving on scene, and soon included CCSO, the CPD, Bandon Police Department (BPD) and other agencies as well. Soon all of the information would be going into the report of the chief investigator of the crime scene, Detective Sergeant Daniel Looney. The information that he notated there was incredible and would soon set off a nationwide manhunt.

CHAPTER 4

Meanwhile, Coquille Police Department police chief Mark Dannels went to talk with Fred and Laura Eschler. During that interview, Fred told the police chief that on the evening of February 8, sometime between 9:00 and 9:30 P.M., Gabriel and Jessica Morris showed up unexpectedly with their four-year-old, Kalea.

Fred and Laura Eschler knew Gabriel well because he had dated one of their daughters, Esther, when he was younger. Gabe had also gone to their church. In fact, Gabe had dated Esther throughout his high-school years. Fred and Laura liked him so much that they considered him to be a part of their family. Gabe had even gone on vacations with the entire family.

Laura Eschler later recalled, "The doorbell rang about nine P.M., and I answered the door. I saw Jessica Morris there and she was carrying Kalea. I didn't see Gabe at first. He was, kind of, back in the shadows. I invited them in, and there was a sense of urgency on Gabe's part.

"Jessica had contacted me in late January and she wanted to do an observation in my classroom. I was a schoolteacher. And I thought Jessica was showing up to talk about that. I wasn't paying too much attention to Gabe at the moment, but I did notice that Jessica and Kalea were in their pajamas and not wearing any shoes."

Laura had the Morrises come into the kitchen, where her husband, Fred, was sitting. Fred was always glad to see them, but almost immediately Gabe told him that this wasn't a social call.

Fred also recounted to Dannels how Gabe had gotten down to business right away. Gabe said that he was working for the government on an antiterrorist operation. Things had gone horribly wrong, and there had been an attack on the residence where he and his family were staying, which was, of course, Bob Kennelly's place. In the cross fire, Bob and his mom had been killed, and Gabe had been able to kill one of the terrorists, who then broke off their attack and disappeared into the darkness. In fear for Jessica and Kalea's safety, Gabe had hustled them over to the Eschlers' home as soon as he could. They had escaped to the Eschler house without even wearing shoes.

Gabe said to Fred and Laura, "We need a ride to San Diego. I have to report to an air force base there."

Both Fred and Laura said they couldn't do that, since they both had to teach classes the following morning. They both worked for the school district and couldn't just take off from their positions at the drop of a hat.

Gabe was calm, but very much in a hurry. He asked Fred for .40-caliber ammunition. Fred said that he didn't have that kind of ammo. Fred did note, however, that Gabe, Jessica and Kalea were not dressed for such rainy, cold weather. The Eschlers gave them warmer clothing and sleeping bags.

Gabe was thankful for this, but he kept insisting he needed .40-caliber ammunition, with which to protect himself and his family. During this conversation, Fred noticed that a pistol fell out of Gabe's jacket onto the couch. Gabe quickly picked it up, and Fred assumed that Gabe wanted the .40-caliber ammo for this handgun.

Fred finally loaned Gabe a 9mm semiautomatic handgun, with three additional loaded magazines, and $150 in cash. He also loaned him a silver Ford Taurus, in which Gabe supposedly would drive to California and report in at an air force base there.

Laura Eschler told Police Chief Dannels that while Fred was engaged in conversation with Gabe, she had tried talking to Kalea. Laura said that a four-year-old's language was hard to understand, but she took Kalea to say, "Something bad happened to Grandma." Laura added that Gabe heard this, and stopped Kalea from saying any more. Then Gabe said, "Kalea, you are not to talk about what happened to Grandma to anyone!"

Just before they took off, Gabe hugged both the Eschlers and said, "Thank you so much." Laura couldn't remember later if Gabe said, "Pray for me," or if Jessica had said it.

Gabe piled their meager belongings into the car; and with Jessica positioned at the wheel, the Eschlers saw Gabe lie down in the backseat with Kalea. And then without another word, Jessica took off. The Eschlers watched their vehicle and the Morrises disappear down the street and into the darkness.

The Eschlers' interview with Chief Dannels really set off alarm bells with DA Paul Frasier. He personally owned a .40-caliber Glock handgun and was familiar with the ammunition that it used. From police reports already coming in, Frasier also knew that Bob Kennelly and Robin Anstey had been killed by .40-caliber bullets.

What had initially seemed to be so random now started to make sense in DA Frasier's mind. He no longer believed in terrorists and some sort of shoot-out between them and Gabriel Morris, where Robin Anstey and Bob Kennelly became innocent bystander victims. Frasier began to believe that the sole shooter in all of this was Gabriel Morris. Just why Morris had done it remained a complete mystery at that point.

Frasier went back to his office and began writing out an arrest warrant. In it he stated: *I have probable cause to believe and do believe that Gabriel Christian Morris is responsible for the death of Robin Anstey and Robert Kennelly. As these two deaths occurred during the same criminal episode, that two charges of Aggravated Murder have been committed and that Gabriel Christian Morris is responsible for their deaths.*

Writing up an arrest warrant was one thing—actually determining where Gabe Morris and his family had gone was quite another. They could have gone in any number of directions, since they were known to have friends up and down the West Coast. And the questions soon became, not only where had they gone, but why had Gabe Morris killed his mother and her boyfriend? And how had this young man, who people said was once friendly, outgoing and very responsible, turned into a cold-blooded killer?

CHAPTER 5

Gabriel Morris was born in 1976, into a blended family. The family initially lived in Pacific Beach, California. This was right on the Southern California coast that has been depicted in so many movies. But the Morrises didn't inhabit a home straight out of some Hollywood depiction of suburban Southern California. Instead, they lived in one of the poorest districts of San Diego.

Gabe's father was Daniel "Danny" Morris. Both of Gabe's parents had been married before and had children from those marriages. Robin had a boy, Jesse, from a previous marriage. He was six years older than Gabe, and Gabe would get to know him very well. Danny had a daughter, who had been adopted out, and Gabe would not know her at all.

With his full bushy head of hair and cherubic smile, Gabe looked the epitome of a happy, carefree 1970s Southern California boy. One photo from that era depicted a smiling Gabe up in a tree with his older brother. They obviously were having fun and enjoyed each other's company.

No one more than Jesse would later tell as much about what life was like for him and young Gabe. Jesse later recalled, "We grew up in San Diego in a very poor, welfare area. It was one of the ugliest places I can remember. It was just tough, mean streets.

"We were a minority there, being white. It was mostly black and Hispanic. Mom had divorced my dad and was married to Danny Morris. I was six years old when Gabe was born. Danny was pretty good to Gabe, but he was rough on me. I always thought he loved Gabe too much. It was more than just a regular father/son love. It was just odd.

"Gabe tagged along with me a lot. Gabe was very, very loving. I always admired how he loved his family. I felt that it was more than I was capable of doing. He always wanted to be with us all, and he particularly loved his mom. Both me and Gabe loved Mom, but he seemed to have a bond with her that was beyond what I was capable of having."

Gabe's relationship with his father was, indeed, noticeably strange. It worried family and neighbors alike. In fact, it rose to the point of obsession with Danny.

A neighbor named Jasmine, who knew the family, called Gabe by the nickname "Gabs." She recalled, "He was a nice kid, who was sweet to my little girls. But he was spoiled by his dad, who gave him anything that he wanted. There was a strangeness about his daddy."

In Jasmine's opinion, Danny was very possessive and protective of Gabs to the point that it made her very uneasy.

One instance of this stuck out in Jasmine's mind. "Gabs was going to spend a night over at a friend's house. It was only to be for one night, but Danny Morris cried because his son would not be home that night."

Gabe's maternal grandmother, Lynn Walsh, also knew the circumstances in which Gabe and his family lived. Years later she said, "My husband and I lived right across the street from my daughter when Gabe was born. I knew my daughter's husband, Daniel Morris, and I had a lot of concerns about him, even before Robin married him. He was untruthful. He was just not the type of person she should have been with. We asked our daughter not to marry him, but she did, anyway. Gabe was a mischievous little boy, as some boys are, but he was a very loving child. We had a close relationship."

The animosity that Gabe would later hold for his mom was nowhere in evidence as a child. Jesse said later, "He was the most loving boy you could imagine. He always needed the attention of his mother. He needed to have affection, to be hugged."

As Gabe got older, Jesse said, "he was never an aggressive or violent kid, but he wouldn't allow himself or his friends to be picked on. He would stand up for himself. He would never start a fight, but he wouldn't allow himself to be picked on. He could handle himself when he had to.

"A good way to describe Gabe was, when you're a kid and get into trouble—well, a kid will fib and tell lies to get out of something. But Gabe wouldn't do that. He was always known for owning up for whatever he did wrong. And then he would get his spanking or whatever."

As Gabe grew up, both he and his mom, Robin, loved reading books such as *The Lord of the Rings* and *The Hobbit.* Gabe had a colorful imagination, and the fantasy worlds portrayed in these books enthralled him. In fact, even at an early age, Gabe sometimes had a hard time distinguishing fantasy from reality. He didn't just read or hear some fantastical stories and knew that they were fiction. He began to really believe that he was somehow part of the story.

Gabe was incredibly enamored with the world of fantasy, especially with Dungeons & Dragons (D&D) and other role-playing games (RPGs). He would play them for hours upon hours. His father, Danny, was also very much into D&D. Jesse later described both father and son as "genius-level smart." But that "genius level" may have been a curse as well as a blessing.

Interestingly, Danny Morris had graduated from high school and had taken a few junior-college courses, but he never earned a degree of any sort. Danny had held many different jobs while Gabe was growing up. Most of these were manual-labor positions, including one stint at a bread factory.

For Gabe, there were times he wasn't just playing the RPG; he seemed to have left the present world behind and actually believed he was part of the imaginary world of his creation. Gabe became a wizard or a warrior. Brother Jesse worried about this obsession in his younger brother.

Jesse later said that he told his brother to go outside and play instead of being so fixated on Dungeons and Dragons. But as in many things Gabe did, and would do later, he seemed to zero in on some task to the exclusion of everything else. It wasn't enough to enjoy it. He felt that he had to master whatever it was. Gabe never felt whole unless he was the best at something. And if he wasn't the best at something, he would invent tales of how he was. These stories were very convincing; but unfortunately for Gabe, he began to convince himself about things that weren't true.

Gabe always seemed to carry situations too far. When he and Jesse "roughhoused," Gabe would push things to another level. Jesse related, "He'd bite, or go for the groin. Mom sometimes called him 'the Devil Child.'"

Part of Gabe's obsessive behavior may have come from the deteriorating marriage of Robin and Danny. Jesse would later say that Danny was abusive to Robin and to him. Gabe would also later relate that he was abused, but it's hard to know for sure, since many things he said later could be proven to be false. It was a fact, however, that his father did obsess on Gabe to the point of mentally disturbed behavior.

Gabe's grandmother Lynn said, "We urged our daughter to separate from her husband and get custody of Gabe. We said we would get an apartment for her, and she should get a restraining order against Danny. We were afraid that Danny would just take Gabe and leave. Robin said, no, that Danny would never do anything like that. But she was working and my husband and I were at home with Gabe. The police came and it was Danny who had gone to a judge and got a restraining order on her.

"Gabe was upset by being taken by the police. And we were terribly upset. We asked the police if we could do anything. And the officer said that if we didn't let Gabe go with them, we would be in contempt of court. So we let him go. His father took him to Escondido, and we didn't see much of Gabe after that."

Robin may have been threatened by Danny, and she would later say that he physically mistreated her. For whatever reason, she was scared enough of him to flee all the way up to Coquille, Oregon. It was a very hasty departure, leaving Gabe with a man who seemed to have a disturbing obsession with him.

CHAPTER 6

The one person who was close to Gabe who still did see him a lot was half brother Jesse. Jesse said later, "I had real concerns about Danny Morris's mental health. I didn't know what he would do to Gabe. When Mom moved away up to Oregon, I stayed near Gabe at my soon-to-be wife's house. It was close to the place where Danny and Gabe lived in Escondido. I actually began working for Danny, and stayed close, because I had concerns for Gabe and wanted to see how he was doing. I'd just go by the house a lot and check on the situation. I stayed near Gabe until I went into the army, when he was fifteen years old."

Gabe would later talk about his father, and much of what he said had to be taken with a grain of salt. When Gabe said these things, he had a very skewed view of his dad. Nonetheless, many of the things Gabe said seemed to jibe with what Jesse McCoy stated about Danny Morris.

Gabe recalled, "My dad was insanely intelligent,

but he was a very manipulative, persuasive and abusive person. Danny was beaten as a child, and so he beat me too. He took offense at every slight. He was very controlling. I basically had a shitty and awful childhood. I didn't know how bad it was until I got older and saw kids in other families. I knew that he sold drugs to make extra money, and he never got arrested for it."

Except for the part about selling drugs, which could not be corroborated, everyone who knew Danny Morris said that he was very controlling when it came to Gabe. James Anstey, a man whom Robin would later marry, related that both Robin and the boys were mistreated by Danny Morris. Anstey said, "Robin was terrified of Danny. She just wanted to get away from him. That's why she came up to Oregon."

Jesse said later, "The split wasn't pretty—no divorce is." But the acrimony on Danny's part went beyond most divorces. He blackened Robin's name as much as he could, and told Gabe that his mother never loved him. Danny painted tales of Robin being addicted to drugs, which was not true. He called her every name imaginable.

Gabe, who was impressionable, began to believe the things Danny was saying about his mother. Both Gabe and Danny had lived in a fantasy world of Dungeons & Dragons; and now Danny was creating another fantasy world for Gabe to live in— one where Robin was the "wicked witch," who had no redeeming qualities.

* * *

Gabe may have ended up with his father, but it was not a bed of roses with him. Gabe claimed later that there was physical abuse and sexual molestation as well. He spoke later of his father as a mean alcoholic with a hair-trigger temper. And the possessiveness of Danny toward Gabe bordered on the psychotic.

On several occasions, Gabe went up to visit his maternal grandmother, Lynn Walsh, in Silverton, Oregon. When Gabe was gone, his father wrote him long, detailed letters. Lynn happened to see some of these letters and later noted about them, "They were letters someone might write to a spouse." The obsessive nature of the letters alarmed her.

As far as her relationship with Gabe at that time, Lynn said, "He was a loving child and very family-oriented. Very much into my husband and me being grandparents. He adored his mother."

Gabe endured this chaos for five years with Danny; and then when he was a freshman in high school, he went to visit his mother in the town of Coquille, Oregon. At the time, Robin was living with a boyfriend named John Lindegren, often called "Big John." Apparently, at that point, Gabe liked the idea of living with his mom and John more than he did with his father. He was placed in the custody of Robin. Gabe's world suddenly changed from the sunny, large-city environment of

San Diego to the small-town, misty and forested Coquille, Oregon.

Coquille, a city of about four thousand people along the banks of the Coquille River, is what is often envisioned when a rural Oregon town is brought to mind. The economy was based upon timber harvesting and agriculture in the farmlands along the banks of the river. It was small enough so that everyone seemed to know everyone else in the area. For someone who had just come from a large city, Gabe slipped into his new role of small-town boy fairly quickly.

John Lindgren, Robin's live-in-boyfriend, later said of Gabe, "He was a nice guy. Real cordial and polite and an all-around good boy. During his high-school years, he never got into any trouble. I was a carpenter and concrete finisher, and Gabe helped me out on work projects once in a while. He was a very good worker. He had a very close relationship with his mother. They cared about each other a lot and he would do anything for her."

Lynn Walsh noted, "In high school, many of Gabe's companions were not popular kids. He would choose them to show friendship because he knew they were lonely." Gabe always did seem to have that aspect about him. He would look out for the underdog when he could.

As Jesse had noted, Gabe was very bright, but he was not particularly ambitious in his studies. At the age of fifteen, Gabe began attending Coquille

High School. He excelled at some subjects, while slacking off in others. He only seemed to want to be proficient in things that interested him and had no time for becoming well rounded on other topics.

John Lindgren later said of Gabe that he was a "smart kid, but did not apply himself in high school. His mom didn't discipline him, and Gabe was free to come and go as he pleased. He frequently skipped school, got into little scuffles, but never anything serious."

One thing that Gabe did get into was smoking marijuana. His mom, Robin, didn't smoke marijuana, but John did. In many parts of coastal Oregon, smoking marijuana is looked on by some people the way that many inhabitants of Appalachia looked upon drinking homemade moonshine. It was just part of the culture.

Half brother Jesse also knew about Gabe smoking marijuana. "I maintained contact with Mom and Gabe when I was in the service. I knew that he used marijuana in high school. It was his drug of choice. He didn't drink alcohol and he didn't do any hard drugs like meth or anything.

"I was a combat medic at the time, and I had advanced infantry and arctic survival training. I was actually on some top secret operations." (Jesse didn't say where, but perhaps it may have been in Afghanistan, since there were cold mountainous regions there, and that was certainly not the case in Iraq, except for up in the Kurdish regions.)

"I would tell Gabe about my life as an army medic, as many details as I could without specifics. And Gabe admired this aspect of what I was doing."

During this period of time, Gabe had a renewed respect and love for his mother as well. John Lindgren noted later, "They had a very close relationship. She would have done anything for Gabe, and Gabe would have done anything for her." In fact, Gabe could be very affectionate at times. He'd go out of his way to tell his mom how much he loved and appreciated her.

Gabe enjoyed martial arts and would eventually gain a black belt in karate. Karate became another one of those subjects where Gabe was obsessive. Despite this, John said that Gabe was not an aggressive kid. "If pushed into a corner, he would fight back, but he did not pick fights."

Gabe coasted along in high school, but mainly he wanted to get high. With this yen for substance abuse, his choice of a girlfriend was very unusual. He didn't pick some rebel or druggie. Instead, he started dating a Mormon girl named Esther Eschler. This was particularly strange, since the Mormon belief allowed no consumption of alcohol or illegal drugs.

But there was always a strange dichotomy to Gabe: brilliant and motivated when interested and challenged, as well as a lazy, dope-smoking slacker. He seemed constantly balanced on a high wire between these two characteristics of his personality. And there was another aspect about Gabe: he constantly seemed to be reaching for things that might seem unobtainable to others.

To date Esther, Gabe had to convince her and her family that he was a "straight-arrow" guy, not a teen who drank an occasional beer and smoked marijuana. And apparently being with Esther made him stop doing those things. Whenever Gabe got some new idea into his head, he didn't go about it in a halfhearted manner. He threw his whole spirit into the endeavor.

Fred Eschler, Esther's father, recalled, "I first knew about Gabe because my wife taught in the school system. I formally met him when my daughter brought him home for dinner. They became boyfriend and girlfriend, and he had a good relationship with all my kids. I had five daughters, and I knew you can't pick who your daughters will pick as a boyfriend. I tried to be friendly as I could be with the boys they brought home. With Gabe, that was not hard at all. He was personable, friendly and easy to talk to.

"I felt that he went out of his way to be nice to me whenever we met. It was just part of who he was. Eventually Gabe went on vacations with me and my family. He was essentially part of the family. I can't think of a time when I didn't like Gabe. He had free run of the house, and he came and went when he wanted to. Esther didn't even have to be there. He was friends with all my kids. Gabe was confident, but quiet. While seeing Esther, Gabe decided to convert to the LDS Church. I was the one who actually baptized him."

There was a flip side to Gabe, however. It always seemed that Esther had to dance along to his tune. At his beck and call, she was the one who made him meals; she was the one who often paid for their dates. If Gabe wanted to do a particular thing, then that was what they would generally end up doing. Gabe would force her into situations she was not comfortable with. If she didn't comply, he would tell her she didn't love him. It was not always easy for Esther to be with Gabe.

CHAPTER 7

All throughout high school, Gabe dated Esther, off and on, over the years. And through Esther and her family, he was introduced to the Church of Jesus Christ of Latter-day Saints (LDS), more commonly known to outsiders as the Mormon Church. Before long, Gabe absolutely believed in the tenets of the faith. His mother, Robin, did not, but she had no problem with him being a member of that faith.

Despite being very bright, Gabe barely graduated Coquille High School. When Gabe and Esther's senior year was over, she left the area to attend Brigham Young University (BYU) in Provo, Utah. This was in the heartland of the Mormon faith and culture around Salt Lake City. The university was founded as the Brigham Young Academy in 1875. Later it became an accredited university and was sponsored by the Church of Jesus Christ of Latter-day Saints. By Esther's time, its brochure noted that it featured: *esteemed performing arts, famed sports*

*programs, an immense language curriculum, and served
as a center for learning and culture in the Utah Valley.*

Gabe's life after high school went in a very different direction. He left the Coquille area and moved
up to Silverton, Oregon, where his maternal grandmother, Lynn Walsh, lived. This was much closer to
metropolitan areas, such as the state capital, Salem,
and Portland, than Coquille had been. It was also
very near one of Oregon's natural wonders, Silver
Falls State Park. The ribbon of water leaped over a
cliff into an incredibly green world of ferns, shrubs
and pines. Hiking trails led up to the base of the
falls, and countless tourists trekked up to view
them every year.

Gabe began studies at Mt. Hood Community
College (MHCC). While enrolled there, he lived
with Lynn Walsh. She recounted, "Gabe was attending Mt. Hood Community College and working more than one job. He even worked nights at
a restaurant to pay his way through college. And
he was just as nice and helpful as ever. There was
an elderly woman in a wheelchair in the neighborhood. Gabe would mow her lawn and run out to
take care of her needs. Normally, to me, a young
person would be looking for entertainment or
something else."

This was a theme that people over and over
again said about young Gabe. He was willing to go
out of his way to help people. And as Fred Eschler
noted, Gabe seemed to have an innate facility to

start up a conversation with anyone, no matter what their job was or their circumstances in life.

Gabe chose automotive mechanics as his field of study, something that he was good at. Like anything that he was interested in, Gabe studied hard and performed well, carrying a 4.0 grade point average. In fact, he was at the top of that year's class. His instructors commented upon what a good student he was. Gabe even became valedictorian for his graduating class. His speech was full of optimism and hope for the future; it looked as if Gabe was on his way in a promising career.

Gabe was immediately hired as a mechanic at a prestigious BMW dealership upon completion of his courses. Gabe, as usual, was outgoing and gregarious and got along well with his coworkers and supervisors. He was pulling in a good salary and seemed to be adapting to a well-structured, comfortable life.

Michael "Mike" Woods, the manager of the BMW dealership, remembered Gabe as a "great kid." He described him as intelligent, straightforward and honest. Gabe showed up to work on time, never caused any problems and was very proficient. Customers of Gabe were just as enthusiastic about his workmanship. He was always professional, neat and had a certain charisma about him.

Years later, Woods said of Gabe, "We had an agreement with the community college where there was one term in school and one term in the shop. I was the shop foreman who trained a lot of technicians. I had a lot of one-on-one training with

Gabe at the dealership and saw him off and on over that two-year period. He was a paid employee during that two years, and when he graduated, we wanted him to stay on with us.

"Gabe was very competent in his work and a joy to be around. Very uplifting, very sunny, very bright. If you were down, he would joke around and try to bring you up. He didn't use profanity. He was just a clean-cut boy. He didn't use alcohol or do drugs, and I don't think he even drank coffee.

"He didn't brag or puff himself up. It was more like he was there to help you. He was compassionate with others, and when you talked to him, you got a sense that he really cared. While I knew him, over the course of three years there, the one person I felt that he truly loved was his mother. He always talked well about her, and he wanted to work with her and help her in any way possible. I never heard a bad word about her from him."

Gabe, however, was always restless. Once he had mastered a challenge, he began looking for greener fields over the horizon. And in 1999, the new horizon for Gabe included a wish to go on a mission for the LDS Church. Part of this was due to his faith, but there was another aspect to Gabe. He started off doing things well, but he either became bored with what he was doing or succumbed to a restlessness that he couldn't seem to quell.

By now, Gabe's mom had married a man named

James Anstey, and they lived in Bandon. James and Robin managed an antique store in the area, and it fit in well in the tourist seaside community. Gabe went there to live for a while before heading off on his mission. In the process, he got to know his new stepsister, Isabelle Anstey. She was fourteen and had decided to go live with her dad, Robin and Gabe.

Isabelle recalled, "When I was fourteen, I had a lot of issues, and Gabe was someone I could talk to. He helped me out a lot. If anybody needed help with anything, he would be there. He was the kind of brother I never had.

"He was religious, but he didn't push it on anybody. He was extremely honest, and he didn't brag about himself. His mom would do anything for him, and he would do anything for her."

Before going on his mission to Australia, Gabe flew up to Alaska, where Jesse was serving in the army. Gabe and Jesse were a lot closer than many full-blooded brothers. The two half brothers liked and respected each other to a great degree and wanted to see each other as much as possible.

Jesse said later, "I knew that Gabe had picked up the Mormon beliefs from Esther Eschler and her family. But it was his choice to become part of the LDS Church. It looked like at the time he was adhering to the tenets of the Mormon faith one hundred percent."

Gabe told Jesse how excited he was about going on a mission to Australia. Jesse was happy for Gabe and was sure he would do a good job there. When Gabe put his mind to something, he was very upbeat and enthusiastic. Yet, even Jesse knew that with Gabe, it wasn't the initiation of projects that mattered. It was if he could follow through.

CHAPTER 8

Gabe passed all the initial requirements of becoming a missionary for the LDS Church and was assigned to Australia. He was sent to Sydney with a group of other young missionaries. Dr. Terrence Barry and his wife, Matrina Evanoff Barry, were leaders of that group. Dr. Barry was often in contact with Gabe while he was on his mission in Australia. He evaluated Gabe's progress every month.

Dr. Barry later recalled, "I was in Australia from 1998 through 2001. I saw two hundred–plus missionaries there during that period of time. I would evaluate these missionaries once a month to evaluate their spirituality and to see if they were adhering to the mission rules. To see how they were feeling—were they happy, not happy, feel like they were doing a good job.

"It was a very regimented daily routine. They would arise about six-thirty A.M., initiate their Scripture study and work with their companion.

They always stayed within an arm's breadth of another missionary. Once they completed their Scripture study and prayers, they would go out into the populace to proselytize. They'd approach people on the street, in their homes, wherever it might be. And they would try and spread the Gospel. This would go on until almost nine in the evening. After prayers and Scripture study, they would retire at ten P.M.

"The missionaries would rotate around in different areas, and some of these were poor areas. Gabriel was in one of these and he spent time in some rough neighborhoods. He was an exceptional young man among exceptional young men. Every time he entered a room, he would be smiling. He had a very positive outlook. He was very pleasant and always upbeat."

Matrina Barry had an equally positive impression about Gabe. She said later, "The first time I saw him, I saw a very kind, gentle, tender, compassionate and spiritual young man. He was very humble. With his companions, he always showed love and concern. He took every opportunity to build them up. With people in the community, he always looked for those who were lonely or sad. Everything he did was representative of Jesus Christ. That's how I saw him.

"In my position, I emphasized the spirituality of the missionaries. Sometimes they were having hard times, being away from their parents. I would try and stay in close contact with them. If they were sick, I would take soup over or a plant or something like that. Gabe was living in a really downtrodden neighborhood. It was upstairs in a place that was despicable. And Gabe was sick, but he was more concerned about his companion than himself."

A fellow missionary in Australia was David Bastian, who was also stationed in Sydney. David had been in Australia for a year when Gabe arrived, and he met Gabe on Gabe's second day in the country. Bastian imparted to Gabe a lot of wisdom about things that could be useful to him in adjusting to his new life in a land so far away from home.

Over the next several months David met with Gabe quite often. David later said, "He was a sincere, outgoing individual, who cared about others. He lived his faith and enjoyed sharing it with others and seeing the change in their hearts. It seemed like he had a wonderful relationship with his family back home."

And yet there was always something that set Gabe apart from others. He seemed to have an expectation of entitlement or at least a special relationship with God. At that point, Gabe wasn't expressing this special relationship to others, but he definitely felt it.

Gabe would look back on this time and later comment about how he was special in the eyes of God. He said that he felt that he was guided by God to go to certain parts of the city or countryside, where he would perform his mission well. This went so far as God directing him to take certain roads and streets and even which houses to visit. It was never enough to just think that things might have worked out that way, anyway. Gabe saw God's hand in the things that he did, especially missionary work.

When Gabe completed his mission in Australia, he decided to return to his mother's home, which she shared with her new husband, James Anstey. Despite being so talented as a mechanic, Gabe now decided upon another means of making a living. He became a waiter at the Rip Tide restaurant in Bandon and at the Kozy Kitchen in North Bend.

David Grover owned the Kozy Kitchen and recalled of Gabe, "He was a super good kid. Very courteous and very polite. He cared about all his customers and was a hard worker. Just an all-around good guy.

"He never swore, smoked, drank alcohol or any of that. He was religious, but not preaching to everyone about it or bothering them with it. He kept it to himself pretty much. He didn't have a mean bone in his body.

"I was familiar with the relationship he had with his mother. He seemed to have a really good relationship with her and his stepfather, James. They would come in quite a bit and have dinner. When she came in and he was working, they would always hug."

Another person who spoke well about Gabe

was Sandra Johns, who managed the Rip Tide restaurant. She unequivocally said later, "He was the best employee I had there. He was kind, considerate and friendly to everyone. Just a decent, pleasant young man. If you needed anything, you asked Gabe. He helped the customers and gave them extra attention. And he never bragged about what he did.

"He did talk about his religion and being on a mission to Australia. But it wasn't overboard. He talked about wanting to go to college and about his family as well. He and his mother loved each other. Whenever she came into the restaurant, it was like the first time they had seen each other in a long time. There would be kisses and hugs."

A later police report stated that Gabe became a bartender during his stint at the restaurants. Other people who knew him then would say that this wasn't true. In fact, it would have been out of character, with him being a devout Mormon, to be plying that trade. But then again, Gabe was never one to adhere to anything strictly. He seemed to devise his own rules in the way he wanted to live his life.

Gabe certainly had a gift for gab and would have made a good bartender. One reporter who later spoke with friends of Gabe noted, "He could talk to you for hours without really saying much." Talking, planning, dreaming, were all part of Gabe's makeup. So was a restlessness he could not curb.

* * *

Isabelle Anstey remembered about Gabe's return to the Bandon area that he was very caring about others. She said later, "Bob was our elderly neighbor, and Gabe would go over and help him with anything he needed. Yard work, inside the house, moving things for him, whatever."

James Anstey also liked Gabe very much, and the feeling was mutual. James was a good guy and treated Gabe with a lot more respect than his own father had. Jesse McCoy said later, "Gabe called James 'the father I never had.'"

James recalled about Gabe, "He was a very caring person and very smart. He was compassionate with me. We shed tears together. We used to like to hang out and travel around together." James said that Gabe was a very generous person—not only with his money, but with his time as well.

James encouraged Gabe in whatever he chose to do, and the family of four got along very well at this point. But there was one incident that stood out for James during this period of time. Gabe was even-tempered, except for one occasion; he blew up far beyond what seemed necessary.

James had bought some cans of peaches, and Gabe really liked the fruit. Unknown to Gabe, James ate the last can of peaches in the house. When Gabe found out about it, he blew up. Gabe's face turned beet red and he yelled at James, "How dare you!" Gabe looked so angry—it seemed that he might strike James.

That incident, however, was like an island in a sea of calm for Gabe. At the time, to James, it just seemed like a minor tantrum. For the most part, Gabe was likeable and friendly. His patrons certainly liked him at the restaurants and so did his managers there. In fact, many patrons actually asked for Gabe to be their waiter.

It seemed as if Gabe had found his niche as a local, well-liked waiter in Bandon and in North Bend. But then, in a complete change of direction, he decided to attend BYU in Provo, Utah. Whether to meet up with Esther Eschler once again or because of other reasons, he did not later state. The main reason may have been, as usual, he just could not seem to settle down to any one thing.

CHAPTER 9

Gabe may have entered BYU to see Esther once more, but something quite unexpected happened. He met a young woman named Jessica Pope, instead. Jessica had come from the small city of Blackfoot, Idaho, to attend college at BYU. She was a Mormon as well, and she was very grounded in the faith. Jessica was pretty and bright; and she had one more aspect that Gabe may have learned about early on. She was the beneficiary of a large insurance settlement because of an accident she had as a teenager. In fact, by the year that Gabe met her, Jessica had $100,000 in her bank account. To someone like perennially cash-strapped Gabe, that seemed like a huge amount.

Jessica had received her insurance settlement because at the age of thirteen she had endured a terrible sledding accident. It had required a great deal of rehabilitation and she had a permanent two-inch scar on her neck.

Gabe later explained how he and Jessica met,

and many things that Gabe said had to be believed with caution. Gabe recounted, "We were both twenty-six years old. She introduced herself and we went to a Sadie Hawkins dance, the worst date of my life. But she's a wonderful person."

This was odd. At that point he didn't seem to be that attracted to her, or enjoy being in her company all that much, and yet he acknowledged she was a wonderful person.

Gabe and Jessica began dating. Alicia Bitton shared an apartment with Jessica when they were students at BYU in 2002. Both Jessica and Alicia lived in the Cinnamon Tree apartment complex along with many other BYU students. Alicia recalled that Gabe was friendly and a nice-looking young man. She added that he was fun to be around, always willing to help someone out and genuinely seemed to care about others. Alicia noted that Gabe was very active in the same LDS church that Jessica also attended. Alicia thought that Gabe and Jessica were very happy together.

While Gabe was at BYU, he joined the Air Force Reserve Officers' Training Corps (ROTC) program at that university. Part of the reason may have been that by being in ROTC, he received a substantial sum of money from the air force to cover his costs of tuition, food and housing. Another reason was that Gabe liked the idea of being an air force pilot. It fit the image he had created for himself as an adventurous young man. And he also wanted to live up to the image he had of Jesse McCoy, who had been on dangerous missions in exotic locales. Being a member of ROTC, Gabe was expected to keep up his grades at BYU and enter the air force after graduation from college.

Colonel Roger Maher was Gabe's ROTC detachment commander and professor of aerospace studies. Colonel Maher was responsible for 320 cadets that year. Maher recalled later, "I had Gabriel Morris in a class. As a professor of aerospace studies, I realized that Gabriel was one of the most exceptional young men that I had met that year. He was bright and he was positive. Optimistic and very personable. We actually had a great year together.

"Gabe was willing to do anything that was asked of him. A good team player who demonstrated leadership qualities. Gabriel was very humble and even-tempered. He pledged a service organization, the Arnold Air Society, and was very engaged in helping people."

Gabe and Jessica Pope became serious in a very short space of time and Jessica took him to meet her parents, Bill and Rita Pope, up in Blackfoot, Idaho. Bill had some suspicions about Gabe and asked if he intended to marry his daughter. Bill was aware that Jessica had a substantial amount of money because of the insurance settlement. He worried about his daughter being taken advantage of on that account.

Gabe assured the Popes that he and Jessica were

just friends. And then in something so typical of Gabe, he proved how false that statement was. Without Bill and Rita Pope knowing about it, Gabe asked Jessica to marry him. There was whirlwind activity before the wedding and then they were soon married at an LDS temple in July 2002.

Bill and Rita Pope were stunned by this turn of events. Gabe had just assured them that he and Jessica were not romantically involved. Now the Popes had a new son-in-law on their hands. Before they knew it, Bill and Rita Pope were heading out to Bandon, Oregon, where Gabe and Jessica had a reception. Gabe's mom, Robin, was there, as was her new husband, James, and Jesse McCoy and his wife as well. It remained to be seen just how well Gabe would treat the Popes' daughter, Jessica.

CHAPTER 10

Jesse McCoy recounted, "I got out of the service about the time Gabe got married to Jessica. We talked all the time on the phone and he told me all about her before they got married." As to marrying Jessica, Jesse said later, "Gabe was one of those guys who was very charismatic, handsome and well spoken. It seemed like he could have dated any girl he wanted to, but Gabriel seemed to go after the ones who were more intellectual and in tune with him. It was never about how beautiful they might be. When he married Jessica, I wouldn't say for a second what the heck was going on, because she was like night and day to Gabriel's personality. But he really loved her faith and dedication. I drove out to Oregon with my wife to see Mom. Gabe, Jessica and her family drove out there from Idaho and we all had a reception in Bandon."

It wasn't long before Gabe convinced his new wife to use a lot of her insurance money so that they could put a down payment on a house in Provo, Utah, while they both went to college. As it turned out, though, they soon had housemates as well. Gabe asked Jesse and his wife to move into the new house with them. Jesse remembered, "Gabe and I agreed that me and my wife would move in with him and Jessica. We missed all the time we used to spend together. He was a wonderful guy when he was at BYU. As far as I knew, he was no longer using marijuana and he didn't drink alcohol. He was very healthy and seemed very happy."

Jesse liked Gabe a lot, but he did not like his continuous preaching about the Mormon faith. Jesse was not a Mormon and did not want to become one. Gabe, however, would not let up on the subject. He dogged Jesse about it day after day. Jesse said later there were times he would leave the house just to get away from Gabe's preaching.

Another thing that Jesse did not like was Gabe playing video games on his computer into the wee hours of the night. Jesse said later, "I voiced my concern about this and thought it was ridiculous." Gabe responded that it wasn't hurting his studies, but there were times he went into states of denial. Jesse was sure that Gabe spent so much time on there, that it did hurt his studies.

Another person who was in the household for a while with Gabe, Jesse and their two wives was Gabe's stepsister, Isabelle. She was there for a couple of months and acknowledged that Gabe was still a wonderful brother. Isabelle said that it was always good to be around him. He was very positive and helped her in a lot of ways.

One place where Gabe continued to shine was in his studies in ROTC. As far as Colonel Roger Maher was concerned, everything seemed fine in Gabe's family. In fact, years later, Maher recalled an incident that stood out in his mind: "Gabriel did something exceptional, for any of the cadets I ever had. He and his wife, Jessica, invited me and my wife over to his house for dinner. Most people would have been too intimidated. But Gabe was very personable and excited to have us over. He prepared an Australia repast. He made it, not Jessica. We enjoyed a very fine meal and good conversation."

Jessica was smart and persistent in her studies, but Gabe had fallen back into his old ways. Distracted and restless, he was more prone to playing video games than studying. He did have dreams of becoming a pilot in the U.S. Air Force, and his ROTC training seemed a sure route toward that goal. But never one to let the truth stand in the way of a good story or a good presentation of himself, Gabe told Jessica and her parents that he had already been accepted into an air force flight-training program. Nothing was further from the truth. And what exactly occurred next, and why it occurred, became very murky in the years to come.

Gabe's stories always seemed real to the person

he told them to. Especially when they had known him for some time. The one quality almost all of them commented upon was how honest he was. They couldn't perceive of Gabe embellishing the truth about a situation.

As Colonel Maher recalled of the incident, "After what I thought was a very successful year, with great promise and leadership potential, I thought that Gabriel would serve as an officer in the air force. I think he would have served well as an officer in the air force.

"He came to my office in the springtime of 2002 to say he was leaving the ROTC program. When I asked him why, he told me he had to protect his mother. After that first year, he said he knew the military was going to cost him timewise. I asked him, 'Isn't that something that law enforcement agencies would do?' He said, 'No, they can't. I have to protect my mother.' Out of respect for Gabriel, I didn't pursue it. That was the first time his mother came up in conversation with me."

To another person, Gabe said that he dropped out of ROTC because he did not want to kill innocent women and children. And to others, he said that he did not want to drag Jessica around the country and the world as a military wife. Just what the truth really was, Gabe probably didn't even know himself in years to come. He seemed to believe whatever he was telling someone at a particular time.

* * *

Gabe was not accepted into a flight-training program or even the Air Force Academy in Colorado Springs, Colorado, because he had no degree from BYU. His studies there had slackened to such a degree that he didn't finish college. Deciding to cover up this fact, Gabe told Jessica and her parents that he decided not to become an air force pilot because it would mean moving Jessica from place to place, depending upon where he might be stationed. Gabe sugarcoated all of this by stating that he was giving up his dream because he didn't want Jessica to "endure the rigors" of being a military wife. This story became his most persistent one, but he would use the other stories as well, when he could get away with them.

All of that might not have been so bad, but because he had not performed the requirements in college, the air force now demanded that Gabe pay back all the money he had received from them while at BYU. Gabe did everything in his power to dodge and weave his way around paying anything back to them.

By his dereliction, Gabe had squandered his opportunity; even worse, he had no job and no prospects of a good-paying job at any time soon. He began running up huge amounts on credit cards, just so they could stay afloat and pay bills. Gabe talked Jessica into letting him invest funds from her settlement that were not used in the down payment of the house in Provo. She allowed him to do so; he promptly lost all of that money in bad investments.

Jesse noted that around this time Gabe started drinking beers and smoking dope. He seemed to have fallen back into the malaise of his high-school years before meeting Esther Eschler. The sunny, outgoing Gabe was starting to be eclipsed by a restless, sullen Gabe. He even told Jesse not to let Jessica know about his drinking and smoking dope: "It's better that she doesn't know." And since she was the one out working, while he sat around the house getting stoned or drunk, he was able to get away with it.

Life had not turned out as planned for Gabe or Jessica Morris. He had made many, many promises to her, and most of them had been hollow. She was, however, still in love with him. To try and get back on their feet, the young couple sold the house in Provo. They moved up to a place in Blackfoot, Idaho.

Jessica recalled, "We bought a house in Blackfoot, and I got a job working at the state hospital. From selling the house in Provo, we essentially came out even."

The Popes were glad to have Jessica nearby again, but they were much less enthusiastic about Gabe's presence. As usual, Jessica seemed to be the one putting all her energy into the marriage. And it was Jessica who had the energy and drive when it came to anything concerning family finances. Gabe was always drifting off into flights of fancy about what he *could accomplish* rather than sticking to any actual plan to make it happen. Bill Pope had always had reservations about Gabe. As time went on, those reservations seemed to be more accurate than he would have wished.

CHAPTER 11

Looking around for some way to earn a living, Gabe got a job at the State Hospital South, a psychiatric inpatient facility in Blackfoot, Idaho. His title was "psychiatric assistant trainee." Gabe related later that he liked working at this job. A report indicated that Gabe got along well with doctors, staff and patients. Yet, once again, it wasn't long before Gabe was looking for greener pastures. The hospital assignment was only a stepping-stone to something else.

He applied to become a deputy sheriff at the Bingham County Sheriff's Office (BCSO) in the Blackfoot area. Despite squandering so many earlier opportunities, Gabe actually got the job. It looked like he was on his way to becoming a lawman.

As in most things, Gabe started off in fine form as a Bingham County deputy sheriff. He was always good at beginning things, but it remained to be seen if he could finish what he started.

Later on, the sheriff would say that Gabe had done a good job as a deputy and took his work seriously. He took orders well and followed procedures in a manner that was proficient and up to standards.

Then, in November 2005, daughter Kalea was born to Gabe and Jessica. Kalea was a beautiful baby. It seemed that at last the family could settle down to a comfortable and prosperous home life.

As he traveled the main highways and back roads of Bingham County, Gabe performed well at his job. Besides the largest city of Blackfoot, there were the small towns of Rockford, Aberdeen and Atomic City. The main thoroughfare through the county was I-15, but there were also US Highways 20 and 26, as well as numerous back roads. Agricultural land spread along the Snake River Plain and ranches farther away. The southwestern part of the county was dominated by a huge lava bed, with the Craters of the Moon National Monument and Preserve on the distant horizon. Another large sector in the county was the Fort Hall Indian Reservation, which had its own law enforcement agency. It was a very different world from the tall pine forests and rocky seacoast of Bandon, Oregon.

As had happened in the past, Gabe's fantasy life and real life began blending in disturbing ways. To people outside the sheriff's office, he started circulating stories that his job as a deputy sheriff was only a cover for his "real job." He was supposedly with a top secret unit of the air force that did "black ops" work. He claimed that he was sent out on dangerous overseas missions and even worked as an assassin, when necessary. He indicated that these might have been in the Middle East and other world hot spots. Gabe was never very specific about where he would go or what he would do there. It lent an air of mystery about his life; and he, of course, explained being nonspecific about details because of national security. It's quite possible that Gabe was envious of the life that his big brother Jesse McCoy had lived in this regard, and, therefore, he started inventing these tales.

Jesse said later, "When Gabe became a police officer, we spoke all the time on the phone. We were still very close." Gabe wasn't telling Jesse these stories of black ops, with secret government groups, but apparently he started telling some fellow officers. The wool could not be pulled over their eyes so easily, and they derided and laughed at his stories. Unfortunately for Gabe, he half believed these stories himself. In some ways, he still felt inadequate compared to his older brother. These stories were one means of making him feel better about himself.

Gabe should have been happy with his new profession as a sheriff's deputy, but that was not the case. "Good enough" was never enough for Gabe. He didn't want to rise slowly through the ranks, like everyone else. He wanted to be a detective by 2007. He'd only been on the force for two years; and when a position came open in the detective division, Gabe applied for it.

A much more experienced officer was chosen by the sheriff. In disgust, Gabe resigned in a huff. Later he would concoct different stories of why he quit at that point. One of these stories was that he'd been on a raid with other officers and didn't feel that they'd done it properly. He said he felt he'd been put at risk by their actions.

He went so far as to claim that he'd gone to the sheriff about this, and the sheriff had not backed him up on the matter. Feeling that his safety was at risk, Gabe said, he resigned from the sheriff's office. Whether that happened or not could not be verified later.

Another story he put out was that he'd sustained a shoulder injury in the line of duty and could not return to work. As a result, he said, he was let go from the department. And in yet a third story, Gabe said he'd been offered a job at a police department in Anchorage, Alaska, a place where he'd always wanted to live. Later, after he'd resigned from the Bingham County Sheriff's Office, he claimed the job offer in Alaska fell through. In yet another story, he would recount that he was angered by the sheriff's office's treatment of inmates and alleged that the sheriff's office was corrupt.

The Alaska story may have been partially true.

Gabe did go up there and apply for a position in the Anchorage Police Department. He had the understanding that they were going to hire him. However, when he went back for a second interview, this did not transpire.

Most of his stories did not pan out. The sheriff of Bingham County said that Gabe had never come to him about other officers putting him at risk, and Gabe had never sustained a shoulder injury in the line of duty. What seems to have been the truth was that when Gabe did not immediately get what he wanted, he behaved like a spoiled toddler.

Another job had been squandered by Gabe Morris. Searching around Blackfoot, he was lucky to find a job opportunity in a short amount of time. This job was at Gold's Gym as a trainer. Once again, it was a good start for Gabe. The owner liked him, and so did those whom he taught.

Owner Taylor Ball later said of Gabe, "He was very positive and outgoing. He made you feel really good about yourself. He was full of compliments." In fact, Gabe was tailor-made as a personal trainer at a gym. He did have a winning personality, when he decided to let it shine. Likewise, he was muscular and fit, all of which was a good combination for a personal trainer at a gym.

Gabe liked his job at Gold's Gym, and with good reason. He met a woman there named Brenda Owens (pseudonym), and she was very pretty.

Gabe may have been married to Jessica, and had a young daughter at home, but Brenda was alluring and stoked his ego. Besides, it was still certainly galling to Gabe to be living in the Popes' orbit. That was a constant reminder of all his failures.

It wasn't long before the young, handsome former sheriff's deputy had a lot of clientele—especially attractive young women—and Brenda certainly fell into that category. It's not recorded now if Gabe let Brenda know if he was married or not. He was definitely less enthused about his life with Jessica after his BYU days. There had been too many false starts and disappointments in his life by now. In his mind, Jessica was part of that equation. Brenda, by comparison, was attractive and a boon to his ego and self-esteem. She may have been supposedly off limits by all the tenets of his faith, but she was also alluring and someone whom he wanted. They started a sexual relationship around this time.

Taylor Ball not only owned Gold's Gym; he also had an American Family Insurance Agency as well. With Gabe's often-winning nature and gift of talking easily to almost anyone, he seemed like a natural as an American Family Insurance agent. Gabe had the right touch, no matter the person with whom he was talking. It was more than just being a con man, he seemed to believe the things he was saying himself—even when they weren't true, or at least only partially true. Con men are cynical by nature, and they see the rest of humanity as a bunch of suckers. Gabe, however, seemed to con himself into believing whichever persona he chose at the time. He was as persuaded as much as anyone else.

Gabe began working as an insurance agent, along with his Gold's Gym training. Before long, he hired Brenda as an assistant in the insurance business. He had a lot more in mind for her than that, however. He wined and dined her, taking on the aspect of the big man around town. He even took trips to Las Vegas with her.

Gabe opened his own American Family Insurance Company office in Pocatello, Idaho, where Brenda resided. He began making a lot of excuses to Jessica about why he was staying late at the office or going on so many business trips. His new life seemed exotic and fast paced. The life with Jessica and Kalea was weighted down with drudgery and past failures.

Now smitten with Brenda, Gabe moved out of the house he shared with Jessica. Incredibly, she fell for his story that he was going to be away for a while on a secret black ops mission. Even after all the deception and promises on Gabe's part, Jessica still believed him and in him. In many ways, she believed in the aspect of what Gabe could be, rather than the Gabe who was right in front of her eyes.

Half brother Jesse recalled this period in

Gabe's life: "I started noticing a lot of changes in Gabe around this time. It was like night and day. Before, we had not kept anything from each other. I went up there to Idaho and was surprised to find he had quit the sheriff's office and was working for an insurance agency. His marriage was rocky by that time."

Gabe was doing everything he could to live the high life. He gained access to Brenda's credit cards and began running up huge totals on them, unbeknownst to her. He purchased a very expensive BMW and a Mercedes as well, even though he couldn't afford either car. When Brenda asked him how he could afford such vehicles, he lied and said that he was in a business venture with his stepfather, James Anstey. James had an antique store in Bandon, Oregon, and Gabe said that he was helping James sell expensive antiques. Gabe claimed that one sale alone was worth $50,000. Of course, it was all a fabrication on his part.

Gabe also told Taylor Ball that he worked in the very high end of antiques dealing and artwork. He seemed to imply that he had connections to the New York art scene. Gabe mentioned that he dealt art to "really wealthy people." Gabe also claimed that he was getting huge commissions on these sales, which was another lie.

For all his effort at creating a façade as an upstanding, outgoing young man, Gabe could not keep his inner demons in check forever. There seemed to always be a hard, dark core about him. There was an inner anger, which was constantly smoldering. Taylor related that both he and Gabe were fans of martial arts. One time Gabe came up to Taylor and said that he was worried what might happen if he really got angry at someone. He might hurt them badly or even kill them.

Then Gabe showed Taylor a picture on his cell phone with himself covered in blood. He said that had happened when he'd gotten into a fight with some guy. According to Gabe, it was the other man's blood. "I beat him up pretty badly," Gabe claimed. And then he added, "I'm a bad man. I'm a good guy, but a bad man." It may have been the one time that Gabe came closest to the mark in nailing down exactly who he was.

Casey Yeats became a good friend of Gabe's during this time period. Gabe spun his stories to Casey about having only one more year left with his contract with the air force. He hinted about black ops operations and that he would be moving to South America soon. He even indicated that he wasn't supposed to be in the United States at all, because he had missions elsewhere to perform. Gabe was such a convincing talker, he could get people to believe in very outrageous things. One thing that Casey added was that he did not see "a mean bone in Gabe's body. I never saw him raise his voice or become angry."

Gabe might have built up a framework of illusion for ordinary citizens about his supposed black ops, but he was flirting with disaster when it came to trying to fool an insurance company. Gabe's concept of ethics was pretty much gone by this time. He was not only ripping off Brenda, but he was ripping off his American Family Insurance customers as well. He began charging some customers for extra services that they were not receiving. Apparently, Gabe was pocketing the extra money. Customers complained about the discrepancies, and the insurance company began an investigation of Gabe's business practices.

CHAPTER 12

About this time, Gabe moved out on his own, down to Las Vegas. Jesse recalled that he got Gabe to stop off in Salt Lake City, where Jesse lived. Jesse explained, "The changes in Gabe by that time were profound. Mom and I talked about it by phone almost every day. We were both very concerned for Gabe's well-being. We knew he wasn't with the insurance company any more, but we didn't know what was going on with him, or with him and Jessica.

"He wasn't talking about black ops stuff to me, but it was stuff that would cause concern. On the phone he was maniacal on whatever he was talking about, and I couldn't get a word in. I thought he might be bipolar. He would just go on and on about some subject.

"Around this time, he told me some story about his dad, Danny Morris, taking him out to the ocean to drown. He said Mom was sitting on the beach and let Danny do it. Gabe said he was left underwater and went to the bottom of the ocean and had a conversation with God. He said he knew he was special at that point. God gave him the power to breathe underwater. He said he started walking on the ocean bottom, right up to the shore. Both Mom and Danny were amazed when he showed up alive. I told Gabe, Mom would never let anything like that happen."

Despite this story making no sense at all, Gabe started incorporating it into his belief system. Part of the dynamic was the feeling of being abandoned at a young age. The other dynamic was having special powers and a special relationship with God. If God had allowed Gabe to breathe underwater as a child and cheat death, what future miracles might be in store in his life?

One of the murkiest times in Gabe's life occurred when he moved from Idaho to Las Vegas, Nevada. Not even his half brother Jesse was sure what he was doing down there. Jesse recalled that he helped Gabe move down to Las Vegas; and once he was down there, the only kind of "work" Gabe said he was doing was gambling.

Not too long after that, Gabe phoned Jesse and said he had some new "work." According to Jesse later, "It was kind of like robbing from the rich and giving to the poor. He also said he was investing money, but he didn't say how he was getting the money, or how he was even getting money to gamble. He kept alluding to doing 'crooked stuff.'"

Just what this supposed "crooked stuff" was, was fantastic. Gabe later said that he was hired as a bodyguard to protect high-class prostitutes. There was another story that he would break into very rich people's homes and steal expensive items. In some stories, he gave some of his proceeds to the poor. In other tales, he just kept everything for himself, fencing many items for cash.

There was even one very murky story that he killed someone in Las Vegas. Or in a retelling of this, some bad guy killed someone close to Gabe and then was after Gabe as well. After a while, Gabe could not recount with any clarity what really happened, or if this had occurred at all. He was drinking heavily during this period of time and his thought processes were cloudy at best.

What Jessica remembered of this chaotic period was that "Gabe would call to talk to Kalea. And sometimes she would talk to him, and sometimes she wouldn't. He would come up to Idaho and stay for a few hours, get mad at something, and then just leave. As far as what he did down there, I didn't know. But he spent a ton of money in Las Vegas drinking and partying and whatever." This last part, Gabe had to have told her. Jessica never went down to Las Vegas to be with him.

Perhaps knowing that he could be in real trouble, because of playing fast and loose with other people's money—especially when it came to the insurance business—Gabe abandoned Brenda and told Jessica that he wanted to make their marriage work. He even said that his relationship with Brenda had not been sexual. Incredibly, Jessica believed him. She strongly wanted to have Gabe, herself and Kalea as a family, so she was ready to believe anything he told her.

In disgust, Jessica's father later related, "He was able to sell her malarkey. She thought she could make a responsible, hardworking fella out of him. Those two characteristics never seemed to appear."

More incredible news was right around the corner for the Popes. Brenda had found out where Gabe and Jessica were staying, which was the Popes' residence. She called Bill Pope there. Brenda told him that Gabe had run up a bill of $30,000 on her credit cards without her permission. She described him as a liar and a cheat.

With this information, the Popes tried to talk Jessica out of taking Gabe back. They knew he was toxic and would one day drag her down with him in his wild and irresponsible schemes. However, more than anything else, Jessica wanted to keep the family together.

Bill said later, "She had all the faith in the world in God and ability to transform people. The subject of Gabe was kind of off limits in family discussions."

Of course, when it came to God, Gabe had his own flights of fancy about his relationship with the Almighty. This concept did not seem to have a moral code that would be understandable to other people.

And then, for whatever reason, Gabe was the one who filed for divorce from Jessica. It happened in March 2009 at the Bingham County Court. He claimed "irreconcilable differences" as the reason for the divorce. Reluctantly, Jessica signed a settlement that required Gabe to pay $1,000 a month to her. He reported his income at the time as $48,000 a year. This came from working at Gold's Gym and as an agent at the American Family Insurance Agency. It's doubtful he reported the money he was skimming from that company. Jessica was to retain full custody of Kalea.

That should have been the end of it, but there was never a clean ending with Gabe. He changed his mind once again and the divorce was not finalized. Gabe moved back in with Jessica and Kalea. In desperation, he turned to the one source of income that he could still tap: Bill and Rita Pope.

CHAPTER 13

When Gabe had to convince someone, he could do a very good job of it. He told Bill Pope that if he could only get himself, Jessica and Kalea back to Oregon, he could go into business with James Anstey. Gabe swore he could make a good living doing that. It would keep his family together; it would help erase all his financial debts; it would give them a clean start.

As far as Jessica went, she believed things Gabe was telling her about why they were in such financial trouble. She said later, "He just started taking clients out to dinner (clients of the American Insurance Company). And he got the BMW. He said it would help him with getting more clients. And he said he was paying back the ROTC loan." (Author's note: He may not have been doing that repaying.) "He started using credit cards for everything—gas, food, everything. And he got business accounts for the women who worked for him at the life insurance agency. He bought cell phones for them and the accounts. It was all going on credit cards.

"It just got worse and worse. He got the place in Pocatello." (Author's note: He may or may not have rented a place there.) "So there was another rent. And then he picked up a real nice Mercedes. The money would just come in and go out before we could save any. He just kept applying for more and more credit cards. All the money was just going out."

Jesse McCoy also heard this line of reasoning from Gabe. Jesse recalled, "He said he wanted to go to Oregon and be around Mom and the ones he loved. He was having marital problems, but the next thing I knew he was back with Jessica once again. I wasn't aware that he was having any financial difficulties."

Bill Pope had heard this all before, but he loved his daughter. He knew how much she wanted to keep her family as a unit. He very reluctantly agreed to give them $7,000, and told Gabe to declare bankruptcy in Oregon. Since Gabe didn't even have a car now, they had both been repossessed, Bill loaned them the use of a pickup truck. With grave misgivings, the Popes watched as Gabe, Jessica and Kalea drove off and headed westward to Oregon in September 2009.

By the time Gabe and his family reached Bandon, Oregon, Robin had divorced James Anstey and was now living with new boyfriend Bob

Kennelly. Bob owned a place out on Highway 42 South, which was several acres on the south side of the Coquille River, about six miles from Bandon. This was a very pretty area of woods, farms and ranches along the river and rolling forested hills. The immediate area was known as the Flower Hill Ranch. It was a postcard setting for that part of Oregon.

Bob had been born in Los Angeles, California, but the family moved to Redwood City, up in the San Francisco Bay area, where Bob spent his school years. He met a girl named Linda Sellers there, and they got married in San Jose in 1985. They eventually had two daughters.

In the 1990s, Bob and family moved up to Oregon, where he worked for the JGS Machine Shop for many years. He and Linda divorced in 2002, and Bob then married Linda Bray in 2004. In 2008, Linda died of cancer.

Bob and Robin Anstey began dating after she divorced from James. Besides having a nice place up on Flower Hill and raising alpacas, Bob liked hunting and riding his motorcycle. Bob and Robin also liked eating out a lot at the local restaurants. By 2009, Robin was living full-time at Bob's place outside of Bandon.

Bob's property included the main residence, a large shop building, with a second story, and several outbuildings. The main house was a spacious split level. Its setup allowed Robin and Bob to have their own area downstairs, while Gabe, Jessica and Kalea lived in their separate upstairs section. Robin and Bob had a master bedroom on the ground floor, large kitchen, dining room, bathroom and living room. Upstairs was a bathroom, two bedrooms and another small bedroom in a turret. This was only half jokingly called the "Castle Room." Gabe and Jessica had one upstairs bedroom; the second bedroom was used for storage; Kalea slept in the Castle Room.

The main residence had an unusual pattern. The main stairway to the upper rooms led to a balcony, which looked down upon all the open space below. From the balcony and stairway, there was an unobstructed view of the living room and the front door.

Even before Gabe and Jessica left Idaho, an idea had supposedly been floating around that he would go into business with Bob Kennelly and his mother concerning a bed-and-breakfast place. Gabe and Jessica would manage the B and B. At least, that scenario was present in Gabe's mind, but none of that ever went beyond the dreaming stage.

There was also another option that never went anywhere. When Robin moved in with Bob, she had her own house in Bandon, which no one was living in. Gabe and Jessica thought they might be able to move in there. As Jessica explained later, "That house had not been lived in for about a year by the time we arrived. And it needed a lot of work. It was really disgusting. It never got new drywall. And so it never happened."

Gabe promised to go to work in Bandon, but it

was Jessica who got work first. She applied for and got work at Bandon Bookkeeping. Right from the start, Jessica proved what a good worker she was. She was very competent and got praise from the owner of the establishment and from her coworkers.

As far as Gabe went, it was altogether a different story. He did approach his stepfather, James Anstey, with a business proposal. However, it was not one that James wanted to hear. Gabe said he would drive to Nevada, steal items there and secret them back to Oregon, where they could be sold at James's antique store or on eBay. James turned him down flat.

James wondered what had become of the bright, cheerful boy he had once known. Gabe now was very troubled and angry all the time. He seemed to have lost his moral compass as well. It was incredible that he'd been a deputy sheriff not that many years before and still claimed that he followed the tenets of the Mormon Church.

Stymied by James's unwillingness to go along with his illegal scheme, Gabe turned to something controversial that was now legal in Oregon. He proposed to Bob and Robin that he start a medical marijuana–growing operation on Bob's property. Neither Robin nor Bob smoked marijuana, but they agreed to go along with this. It would at least provide Gabe with some income.

In December 2009, Bob, Robin and Gabe applied for, and were granted, medical marijuana cards. Gabe might have been able to do this by citing an arm injury while he was a deputy sheriff. Whether he really had sustained an arm injury was up for debate. They were also granted the right to grow marijuana on the property.

It soon became apparent that Gabe liked smoking his product more than trying to make a living from it. He was also hitting the booze very hard. He even bragged during this time period that he was drinking a bottle of hard liquor per day, along with countless beers. For someone who still professed to be an active member of the Latter-day Saints Church, he certainly wasn't acting like a responsible member of that faith.

Even worse, Gabe was the caregiver of Kalea by now. He constantly smoked dope around her, and he kept marijuana paraphernalia in her room, as well as "roaches," the burnt remains of marijuana cigarettes. Gabe's main "job" became sitting around the house, getting high and playing computer games. He was as addicted to those games as he was to booze and dope. He could barely be pried away from the computer screen to eat or take care of Kalea. It was an irritant to Bob that Gabe couldn't seem to tear himself away from the games to help around the place.

One of the games that Gabe was addicted to was called Perfect World. It was a game where people socialized and tried to create their own alternate reality of life, as compared to the one they were actually living.

* * *

One of the people with whom Gabe interacted a lot in this game was a young woman named Judy Ward (pseudonym), who lived in Dumfries, Virginia, just across the Potomac River from Washington, D.C. Judy later spoke of how she met Gabe: "We met through one of the servers, and we just happened to get in a group together. And then he started talking to me more, and we joined a guild. Not his, but just a guild. When we left the faction, he wanted a way to contact me. We needed a way of contact for this other project he was working on. It was just a project to bring people together for graphics work, stuff like that. Just to help inspire people.

"He told me he worked for the air force, with the OSI or something like that, and that he had a team who tracked and caught terrorists. I don't know how it worked, but that's the impression I got. So that's what I thought he did."

While Jessica earned her keep, Gabe was nothing but a freeloader in the household. His caregiving toward Kalea was worse than useless; he'd become a burden to Robin and especially to Bob. The money that Bill Pope had loaned him was long gone, and it appeared that Gabe had no intention of finding any productive job in the area at all. Gabe and his family were using Robin and Bob's food, using their water and using their electricity. It's not recorded if Jessica was paying them something, but Gabe certainly was not.

When he wanted, Gabe could still be charming and personable. When Gabe's stepsister's husband, Robert Hayden, first met Gabe, he thought he was a "cool guy." Gabe was friendly and did not act weird around Isabelle's husband.

But he was slipping a lot in other aspects of his life. Incredibly, he now pronounced that he didn't approve of his mother living in sin with Bob Kennelly. This was incredible—in light of the fact that he'd just cheated on his wife and had done a myriad of other illegal acts.

But Gabe told Robin and Bob that he was a "spiritual man." And then he absolutely floored them with his next comment: "I'm the forerunner for the Second Coming of Christ."

Gabe did not explain how a boozing, dope-smoking, wife-cheating slacker was somehow the forerunner of Christ. Robin didn't know whether to laugh or cry at this outrageous statement.

When Robin and Bob refused to acknowledge his wild claims, Gabe became angry and visibly upset. By now, Gabe was not just telling them that he was the forerunner of Christ's Second Coming; he had started telling others in his church as well. In fact, it became his new mission to tell others exactly how the local church should be run.

Gabe started to fall prey to rumors that some folks gossiped about and spread—claims that Bob's previous wives had not died natural deaths. None of these charges were true; but since Gabe was already antagonistic toward Bob, he began to believe in them wholeheartedly. In fact, this belief began to take on darker and more sinister tones in Gabe's mind as time went on. What had only been rumors in some quarters became a matter of faith in Gabe's mind.

Gabe had believed a lot of things about himself over the years, but now his beliefs bordered on madness. It wasn't some con, some artful duplicity. No, he actually believed his wild claims. He caused scenes around town and even at his church. He said that he had the true faith, and the leadership at the local LDS church did not.

Pamela Hansen, who lived in the area, had known Gabe for sixteen years by 2009. Often called "Pam," this young woman originally knew him as a person who was "extremely bright, energetic and smart. All the world was his stage, and everyone liked him."

Pam recounted, "We were teenagers when we first met, and my family hadn't moved to Bandon yet. We just went to church there whenever we were in the area. Later, Gabe was friends with me and my husband. He visited us more after he came back from his mission to Australia. Gabe always had big ideas and hopes. He didn't brag about them, but he was excited about going to BYU.

"Gabe always showed compassion to others. He was interested in what other people were doing, and it wasn't all about himself. He saw good in other people and considered them to be a child of God.

"Robin and James Anstey had a shop in Bandon and thought very highly of Gabe. He was full of life and ready to take on the world. He loved the Gospel and liked to have discussions about it. My husband was an avid outdoorsman, and he and Gabe liked those kinds of things.

"I attended the reception in Bandon after Jessica and he were married. They were very happy together. Later I met Kalea. He seemed to be a good husband and father. Gabe had a good relationship with Kalea, and she was well-behaved, loving and happy."

Pam once again became acquainted with Gabe when he, Jessica and Kalea moved to Oregon in 2009. "When he came back from Idaho, he reinitiated contact. He was a little less enthusiastic about life, but not out of the ordinary. He had responsibilities as a husband and father. We had them over for dinner and the only thing that stood out was that he seemed stressed out about getting work."

And then things started to change: "Gabe came over in the afternoon one day between Christmas and New Year's Eve, 2009. He spent a long time [here] and did most of the talking. He was talking about mystical, magical kinds of things. He said he was a forerunner of Jesus Christ and that these were the Last Days. In other words, the Second Coming of Christ.

"He talked about a pre-mortal existence and he had been a dragon rider. Whether he was fantasizing or not, I'm not sure. But he said we had been together in the pre-mortal life and I had been his queen. Together with an army of Heaven, we had expelled Satan and his hosts from Heaven.

"He then told me he had done some things in this life that he wasn't proud of. I told him we can be forgiven. Through repentance he could go forward and live a good life.

"He was very excited when he told me this. I kind of went along with him, and I asked what color dragon he rode. He said it was blue, so I asked him what color mine was, and he said he didn't know.

"He was very serious about what he said. Gabe told me that I was his queen, and he knelt before me with tears in his eyes. He said that he would do anything for me. Then he said, 'Please, just tell me what to do.'

"Certainly, I thought that Gabe was under some kind of distress. So I reiterated that he should ask for repentance and lead a good life in the future. To this, he said that he liked coming over and talking to me. It made him feel calmer.

"He told me I needed to leave Bandon because it was going to become a dangerous place. It was an apocalyptic end-of-time kind of thing. I needed to leave the area to be out of harm's way. I thought a lot of what he was saying was gibberish. It was very random and hard to follow.

"This whole visit lasted about three hours. When he left, he seemed to be much calmer. He gave me a big hug and said good-bye. When he left, I thought he had an emotional breakdown. I was concerned for his well-being."

* * *

Jesse McCoy saw Gabe around this time and said later, "I saw him at Mom's house and he was drinking a lot. He was more than just drinking—he was belligerent drinking. He would drink a whole bottle of hard liquor at one time and get drunk. He was also openly using marijuana, even in front of Jessica. He did not give me a reason why he was doing these things.

"He was also addicted to video games. When I left there, he would call me on the phone and say that he was spending endless hours playing them. He even called up once and said that he had special powers from God. It was very alarming to me."

Boozing, smoking dope, addicted to video games, Gabe's tenuous grip upon reality was becoming frayed to the breaking point. He'd always had a hard time telling fantasy from reality. Now the two had blended as one in a toxic mix of anxiety, grandiosity and paranoia.

Gabe had been playing Perfect World constantly on the computer in 2009; but by that point, his real world was anything but perfect.

CHAPTER 14

To what depths Gabe had descended into paranoia can be ascertained by his remarks to his wife in January 2010. He began telling her that Bob Kennelly was trying to poison them. Gabe said that Bob was putting rat poison in their food and was also wiping it on their plates.

By this point, Gabe was so delusional that he later claimed that he absolutely knew he was being poisoned. He said he purposefully imbibed the rat poison, knowing that it would kill an ordinary person, but that he was *no ordinary person*. According to Gabe, because of his extraordinary powers granted by God, he was able to heal himself.

Around that same time, Dillon Hogan, Bob Kennelly's son-in-law, had dinner with Robert and Robin at their house. Robin told Dillon how Gabe was claiming that he could run through the trees of the forest at night, at full speed, and see God and hear His voice. Gabe claimed he never hit a tree or stump because God was guiding him.

Robin was so alarmed by this that she said she thought that Gabe was psychotic now.

James Anstey was equally alarmed. He later said, "He was no longer the Gabe I knew. He thought he was some kind of superhero. He spoke of scams in Las Vegas and all kinds of crazy things. He was totally irrational. Something inside of him had broken."

Around that same time, Gabe went to visit his old boss David Grover at his restaurant the Kozy Kitchen, in North Bend. Grover recalled, "Gabe stopped by the restaurant with his wife and daughter. In the beginning, he was very cordial, as he always had been. He was a lot thinner than I remember him being.

"As the conversation went on, he told me he knew I was a good person, and he said he knew that because of my smile. He went on to talk about some kind of mission he was on. He said that if there were any people who were giving me problems, he would help me out on that. He added that he was on some kind of military mission and there were other people in the area helping him out. It was like secret agent stuff, black ops kind of things.

"He had always been honest with me in the past, so it was hard to discount these stories, but it was all very odd. I hadn't seen him in six or seven years and I asked him what he was doing back in town.

Then I said to him, 'Oh, right. Your mom lives around here.'

"He said he wasn't seeing her or her boyfriend. 'They're bad people! I love my mom very much, but I can't be around her.'"

In January 2010, Gabe and Judy Ward, who lived in Virginia, met each other in a Skype chat room. That was the first time she had seen his face. She recalled, "On Skype, we never talked about his real life. It was all about either the game or working on a website and getting it up and running. He just seemed like a caring person."

Around that same time, Gabe began going over to his stepsister Isabelle's house more often. Now married, she and her husband, Robert Hayden, lived in the Bandon area. Isabelle recalled, "Gabe began stopping by once a week. I started noticing there was a big change in him. It was the way he would talk and preach to us. His conversations were more intense and his stories were more wild.

"He started talking about God giving him missions. He was preaching about a lot of things he could do. He said he was in special operations— secret agent stuff. It got progressively worse. It got to where I didn't even want to come to the door when he showed up. But I'd open the door because it was Gabe.

"He would just ramble on and on, and I couldn't follow what he was saying. I would just nod my head. I felt like he was trying to recruit us for whatever trip he was on. He acted like he was some kind of prophet. His conversations were so out there, I would just say, 'Uh-huh, uh-huh.' But I really didn't understand what he was talking about."

Isabelle's husband, Robert, remembered, "Gabe came over to visit a lot and his demeanor had changed. When I first met him, we had all sat around a table playing cards and drank a few beers. This had been over James Anstey's house. Gabe and I sat in a hot tub for a short time, and I thought he was hip and cool.

"By late 2009, he was generally panicky and stressy. I wouldn't say 'paranoid,' but 'anxiety' was a big word for him. He lost a lot of weight. He started talking about religion a lot and secret odd jobs for the government black ops.

"He said he was getting phone calls all the time to do missions. I had some concerns about these stories. I didn't really understand why he was telling me these things. It was like he wanted us to join his group or something.

"With religion, he said he would wake up in the morning and receive his orders from Him. I asked him who 'Him' was, and he pointed straight up at the sky. So I took it to mean God. A lot of the conversations were his philosophy about how the world should be. It seemed like he was trying to convert us."

* * *

Gabe was becoming very worrisome to all of his family members. His maternal aunt, Laurel Carmack, even wrote down, *Gabe is ill and has delusions about himself. He views himself as a prophet.*

And Gabe's maternal grandmother was alarmed by his long, rambling letters to her. They made no sense at all. She feared he had become a religious zealot and conspiracy kook.

Gabe also called Jesse on the phone and started saying he was a prophet of God. His half brother recounted, "He believed God had given him the power to heal and to see the future. In regard to the future, he began saying Mom was not in a good place. And he started giving off a sense of how he had been wronged in his early life by everyone around him. He still loved Mom then, but he felt like she had abandoned him with Danny when he was young.

"He talked a lot about getting her away from Bob Kennelly. He was so manic. I would listen to him talk on the phone and I couldn't get a word in. I could only follow bits and pieces of what he was saying. None of it made a whole lot of sense, but I would listen, anyway. Many of the conversations had religious overtones. In January, he said he was on a special mission to put all of our family together again."

More than anything, Gabe seemed to be reaching out for a golden past that may never have existed in his life. It was a past where his mom, Jesse and Gabe's grandmother could all be together once again without all of the troubles of the outside world closing in. It was a world that didn't include the chaotic years of his youth, nor did it contain all of the frustrations and false starts in the plans he had dreamt of in his twenties.

A person who saw Gabe around this time was Mike Woods, the man who had trained him at the BMW dealership in Portland and had become friends with him. Woods related, "Gabe stopped in the shop one day in early 2010. He was in the area and said he had to go back down to Coquille soon. He was staying in a nice hotel I knew around here, so I went there and spent some time with him.

"He was a totally different person. He was telling stories about military black ops. He said he was in some kind of group that he would do these deeds for—some kind of group with the government. He had a bunch of marijuana with him, and he was smoking pot and drinking beer. It wasn't the Gabe I knew."

When Woods left Gabe's presence, he said, "I was confused about this whole thing. I didn't understand how he had become that way. When he was the Gabe I knew, he was truthful and honest. I knew that he had been in ROTC, but this was like out of the movies. He still did have some positive qualities, but he seemed troubled. His speech didn't flow like it used to. It was like he was struggling."

In fact, Gabe was struggling a lot, just to maintain even the approximation of a normal life. Whenever Robin got on the phone with Jesse, she would tell him about just how worried she was about Gabe. Gabe's stories just kept getting wilder and wilder, and he was more sullen and at odds with Bob all the time. Robin didn't know where all this was headed, but she felt that Gabe needed help.

CHAPTER 15

The local church that Gabe attended should have been a refuge for him and his family. But Gabe was making more and more outlandish comments to people there all the time. These comments would just seem to come out of left field.

Gabe's remarks to Michael Stockford, LDS branch president in Bandon, took the cake. Stockford had asked Gabe to meet with him because his recent comments were making people in the congregation very uncomfortable. While listening to this, Gabe paced up and down and rambled about things that made no sense to Stockford. Finally the LDS leader asked him to leave.

Gabe was only gone a few minutes, and then returned, claiming, "I am Jesus Christ! There is evil that needs to be taken care of! I can heal people. I can see into the future."

Gabe was asked to leave once more, which he did.

* * *

In late January, Gabe phoned Pamela Hansen. She recalled, "He had some issues with the local leadership in the church. He said they had not handled some things in the correct way. He said I shouldn't go to church in Bandon anymore.

"When I defended our church leadership, he got very agitated. His thoughts were random and incoherent. It was very hard to follow. Then he said I might not see him for a long time. He said there were enemies looking for him and it had something to do with when he worked in Las Vegas. There was something about a ring of prostitutes. It was not clear. But he did say I would see him again."

Also in January, Robin's old live-in boyfriend, John Lindgren, came by Bob Kennelly's property to make a bid on some work that needed to be done. Gabe had always liked John. John recalled later, "I got a call to come out to Flower Hill to make a bid on a drywall job on Bob Kennelly's house. I went out and measured it and noticed that Gabe was not the same old Gabe I had known. He was bouncing on his heels and real agitated.

"I shook his hand and gave him a hug and we talked for a little while. He asked, if I got the job, if he could help me, and I said, 'You bet!'"

While he was there, John noticed that there was real tension between Gabe and Bob Kennelly. They didn't speak to each other at all. In fact, they were practically glaring at each other. John wasn't sure what all this was about, but he definitely felt something was wrong.

* * *

On top of his troubles with the local branch of the LDS Church, Gabe kept upsetting Isabelle and her husband, Robert. His stepsister recounted, "I hadn't talked to Robin for a while and I wanted to go over and give Robin some photos. And Gabe told me, 'No, just leave her alone.' I didn't know why he told me that. It just sounded like she and Bob needed their space."

Robert Hayden knew that Gabe was smoking marijuana. One day, Gabe told him a story about marijuana and Idaho. Robert recalled, "He said that when he was a sheriff's deputy, he would pull people over, jot it down that they had already been pulled over and then let them go. That way, they could transport marijuana through the state without being pulled over again. It was basically that he was helping people run dope through the state of Idaho."

After that, Isabelle and her husband invited Gabe, Jessica and Kalea over for a spaghetti dinner at their house. It was a meal they would never forget. Isabelle recalled, "Gabe just sat there and didn't eat anything. He was a lot scruffier and a lot skinnier than he used to be. He was wearing more raggedy clothes."

Robert remembered this visit: "The spaghetti dinner was the peak of his preaching to us. After dinner, Gabe sat on the couch with me talking about different opportunities. It was basically about opportunities in ways to make a lot of money fast, but he wasn't specific about how the money would be made.

"It was kind of scary for us. We'd ask how it was supposed to happen, but all he would answer was 'You can have it, if you want it.' Stuff like 'One hundred twenty thousand dollars by tomorrow morning.' He kept saying, 'You can have it, if you want it,' and then it was very strange. Jessica said the same thing, and so did Kalea.

"While sitting on the couch, he started tearing up and said, 'I have to stay on this path. And if I don't stay on this path, I'm gonna fuckin' break! And it will all be over!'

"And then he added, 'Robbie, do you ever get the feeling that you could reach over and just rip somebody's throat out on the spur of the moment? Do you think you could ever lose control like that?'

"I said I didn't know. And I looked over at my wife, like *what's going on here?*"

Gabe's emotions were all over the place that evening, and so were his rants. When he and his family finally left, Robert turned to his wife and said, "He's crazy!"

As if the night of the spaghetti dinner wasn't strange enough, Gabe showed up at Robert and Isabelle's home on another night, unannounced, between eleven and midnight. Robert Hayden noted later, "It was just out of the blue. We were already in bed, and Gabe came over just to give our daughter a little green scrunchy for her hair."

A few nights later, Gabe came over to their house very late to borrow a didgeridoo (an Australian Aboriginal musical instrument). Robert noted, "Once again, I could hardly make sense of anything that Gabe was saying. I did know that two of Bob Kennelly's wives had died, even though they were relatively young. (It may have actually been one wife, but Gabe kept saying there were two deceased ex-wives). Gabe and I had talked about how weird that was. Among the people I knew, there was some speculation about whether those had been natural causes. I know that Gabe was worried about something bad happening to his mom. He did say that he did not approve of Bob, and he didn't think Bob was a good fit for his mom."

CHAPTER 16

Jessica was still the only one in their household making a decent living; but near the end of January, Gabe insisted that they suddenly leave his mother's house. His delusions about being poisoned were at full throttle. In the middle of the night, he convinced her that they were in danger. They packed up Kalea and went to Medford, Oregon, about 120 miles away. Neither Gabe nor Jessica told Robin or Bob that the family was going. Like so many things that Gabe was now doing, his impromptu trip didn't seem to have any plans about what they would do once they were actually there. Irrational movement was becoming just as commonplace for him as irrational thought.

Jessica recalled of this trip to Medford, "We drove to Medford because the night before I had been doing the dishes and I felt kinda sick. And I was doing the dishes and I could see them, but I couldn't see what else was around me. And Gabe looked over at me and said, 'Do you feel sick?' And

I said yes. And he said, 'I feel it too. I think we need to leave.' And I said, 'I totally agree.' So we jumped in the truck and took Kalea with us. And we stayed there in Medford.

"The next morning, we talked about it and we felt like Bob was trying to hurt us—to poison us with rat poison by putting it on the dishes. They ate out every day. They would come in to have toast and coffee in the morning, but then they would eat out somewhere. And they'd go out to eat every night. But we'd always fix food there at the house. And I don't know if Bob put it in the food or on the dishes. We had a feeling he was doing that. We both did.

"And Kalea was a lot more agitated than usual. And Gabe even commented that Kalea was fine all day long. But then I'd come home from work and then all of a sudden she wouldn't listen to anything. We were in Medford and we hadn't grabbed anything other than just ourselves and our clothes. And I had to sleep in my contacts because I didn't have my glasses, and that was kind of painful. I was hurting, and he knew it. He said that we needed to go back so that we could get some stuff to live on."

The trip to Medford was just the beginning of their sojourn. They soon returned to Bob's house and quickly gathered some more belongings. Robin and Bob kept asking them what was wrong and where were they going. Neither one would say why the sudden rush or where they were going.

Jessica recalled, "We came back to the house and Gabe told me to go upstairs and start packing.

And Kalea came with me, because she always comes with me when I'm around. And Gabe went to the Castle Room and started packing up his clothes and toothbrushes and that sort of stuff. And the whole time, I didn't know where we were going to go or what we were going to do.

"I knew that I had my job and they were expecting me to be there, and I would be letting Mary Ann down because tax season was coming up. And every day she had been saying, 'You're not leaving, are you?' And every day I'd been telling her, 'No, I'm not.' But my family's safety trumped that job.

"So we packed up as much as we could, and Robin and Bob were there and they just kept walking around and asking, 'Why?' Bob usually doesn't talk to me except about the weather. And I didn't want to say to Robin, 'Because I think your boyfriend's hurting us.' Because he was standing right there. So I just shrugged my shoulders and we took probably about forty-five minutes to an hour packing up.

"Robin didn't want us to go. But Gabe told me to drive, and he said, 'Get in and don't look back.' And so we did. We didn't know where we were going or what we were going to do. But Gabe's grandmother always liked to see him and was excited about seeing Kalea. So we headed there."

Perhaps to try and alleviate his growing paranoia and agitation, Gabe decided to visit Lynn Walsh, who resided in Silverton. Once Gabe and his family arrived, his grandmother was very distressed by his appearance and the way he acted. She said later,

"My grandson was sick. He was under so much stress. There was fear and anguish in him, and there was concern for his mother. He wanted to bring her up to Silverton because he thought she was unsafe in Bandon.

"He was physically suffering from the condition he was in. He was very thin, and when I put food on his plate, he wouldn't eat it. I don't recall him eating anything the whole time he was with me. He began telling me things that weren't logical. I tried to counteract those things by telling him he wasn't making sense to me. He said he engaged in secret activities and that he had one more trip to make to China. I was very concerned for him—concerned for his mental health.

"He said his family had fragmented. He said that he had enjoyed family life when he was living with me. He thought if his mom could come up here to Silverton as well, we could all be a family again."

Gabe also said he needed to protect his mother. He seemed to insinuate that she needed protection from Bob Kennelly. And yet, as time went on, the one person it seemed that she needed protection from was Gabe.

While in Silverton, Gabe showed up one day at the LDS church there with Jessica and Kalea. David Bastian, his old friend from missionary days in Australia, went to that church. David recalled, "It was a Sunday and Gabe came to church with his wife and daughter. There was a break between some Sunday classes and I invited him and his family over for dinner. I was excited to see a friend I hadn't seen for seven years or so.

"Everything seemed normal, although he was running a little late. When he showed up, he was wearing what he called his 'thinking cap.' He sat down on the couch in the living room and we talked. It was soon apparent that Gabe was very different. I don't know what happened to him. It didn't feel right. He would get excited about something and his wife would reach over and kind of rub his back to calm him down.

"Then my wife and I thought it was kind of strange because he wanted to meet with me in private. I invited him into my office, and we just sat down on the floor. We talked a little bit, and at that point, Gabe started doing all the talking. He would be all excited one moment, and then angry, and then he'd have tears in his eyes.

"I looked at his face and I didn't recognize him at all when he was angry. He didn't look like the Gabe I had known. He was not consistently coherent. At one point, he looked over at some Pixar videos I had for my kids, and he said that the people who made those were prophets.

"He started telling me stories about being in black ops. He said he had a two-hundred-thousand-dollar car so he could outrun the police if he had to. He wasn't very clear, but he said that he was working for some agency, but he couldn't go into detail. I took it all with a grain of salt, and just let him talk.

"He brought up about working for some company, and someone was stealing money from the agency and he had the inspiration to help the company crack the code of some numbers. It didn't make a lot of sense. He became more and more agitated while he was there, and that was about two and a half hours. He would take less and less breaks while talking.

"I didn't have much opportunity to change the direction of the conversation. I felt that he had fallen off the horse or was a couple short of a dozen. I was worried about him when he left and I had a hard time sleeping that night. I was stirring in my bed, and I told my wife, 'Something's not right with Gabe.'"

Ray Wetzel, who knew Gabe through the LDS church in Silverton, had been an acquaintance for ten years. Wetzel later said that the Gabe he knew as a young man "was easygoing, polite and positive. He became a friend of my children and spent time at our house. He would come over for dinner and have interesting conversations. He always spoke about his mother with a lot of respect and love."

That was not the case when Wetzel saw Gabe in 2010. Wetzel recalled, "Gabe was talking about Salt Lake City and that it was going to erupt in riots. Gabe said it was a disaster waiting to happen. You need to get your kids out of there. He based all this allegedly on his background as a police officer. I held up my hand and said, 'Gabe, my kids are fine.' When I told him my kids were fine, he calmed down and changed the subject."

The subject change concerned Gabe going overseas on a job. Wetzel recalled, "He said he had an opportunity to go to China and work on some virtual-reality program. I wondered why he wanted to do that. Then he started talking about his grandmother and her house. He thought it belonged to the family, but she was going to give it to someone else.

"Gabe was all over the place and very agitated. Right after he left, my wife and I turned to each other and wondered what it was all about. We wondered if he was on drugs or hallucinating. His manners were very unusual. He still had a way of expressing himself, but he'd lost a lot of weight, and his wife had lost a lot of weight also."

After Silverton, Jessica recalled, "We started heading north on I-5 to see a friend of mine named Diane. So we drove up to Seattle to see Diane. We switched drivers several times, because I was getting so tired I would practically fall asleep at the wheel. Gabe pulled off at an exit, because Kalea would always get hungry before I did. He got off at a random exit and just started looking for a food place. And then, all of a sudden, we pulled over and he said, 'Can you believe it!' And I'm like, 'No, what are you talking about?' And the restaurant he stopped at was a McMenamins. And we'd just had dinner at a McMenamins restaurant the night before."

Gabe seemed to attest showing up at this second McMenamins restaurant as his special relationship with God, and Jessica went along with this. And then Jessica really believed this when she saw a man there who had dark hair and was wearing a beret. She was sure she had seen the same man in the Portland area restaurant. It was like a sign for her.

Jessica said, "This man was in front of the restaurant smoking a cigar again. And Gabe went up and talked to him. And this man said a prayer for us and we left. We drove up to Seattle and got there during the daytime. It was near an Indian reservation or something. There was a big totem pole there.

"I knew that Diane worked, so I was going to wait until later to contact her. We walked around Pike Place and took Kalea on a boat. I think we went over to Whidbey Island. Just went on it, walked on and walked off. But Kalea was able to go on the ferry ride and thought it was really cool.

"I had served my mission for the Church of Jesus Christ of Latter-day Saints in the Seattle area, so I was semifamiliar with the area. I contacted Diane around four-ish and she was out of town. She was in Florida. She had been there for a few days and was going to be there another week and a half.

"I asked her if we could possibly stay at her apartment that night. She said she'd have to check with her roommate. So we were around there, waiting for her roommate. And we tried calling her a couple of times, but her roommate never got back to us. It was getting late, and I told Gabe I thought there were a couple of places we might stay at, up in Lynnwood. We got up there and went to a church. Guys were playing basketball there and we asked them for a directory and ended up calling some people I knew. They said we could come over and crash on the floor. They didn't have any extra beds, so we ended up staying there one night.

"We just slept in sleeping bags. They had a bunch of dogs, and Kalea ended up playing with the dogs. She was ecstatic about that. I tried calling Diane again, and asked her about wiring us some money. She said she was working and wouldn't be able to do that. So we decided to leave the area."

It wasn't just leaving the area on a short trip. For whatever reason, Gabe now thought they should go to Southern California, where he had grown up. That was more than one thousand miles away.

Movement and traveling, for its own sake, seemed to be a part of the equation. He was seeking some kind of refuge, which did not exist. The refuge was from his personal demons, and there was no such place on earth where he could keep them quiet.

On the way to San Diego, Jessica recalled, "We stopped at a gas station and there was a mechanic shop with it. Gabe wanted to know if the guy wanted to buy the camper shell on the pickup. And the guy did and we got thirty bucks for it, and the pickup got a lot better gas mileage after that. The whole goal of the trip was to find a new place to live because of Bob. And we stayed at a place near the marina and it had two rooms. There were three beds and a fridge and a stove."

They stayed in these motel rooms in Oceanside, near San Diego, until February 7. Apparently, Gabe was not able to raise any funds, as he'd hoped. And whatever relief Gabe got from being back in the place of his youth, it did not last very long.

While in San Diego, Gabe told Jessica that they needed to return to Bandon and have it out with Bob about trying to poison them. Later, Jessica would say it was a joint decision; but by now, she was going along with just about anything that Gabe said.

Jessica recalled later, "We woke up in the morning and Kalea was still asleep. We woke up early and Gabe said that we should go back and see Bob and Robin and talk to them. And I said, 'Okay.' It was going to be a long drive, so we got going, got everything packed, showered and got Kalea up. We had breakfast and then got on the road."

The long drive began once again, back north to

Bandon. On the way, the pickup truck that Jessica's father had loaned them began having problems with the clutch. Up through California's Central Valley, through Sacramento, Redding and over the mountains into Oregon, they just hoped the pickup truck would last long enough to get them back to Bandon.

Despite the mechanical problems, the pickup truck made it all the way back up to Bandon on the morning of February 8. Jessica recalled, "We had missed a turn at Drain on I-5 and ended up having to go to Coos Bay. And so it took extra time and we drove through Coos Bay down to Bandon and then on 42 South. There was a little pull-off past Bob's driveway and that's where we pulled off. We got some rest there. It was just before the sun was coming up."

Gabe purposefully had Jessica and Kalea wait in the pickup while he made his way up the hill. Robin and Bob generally slept late in the morning, and Gabe did not want to have them hear the pickup approaching the residence. Jessica recalled, "Gabe said that it would be best if we did not let them know that we were there. Just because of what happened previously, we didn't know how Bob would react to us."

Gabe made his way stealthily into some brush, where he could watch the house, unobserved. Incredibly, Gabe took a portable radio set along with him; he had given Jessica another one. By this means, they communicated with one another about what was happening.

One of Gabe's messages became garbled, and Jessica understood him to say that he wanted her to drive the pickup truck up the hill. She started up the driveway. Gabe came tearing out of hiding and told her he didn't want her doing that. Rather than drive the pickup back to its original spot, however, he had her pull it off on the side of the driveway, partway up the hill.

This did not seem to satisfy him for long, so then he had her pull the pickup truck behind a barn and hill so that it couldn't be seen from the house. Gabe returned to a place of hiding, this time behind a group of trees. And once again he watched the house and communicated by hand-held radio with Jessica. Perhaps in Gabe's mind, this was like a secret operation he had talked about so much. To him, he was scouting out the "enemy"; and in his mind, Bob was that enemy. He even perceived Bob as being armed and dangerous, since he knew that Bob had a permit to carry a concealed weapon.

After watching the house for several hours, Gabe saw Robin and Bob leave the residence. Gabe walked over to the house and checked out all the rooms, making sure that they were empty. When Gabe determined that things were the way he wanted them in the house, he went and got Jessica and Kalea. Then all three of them went into the house. There they showered and got something to eat. Once this was accomplished, Gabe walked Jessica and Kalea back to the pickup truck and had them wait once more. And Jessica later admitted that Gabe smoked a couple of joints while he was up on the hill. He also apparently drank a beer, because she found an empty bottle of Heineken later. He even told her to take a swig, because she'd had nothing to drink for hours. She did as instructed, but she didn't enjoy it.

Jessica recalled, "Gabe went back in the house alone, and Kalea and I sat there in the pickup and she played with her toys and she was watching a movie on Gabe's laptop and she calmed down. I was on the passenger side and she was on the driver's side, and she had brought some stuffed animals with her that had been inside the house. She put them on the dashboard and watched a movie. And I could tell she was tired, so I laid a sleeping bag out on the front seat. And we covered ourselves and took a nap."

Jessica and Kalea stayed in the pickup truck for hour after hour as Gabe roamed around inside the house. Just what he planned to do when Robin and Bob returned, he did not convey to Jessica. Then once again, Gabe came and got them and escorted them to the residence.

Jessica remembered, "Kalea and I were both ecstatic because we could actually eat again. We had no idea where Bob and Robin had gone or when they'd be back. After we ate, Kalea and I got into our pajamas."

Jessica remembered, "It was about seven P.M. when Kalea and I got in our pajamas and we went to bed. We went to sleep in our room upstairs. Gabe stayed awake so he could talk to Bob and Robin when they got back."

Meanwhile, Gabe kept his vigil—waiting and watching for his mom and Bob to return. By now, he was primed and ready. He had discovered Bob's .40-caliber handgun, and he had at least two full clips. That meant he could get off twenty shots in very short order.

Robin and Bob finished their activities in North Bend and around Bandon, where they had dinner. They finally arrived back in their driveway at some time after 8:00 P.M. At that time of year, it was very dark outside the home. Unbeknownst to them, Gabe was watchful and waiting on the upper balcony, which had a commanding view of the front room.

Robin and Bob entered their home and walked toward a couch in the living room. Robin even managed to put her purse and some items down on the couch. Who knows what thoughts were racing through Gabe's mind at that point? All his failures, anger and frustration had boiled down to this one moment. And in his delusional mind, he may have thought that Bob was reaching for a gun in his coat pocket.

In one version that Gabe later gave, he said that he yelled at Bob to take him seriously. Most likely, however, without a word, he began firing. Bob was hit multiple times and made it as far as the door before collapsing. Robin was also hit multiple times. Wounded and in shock, she still managed to make it outside the front door, before Gabe followed her, took aim and shot her in the head. Mute evidence was left near her body. It was a spent shell casing from the pistol. Gabe had to have followed her outside and shot her to death at close range.

CHAPTER 17

After Gabe made sure that his mother and Bob Kennelly were dead, he riffled through Bob's wallet and got a little bit of cash and Walmart gift cards. Then he ran upstairs, where Jessica and Kalea were now awake.

Jessica recalled, "I woke up to the sound of gunshots. Kalea had woken up first. She was crying and scared. I think I heard Robin's voice, but it was really, really, really distant. It was extremely muffled and distant."

Jessica was groggy and confused. She continued, "Gabe came up to the room and ran in and said, 'Let's go!' Then he ran back out. I had been wearing my glasses, and they were on the counter. I stood up, and then I grabbed Kalea. I didn't have shoes on, so I grabbed some shoes out of the closet. They were Gabe's shoes. I couldn't find any that matched. So I just wore Gabe's mismatched shoes. I carried Kalea. I ran down the hall with her, went down the stairs, stopped at the bottom of the stairs, and that's when I saw them. I told Kalea to close her eyes and not open them for any reason. And I ran out and stepped over Bob and Robin. She was outside. Bob was bloody. He had blood behind his head. I didn't look at Robin.

"Gabe was in Bob's truck and I ran up with Kalea. And we got in and he had the truck started. He took off and sped down the driveway. We hit the embankments and I thought we were going to tip over and go down onto 42 South, but we didn't. It was very dark outside on the road."

It was from there that Gabe made the drive to Fred Eschler's neighborhood and concocted his story about terrorists. Of this whole incident, Jessica's recollection was "He told me when we went up to the Eschlers' door, 'Follow along. Do what I say.' And he went in and he told them that we were part of the air force and that he was like an air force special ops, or whatever it's called. And there had been terrorists that had come and just murdered his mom and her boyfriend, and that Gabe shot one of them. And we needed help.

"Fred told Laura to go clean out the car. And I think Gabe asked Fred something about borrowing it or having to drive us. But Fred said he couldn't do it because he had to work in the morning. Fred put together a bag of food for us. Some cottage cheese, apples, other things, and I was holding Kalea the whole time.

"Fred gave Gabe the gun and they put the bullets in the slidey thing. I don't know what it's called for a gun. And Fred gave him that gun. I asked for a car seat for Kalea, but Gabe said it wasn't necessary. And I wasn't sure how this was going to work. I wasn't sure if he was going to drive. So Kalea was put down in the backseat and he wanted me to drive. I got behind the wheel and we drove off."

As Gabe and Kalea hid in the backseat of the Eschlers' Ford Taurus, Jessica drove down the darkened road away from Coquille. She already knew there were no terrorists, nor were they fleeing for their lives from some radical cell of killers. She had seen no one else in the house, no other dead bodies except those of Robin Anstey and Bob Kennelly. She surmised correctly that Gabe had killed them.

Jessica recalled, "I drove to Roseburg (on Interstate 5) and I asked him which way we should go. Then I said, 'South?' And he said, 'I totally agree.' And so I turned south."

Working up her courage, she asked why he had killed them. Gabe didn't even try to lie to her. His answer was "It had to be done." He gave no further explanation than that.

Once again, on a darkened road, they were heading south. This time it was not to collect money or to look for new job opportunities. It was to try and get beyond the reach of the law. Behind them they had left two bodies lying in pools of blood at a hillside residence on Highway 42 South.

* * *

No one except for Gabe, Jessica and Kalea knew about Robin Anstey and Robert Kennelly lying dead at their residence. This state of affairs went on for two days, until the afternoon of Wednesday, February 10. A citizen of Coquille complained to the Coquille Police Department about a pickup truck parked in front of his home on Dean Street. The police checked on this pickup truck and ran the license plate number. It turned out to be a pickup owned by Robert Kennelly, of Highway 42 South.

Since the address was beyond the CPD's jurisdiction, they asked the Coos County Sheriff's Office to make contact with Kennelly about the pickup truck. Deputy Adam Slater pulled the assignment.

Deputy Slater arrived at Kennelly's place at around 1:45 P.M. on February 10. He thought he was there just to check on a very minor infraction. He drove up the hill from the highway and parked his vehicle where everybody else parked their vehicles, behind the residence near a shed. Slater walked down some steps toward the house and was stunned to see a body lying on the deck in front of the house. It was the body of Robin Anstey. As Slater moved up toward the house, he saw a second body sprawled on the living-room floor, near an open door. This was the body of Bob Kennelly.

Deputy Slater confirmed that both victims were dead, pulled back from the scene and called for help. This was obviously something far beyond a deputy's duties. A detective and other sheriff's officers were going to have to be called in. As it turned out, CCSO detective sergeant Daniel Looney was about to get a case that surpassed anything he had ever seen before.

Looney had been in the sheriff's office for twenty-six years by 2010 and had been a detective for twenty years. As he recalled later, "We received a call from the Coquille Police Department about a white Dodge pickup truck illegally parked on Dean Street in Coquille. They advised us that the registered owner was Robert Kennelly and his residence was out on Highway 42 South. That was in the Coos County Sheriff's Office jurisdiction.

"Deputy Slater's job was to drive out to the residence and make contact with the registered owner and ask him to move the vehicle. About one forty-five, he arrived on scene, found the bodies of a deceased male and female there and called it in."

Soon Detective Looney was on his way; and when he arrived, he noted that this location was known as the Flower Hill Ranch. A steep driveway wound up the hill from the highway, and it was wooded along its side. Pampas grass grew along two small spur roads, which were parallel to the main driveway. The main driveway eventually led to a garage area and shed. There was also a barn off to the side and a large two-story main residence.

When Sergeant Looney got to the deck area outside the back entrance of the house, he noted a middle-aged female lying faceup. He immediately looked for blood in that area and noticed blood smear marks and lots of blood, where she had bled out. There were also small, scattered droplets of blood on other areas of the deck.

And then something really caught his eye. It appeared to him that initially she might have been facedown in a planter box. To his eyes, it seemed as if someone had dragged her to the position where she now lay on the deck and positioned her faceup. Near her present position, there was a spent bullet casing and a pair of glasses.

The deceased male was lying in the living room, faceup. It appeared that he had been running for the door when gunned down. Since Sergeant Looney had concern about the increasing clouds and threat of rain, an awning was placed out on the deck area to cover the female's body and other evidence, but not contaminate the scene. Then Looney closed the French doors to the house to keep any rain out.

As part of the investigation, Looney tried to determine when the crime had occurred. One thing that helped him in that regard were several bags from a convenience store, with a receipt inside one bag. In the living room on the couch was also a purse. When Looney looked inside the purse and a wallet there, he found a driver's license for Robin Anstey, aged sixty-two. Nearby was also a bag from Ross Dress for Less in North Bend. The receipt was dated 5:24 P.M. on February 8. Another bag was from a drugstore in Bandon, with a timed receipt for 8:02 P.M. on February 8.

Moving back to Robin Anstey's body, Looney and the other investigators set up strong lights and found a shell casing for a .40-caliber Smith & Wesson handgun. Nearby was an upside-down plastic pot with a bullet hole through it and a bullet fragment in the pot. Also there was a human tooth lying on the deck and an ammo clip, which was empty. On the French doors, there had been a bullet strike, where the bullet had hit and glanced off.

Moving inside, law enforcement noted that when people entered through the French doors, they were greeted by an open-style living room, which went clear up to the ceiling of the second story. Around this second story was a balcony, which ran around the open area. A stairway to the balcony was on the right side of the living-room area, and to the left were the kitchen, dining room, pantry and laundry room. There was also a master bedroom and a small office on the first floor of the house.

It began to be apparent that whatever happened here had begun inside the house. There were two spent shell casings near a kitchen counter on the floor, and one more near a table. A candle in a dish was near the stove, and right next to that dish was another spent shell casing. There were shell casings on the kitchen floor, in the sink and under a couch in the living room as well. In all, thirteen expended shell casings were found in the area.

What caught Sergeant Looney's eye was the fact that an empty ammo clip that could hold ten bullets was found. That meant the shooter had to reload at some point to keep firing.

Trying to determine angles of trajectory and

where the shooter might have been standing at different times, Looney and the others looked for where bullets lodged and for strike marks as well. There was a bullet hole in the edge of a chair near the right side of Bob Kennelly's body. There was also a bullet hole in the leaf of a plant in the living room. A dowel was placed in one of the wounds on Bob Kennelly's body. Using a laser, the beam shone from the wound, through the plant leaf and up to the balcony area. Apparently, the shooter had begun shooting there and then had come down into the lower portion of the house.

A bullet strike in the French doors confirmed that theory. The angle of the strike mark proved that particular bullet had traveled in a down-ward angle from the balcony area. In fact, a .40-caliber bullet was found in a door when the molding was removed.

There were bullet strikes all over the living room. One was found in a chair near the French doors and another on the floor. The flooring was removed and a bullet found in the subfloor.

As they looked around for paperwork in the house, it was determined that not only did Bob Kennelly and Robin Anstey live in the house, but so did a man named Gabriel Morris, his wife, Jessica, and their daughter, Kalea.

Moving up to the second floor, Sergeant Looney noted a room that "looked like the spire in a castle." He notated it as the "Castle Room" on the diagram of the house and in his report. Looney added, "There was a lot of kid's stuff in there. It was apparently where the daughter slept."

In that room were some things that were very jarring for a child's room. Looney noted in the room an ammo clip with bullets in it, a flare and a plastic bag of marijuana. There was also a bong in the room for smoking marijuana. Near the bong was a matchbox, which contained marijuana residue.

A middle bedroom was used as a storage room, and the bedroom at the end of the balcony was used by Gabriel and Jessica Morris. There was a gun safe in a walk-in closet, where Looney found a clip for a Heckler & Koch pistol. This was sometimes referred to as an HK pistol. There was also a box nearby with a receipt in it; the pistol had been purchased by Robert Kennelly in December 1995. A search all over the house and property did not turn up the pistol.

What was very interesting to Sergeant Looney was a photo found in the bedroom of Gabriel Morris in a sheriff's deputy uniform. Also interesting was a plaque for Gabriel attesting to his fine performance as an LDS Church missionary in Australia. And further investigation around the house turned up a passport for Gabriel Morris in the Castle Room.

Taking the investigation back outside, Sergeant Looney's trained eye noted something very interesting. Looney was a firearms instructor and range master for CCSO. Part of his duty was to train officers what to do if they got into a firefight with an individual. What he noticed on the deck was the position of the empty clip in relation to the dead body of Robin Anstey and what he now knew about Gabriel Morris being a deputy sheriff. Looney said later, "In regard to ammo clips, what you are trained to do as a police officer is, when you've emptied the clip and change magazines, you drop the clip and don't touch it. Because touching it takes time. You let it drop where you're at. You immediately put in a new clip and keep firing." That could explain why there were no fingerprints found on the empty clip on the deck.

Moving out back, the officers found a red GMC pickup with Idaho plates. This was behind a hill in back of the garage area, hidden from view of the house. The pickup truck most likely got there by using a small spur road that ran off from the main driveway. The pickup truck was registered to William Pope, of Blackfoot, Idaho.

Sergeant Looney related later, "When I walked up from the bottom of the driveway, it's a steep driveway, and people who drive up from the bottom can cause spinout marks. That's from trying to get traction. But I found spinout marks that weren't going uphill—they were going downhill. A spinout on the way down is a dangerous and silly thing to do. I thought it might have something to do with the crime. It appeared like someone trying to leave the scene in a hurry."

The tire spinout marks were sheltered from the rain for later analyzing. There were also spinout marks that went down through a grassy area. In fact, at one section on the driveway, a vehicle had lost control and actually slid into the bank of a hillside before continuing on down the hill. Once again, it looked like someone had left the scene in a great hurry.

Besides the Coos County Major Crimes Team being involved, the Oregon State Police (OSP) Crime Laboratory and its agents became involved too, along with the police departments of Coquille and Bandon. One thing the officers discovered was that Robert Kennelly had owned a .40-caliber handgun, which was now missing. Both he and Robin had been killed with .40-caliber bullets, and it appeared that they were probably murdered by the gun that Kennelly had owned.

Sergeant Looney entered the information about the gun into the national crime information computer system. Within a short period of time, the gun in question came back with some very interesting information. It had been picked up on a street in San Diego, California, and was now in the possession of the San Diego Police Department.

A San Diego police officer had found the gun on Genesee Avenue, near April Court, in some bushes. This was an area where there was substantial crime. It was absolutely Robert Kennelly's gun—serial numbers proved that. How it got to San Diego was still a mystery at that point.

* * *

At first, it was not apparent who had murdered Robin Anstey and Robert Kennelly. Then the contact from the CPD to CCSO revealed all of Gabriel Morris's actions at Fred Eschler's home on February 8. Also the information that investigators got from Jessica's parents in Idaho was factored in. Because of this, and other questioning of individuals who knew Gabriel Morris, and his increasingly erratic behavior over the past few weeks, an arrest warrant was drawn up by DA Paul Frasier. Gabe was the main focus in this warrant; Jessica was listed as a material witness.

The warrant stated that Gabriel Christian Morris was wanted for the murders of Robert Kennelly and Robin Anstey, and that the murders were aggravated. This was a class 1 felony.

CHAPTER 18

The news of two murders near the quiet seaside town of Bandon absolutely rocked the community. A local newspaper, *The World,* ran the headline POLICE SEEK DOUBLE HOMICIDE SUSPECT. The article began: *Police are asking for the public's help in tracking a murder suspect and his wife, tied to a double homicide, near Bandon.*

The article went on to show the location of the crime on the Coquille River between Bandon and the hamlet of Riverton. A photo of Gabe and one of Jessica was next to the map. The article gave out the license plate number of Fred Eschler's silver Ford Taurus and reported that the couple's four-year-old daughter, Kalea, was with them. In addition were the lines: *Gabriel Morris is reported to be armed with two handguns. The couple has friends and family in Idaho, Portland, Salem, Seattle and San Diego.*

A reporter talked to DA Paul Frasier about where the couple might have gone. His answer was "Your guess is as good as mine as to which way they went." Then he added that he was seeking Jessica Morris as a material witness to the murders. And already he let out that evidence at the scene pointed to Gabriel Morris as the shooter. Just what evidence this was, Frasier would not say.

Frasier did say that Jessica, until recently, had been helping with a fund-raiser for the Women's Safety & Resource Center. And Mary Ann Donaldson told a reporter that Jessica was "vivacious, outgoing, intelligent and a really sweet person who also appeared to be a great mother. We were worried about her. She just disappeared. She was really a great, reliable worker and we really liked her." Donaldson added that they were all concerned for Jessica's safety and that of her daughter.

The next day's newspaper ran a headline that stated: POLICE SAY FUGITIVE IS DANGEROUS. At a press conference, DA Frasier confirmed that the victims were Robert Kennelly and Robin Anstey. A photo was shown of Gabe, Jessica and Kalea in happier days. About the dangerousness of Gabe, Frasier said, "If he, Jessica Morris, their child or automobile is located, citizens are strongly cautioned that they should not approach them or the car and should immediately call nine-one-one."

To another reporter, Judy Moody, the director of the Women's Safety & Resource Center, said, "Jessica was very enthusiastic and engaged in the process of creating a fund-raiser." But the Soup Bowl luncheon fund-raiser, which was meant to be held a day before the Super Bowl, never happened. Jessica had not collected donations for the fund-raiser and had not purchased bowls and spoons from her own money, as she had promised. As far as being involved in the crime, Moody said, "I don't think she's involved. That just doesn't fit."

By now, Oregon State Police detectives from Central Point, Roseburg and Coos Bay joined other officers in searching for the trio. These law enforcement agencies basically covered the southwestern portion of the state. Of course, this area was mountainous and very forested. Gabe and his family could be hiding in any number of places.

Autopsies were performed on Robert Kennelly and Robin Anstey by Kristine Karcher and Dr. James Olson. Karcher was the chief medical examiner (ME) for Coos County. She had a master's degree in forensic nursing from the University of Colorado. By 2010, she had been chief medical examiner for Coos County for twelve years.

As she explained later, "I deal with victims of violence, and half of those are usually victims who have died. In dealing with my job, I have forensic training in homicides and autopsies, and sometimes I would be assigned to the major crimes team in Coos County."

That is what happened for Karcher on the Kennelly/Anstey case. On February 10, she was contacted and told to respond to a residence on Highway 42 South, outside of Bandon. When she got there, she observed the bodies in place, and drew diagrams of their locations and positioning. She also supervised their removal from the scene.

When the autopsies occurred, it was in conjunction with Dr. James Olson from Jackson County, who contracted with Coos County. As Olson performed the actual autopsies, Karcher took notes and made trauma diagrams. On a front-view diagram of Robert Kennelly, she noted a wound to the abdomen that crossed his chest and went all the way to the left armpit. There was another wound in his left side, which went in a straight direction, and the bullet embedded in a hip bone. There was a third wound in the right leg, near the knee.

In a back view, Karcher related what she called "a very impressive gutter wound that crossed the back of his head and neck and grazed the shoulder. It entered left to right, traveled downward and ended up underneath the skin." There was another wound on Kennelly that went through his leg and exited the calf area. The fatal wound was the one that entered his chest and perforated his right lung and liver.

As for Robin Anstey, she had suffered a gunshot wound that entered near the left ear and exited the right cheek. There was also a wound to her upper left arm, which entered the back of the arm and exited the front. It shattered the humerus bone of her upper arm. There was a graze wound on her shin and a gunshot wound to her buttocks, which exited near her knee. The fatal wound was one to her left temple, through her brain, which exited her cheek and knocked one of her teeth out. This was the tooth found on the deck near her body by investigators. The fatal wound had been delivered at fairly close range.

Karcher had been at the scene and noted bullet holes in plant leaves there. The wounds on Robert Kennelly made sense in light of those bullet holes in the leaves. Karcher believed some of the bullets that entered Kennelly's body had been fired from a steep angle downward. This was especially true of the wound to his lower leg. The gunshot wound to his neck was also in a downward angle. She surmised someone had started shooting at Kennelly from the balcony as he tried running out the door. When Bob was already on the floor, the abdomen wound occurred when he was lying prone.

For that wound, the shooter had to have been standing over Kennelly and firing at a downward angle. All of this pointed to the fact that the shooter meant to kill his victims and was not content on just wounding them. It had taken at least thirteen shots to accomplish this. Not only that, he had time to think about what he was doing, since he had to reload a clip into his gun to accomplish the task.

CHAPTER 19

While law enforcement was trying to figure out what had occurred at Bob Kennelly's residence, Gabe, Jessica and Kalea were on the run. In another mad dash to San Diego, they drove more than eight hundred miles down the highways. Most likely, they cut across to I-5, which ran down through Oregon and Central California. Taking Highway 101 out of Bandon and down the coast took a much longer period of time, since it was not freeway all the way. For anyone trying to cover a great deal of distance in a hurry, I-5 would have been the way to go.

Jessica did not go into great detail about the initial route they took, but later she did say, "We didn't have our IDs, our driver's licenses, so we had to be very careful. We couldn't be pulled over. We drove all the way back to the same hotel in Oceanside, because no one will let you rent a room unless you have an ID. And so we went back to the same one, and I asked the woman there if she remembered me and if we could have a room, and she gave us one. I thought we would stay there for a couple of days, but the next morning Gabe said no."

While they were in that area, they went to Escondido, where Gabe had lived with his dad. Jessica recalled, "We stopped at a pet store. Kalea had been through a lot. Gabe took her in there so she could hold a couple of animals. He thought about getting her a turtle. She cried when we left because they didn't have any turtles. And it was in Escondido that we pawned our rings." By that, she meant their wedding rings.

A rational person would have kept a low profile at this point, but Gabe was anything but rational. With gun in hand, he robbed a convenience store to obtain more cash. In this robbery, he had the car away from any surveillance cameras and it could not be connected to him. Jessica did not go into the store while he was robbing the place. She recalled later, "Gabe said wait, and Kalea and I stayed in the car. And he left and returned and gave me a bunch of money. They were mostly in ones, but there was [a] fifty."

In another irrational move, Gabe was about to lose that gun. Jessica recalled, "We had gone to a friend he used to know in the area and knocked on the door to see if he still lived there. He didn't, so we were driving around looking for a hotel. I couldn't find it and flipped a U. Gabe was drinking gin and got really drunk. He must have had the gun in the bag with the bottle, because he threw the bottle out the window, and the gun was gone after that."

Actually, the gun that Gabe had tossed out the window was soon found by a San Diego policeman, even before the bodies of Robin and Bob were discovered in Oregon. The policeman took the gun into his department and it was kept in storage to see what might turn up about it. For a handgun just lying on the street like that in a rough neighborhood suggested it had been used in a crime scene somewhere.

Gabe, Jessica and Kalea could have made their way into Mexico at that point, since the bodies of Bob and Robin had not yet been found. But in their haste to flee the scene in Oregon, neither Gabe nor Jessica had taken their passports with them. Rather than chance a border crossing, they headed east on I-8. In some places along this route, Mexico was only a few miles away. In fact, past El Centro, the route practically skirted the border.

The family crossed the Colorado River and entered Arizona at Yuma. Later, Jessica spoke of going to a mall or a Walmart around there. Her recollection was hazy as to where exactly this occurred. But she did remember, "Kalea and I were still in our pajamas. We didn't have any clothes. We didn't have anything with us at all. We didn't have soap or anything. So we went to a mall and it was about nine-thirty in the morning and Gabe went in and got us clothes. And we got a swimming suit for Kalea, a car seat, hair spray, soap and a brush. And he came back and we got dressed. And from there, we headed for a friend of mine in Mesa, Arizona."

But before visiting the friend in Mesa, Gabe had other business to take care of first. Jessica recalled, "He was driving around and it was a relatively new little shopping area. And we thought it was kind of ironic because there were a lot of police cars around, like they were on a break together. He drove around several times and circled and then stopped the car and got out. And when he came back, he gave me a whole bunch of cash and told me to count it. And there was like three hundred dollars." By now, Gabe was so audacious or crazy, he robbed a business in an area where there were police cars in the parking lot.

After that, Jessica continued, "We called my friend's house from a grocery store, once we were in Mesa. Gabe told me to tell them we were coming from Louisiana and going to California. Going to San Diego. And that was our story. We were just traveling through and needed a place to stay for the night. And so we did, and Kalea was able to play with their daughter."

Once again, Gabe should have kept his mouth shut. Instead, he rambled on about secret ops missions and working for the government. Jessica did nothing to keep him from talking about those kinds of things.

Jessica related, "The next morning, we got up

and drove again, and there were lots of border patrols around, so we decided to head a little bit north." This took them up I-17 to Flagstaff, Arizona. From there, they headed east on I-40, through Winslow by the Painted Desert and the Petrified Forest.

"We were driving all day and into the night, and Gabe talked about heading up to Mount Rushmore in South Dakota." Just why he wanted to go there remained a mystery. "And we were heading toward Colorado, but then I realized a friend of mine I talked about was out of the way in Grand Junction, Colorado. That was back west. So we decided to head east. We drove all day and night, heading across New Mexico to Albuquerque."

They drove past Gallup, the Malpais Badlands and through Grants. With a journey to Mount Rushmore now out of Gabe's plans, he next thought of a girl he knew from the Internet, with whom he played Perfect World. She lived in Michigan. With that in mind, it became their next destination, even though it was more than one thousand miles away.

During this time period, law enforcement was trying to figure out exactly where Gabe, Jessica and Kalea were, and where they were headed. What they didn't know was that Gabe and his family were now heading due east on I-40. This took them across the Pecos River and into the Panhandle of Texas. It was a bleak wintry landscape out on the plains, and the family lived on fast food and little sleep. In fact, Jessica remembered, "I was dragging at that time, and I fell asleep at the wheel. So I kept pulling over so that we wouldn't crash and die."

The one thing that kept pushing them onward on this marathon trek was the knowledge of what was being left behind in Oregon. The road took them onward to Amarillo, Texas, and Oklahoma City. From there, they began to veer northeast on the Will Rogers Turnpike across Oklahoma. Then it was on I-44 to St. Louis, Missouri.

The murders made front-page news in Blackfoot, Idaho, where Jessica's parents lived. The *Blackfoot Morning News* initially reported a few details of the murders and described Gabriel Morris as a "dangerous double-homicide suspect." It showed a photo of Gabe and Jessica and related that Jessica was a "material witness" in the case. The article stated that Gabe might have two handguns with him and should be considered armed and dangerous. Then it gave out phone numbers to call, including one to an Oregon State Police tip line.

What the *Morning News* didn't know yet was that law enforcement was so concerned that Gabe might be headed to Blackfoot, Idaho, to harm Bill and Rita Pope, they had that couple leave town. Only later would Bill relate, "When we got to our daughter's house in Boise, we ended up outside with officers around us with guns drawn because they had the home under surveillance and saw our car pull up with Blackfoot plates." Gabe, of course, had borrowed one of Bill Pope's pickups and it had Blackfoot, Idaho, plates on it as well. After the cold-blooded murders of Robin Anstey and Bob Kennelly, the police were taking no chances.

The article went on to say that the Morrises might be heading to Seattle, Salem, Portland or San Diego, where they were known to have friends. Readers were cautioned not to try and confront this couple directly, but to call police immediately if the silver Ford Taurus they were known to be driving was spotted. And then it gave out the Oregon license plate number.

The next day's edition of the *Morning News* had little in the way of new information, except to state that Jessica had suddenly disappeared from her job at Bandon Bookkeeping. And DA Paul Frasier was quoted as saying, *"The Morrises were up to their eyebrows in credit card debt. They had returned to Oregon to declare bankruptcy."*

In a later local edition, Jessica's parents had given the newspaper a more recent photo of Jessica and Kalea. Rita Pope stated that she wanted people to know that Jessica looked different than the older photos being shown around the country.

Rita stated, "Jessica weighs forty pounds less now and her hair is cut about chin length. She doesn't wear makeup. She will probably be wearing glasses and she has a two-inch scar in the middle of her neck from a serious sledding accident when she was thirteen years old."

The photo provided depicted a smiling Jessica,

wearing glasses, and Kalea, who beamed for the camera. It was obviously taken in happier days for the family.

Authorities were giving out a little bit more information to the newspapers, and *The World* noted, SHOOTING FUGITIVES HEAD EAST. The article related that investigators had tracked the missing trio to Mesa, Arizona, via San Diego. DA Frasier added that the pattern of travel indicated that they might be heading for Louisiana or Florida, where Gabe had family.

Because of the nationwide search for Gabe, Jessica and Kalea, *America's Most Wanted* television program agreed to run a segment about them. Part of the reason was a fear of what Gabe might do to Jessica and Kalea if he felt backed into a corner. Rita Pope said, "I pray this will help them be found."

A film crew from *America's Most Wanted* went out to Coos County, Oregon, and filmed a segment of the show. During the filming, DA Paul Frasier let it be known, "My biggest concern with the case right now is the safety of Jessica Morris and Kalea. I am very much concerned about what might happen if there is some confrontation at gunpoint, if the police should find them."

And Frasier told a reporter that *America's Most Wanted* gave the case nationwide exposure, which was needed. "We'll take every little bit of help we can get," he said. And he added about the Morrises' unknown journey that if they were trying to cross into Mexico, customs agents and border patrol agents had been given information about them. Then he related, "If they were trying to cross the border, they could have done so in San Diego."

Based on perhaps a surveillance video from Mesa, Arizona, where Jessica was just sitting in the car, while Gabe went inside a convenience store, Frasier stated, "I do not believe, based on that, she is being held as a hostage."

A later issue of the *Morning News* ran the headline FAMILY ASKS WHERE IS FBI? It noted that days had passed since the murders in Oregon and the Morrises had gone on the run. Rita Pope told a reporter, "We have never heard from the FBI, so our family contacted them last week and asked them what they were doing to find Kalea. We were really surprised when they told us they weren't involved."

That news was stunning in light of the fact that law enforcement had proof that the Morrises had headed out of state. The FBI had much greater expertise and resources in cases like these that crossed state lines.

The Popes were also disappointed in the tips that had been generated by the recent segment about the case on *America's Most Wanted*. They worried that the Winter Olympics had drawn many viewers away from that program. By week two of the ordeal, they were no closer to knowing where Gabe, Jessica and Kalea were than when they'd first been told about the incident.

The Popes' contacting the FBI worked, however.

Within a short period of time, that agency issued a federal arrest warrant for Gabriel Morris on charges of unlawful flight to avoid prosecution. This was on top of the Oregon arrest warrant, already in effect.

Bill Pope told a reporter, "Gabe has succeeded in completely isolating Jess from us. We were very concerned about her and Kalea (before the murders). We had just talked to Robin, Gabe's mom, before all this happened."

Rita Pope was sure that the murders had something to do with all of Gabe's financial problems. And she surmised he had talked Jessica into fleeing with him, and taking Kalea along, because he'd convinced Jessica that bad people would "get them" concerning those financial problems. Rita said, "I know that Jessica would do anything to protect her daughter. Kalea is just like Jessica. She is vivacious and fun. She was almost raised here with us. We have to get her back safely. We know that if we can find Kalea, we will find Jessica."

Rita also let it be known that Jessica had an asthma problem and might be without an inhaler. For that reason, Rita thought that law enforcement agencies should keep tabs on hospitals and medical clinics, where Jessica might show up.

Because of the fear that Gabe might still be heading out to Idaho to harm various members of Jessica's family, all of those individuals were now under police protection. Bingham County sheriff

Dave Johnson told a reporter, "At this point, we are going to continue checking the different residences. We will make sure that everything is sound. Our concern is still the same today as it was the first day. The situation hasn't changed."

Since Jessica was going to be taken in for questioning as a material witness when the trio was found, Bill Pope let it be known that he and his wife would take custody of Kalea as soon as that occurred. In the meantime, all he and Rita could do was pray, hope and wait. He said, "It's out of our hands now."

Rita Pope's information was not only being disseminated in the Idaho media, but in Oregon media as well. She said about Jessica, "She loves her husband. I know she does or she wouldn't be with him. But I don't think she knows what he did. And our baby granddaughter is in the middle of it, and I'm afraid we won't see her again."

In a different interview, Fred Pope said, "I spoke with Jessica one week before the shooting. I asked her if she was all right and she said that she was, but I could tell in her voice that things weren't right."

Rita added, "If Gabe did this to his mother, I'm sure that he didn't tell Jessica that he did it. I'm sure that he told her, 'Somebody else did it to my mom, and they're coming after us, and we've got to get out of here.'" Rita was right on target with this remark.

And around this time, the people in the Bandon area had a new revelation through the media. It was the first time they heard about the Morrises' connection to the Eschlers. *The World* ran a story with the headline COQUILLE MAN GAVE FUGITIVE GUN. The article related that Gabe had once dated the Eschlers' daughter and had gone to their church. Gabe and family had shown up on the evening of February 8 with a story of terrorists, murders and working for the government. The article went on to relate about Gabe's request for .40-caliber ammunition, Fred giving him a 9mm Beretta handgun and loaning him his car. Also in the article were references to the Morrises' financial woes.

A reporter wanted to know if DA Frasier was going to file charges against Fred Eschler. Frasier responded, "I don't see how I can. He didn't know about the murders." And as far as Jessica Morris went, Frasier explained his reason for a material witness warrant. "Just because you are at the scene of a crime doesn't mean you're guilty of a crime. I don't know what she knows. I can't charge her with anything until I know what she knows."

By now, the Coos County Sheriff's Office had the story up on their website. They also let the Popes know that if Gabe, Jessica and Kalea weren't tracked down before Saturday, February 20, another segment would air on *America's Most Wanted*. Justin Pope, Jessica's brother, reacted to this by saying, "This is such great news for our family. If we can start to get some national attention, hopefully, we will be able to find my sister and Kalea."

Unfortunately, much of the nation was still glued to their television screens watching the Winter Olympics. And despite law enforcement's concerns that Gabe might be heading to Idaho to harm members of Jessica's family, he was, in fact, more than a thousand miles away, heading in another direction.

CHAPTER 20

One of the constants in Gabe's life was that he was addicted to online video games. That was particularly true of the game Perfect World. And this addiction actually helped him in keeping one step ahead of the law. Most investigators believed he might be heading to some relative's home in either Louisiana or Florida. In fact, Gabe was using a network of people he played online video games with to make his cross-country journey.

The route from St. Louis took them on I-70, across the Mississippi River, through Illinois, and to Indianapolis, Indiana. They headed from there onto I-69 to Fort Wayne, Indiana, and into Michigan. Jessica recalled, "I tried to make it so when we arrived in Michigan, it would be morning, and we wouldn't need a place to stay."

Jessica recalled, "We were looking for a library, where he could get on a computer, but I think it was a Sunday and we couldn't find one that was open. We were driving though Detroit and asking for directions. Gabe had me stop at a comic book store and he asked a guy there where he could get online. And the guy said that a library was open down the street. So Kalea and I dropped Gabe off there and we went to get some gas, and then we went back and picked him up. He said he had sent an e-mail to someone named Judy, who lived in Virginia. And she responded right back to him with her phone number. And he said that he would give her a call, and then he and I and Kalea went and ate dinner. Afterward, we went and found a telephone and he got the number for the lady in Michigan and she didn't want to help us." In fact, this "lady" was only in her midteens, but Jessica probably didn't know that. In essence, they had driven all the way to Michigan for nothing.

Jessica continued, "So Gabe called Judy back and asked if we could come down there to Virginia and meet her and her husband. And she said yes. So we got on the road to Virginia. I started begging at places for gas money."

The route took them across Ohio. Jessica recounted their experience there: "We were in a residential neighborhood. We pulled off on an exit, and I didn't know what he was going to do. He stopped and pulled out the gun, and there was an embankment and a house, and he shot at the embankment. He shot three times. Then we got back on the interstate and he was driving. And a police car went by really fast with its lights on. And

Gabe said, 'See, that policeman is now going to where we just were.' He said it was so the police wouldn't be where we were going."

This was just one more example of Gabe's irrational behavior. All it did was alert police to the fact that someone had discharged a gun illegally in a residential neighborhood.

From Ohio, the route took them to Pittsburgh, Pennsylvania, and on the Pennsylvania Turnpike to 1-70, through Maryland and finally Washington, D.C. Judy's house was right across the Potomac River, in Dumfries, Virginia.

Judy recalled, "Gabe called to arrange a meeting and he was calling from a 703 area code. He said that he was in Arlington, Virginia, and we arranged to meet at an Uno's restaurant in Woodbridge, Virginia. We went there and waited there forever, and he called back a couple of hours after we got there. He asked where we were, and we said we were waiting for him at Uno's."

Jessica said about all of this, "We called them in D.C. and they gave us directions, and we didn't know where it was. We took a wrong road. So we drove down into a neighborhood and there was a guy who was standing there waiting for a bus. And Gabe asked him if he needed a ride, and so we gave him a ride. And we dropped him off at a roundabout near a hotel or something.

"We pulled off at an exit too soon, and we were

lost and ended up driving around for three hours while Judy waited with her husband at the place they told us about. And we finally found it. And we went to a wrong one and Gabe called Judy. So Kalea and I went and used a restroom, and when we came back, Gabe said they were at a place about forty-five minutes away. And we finally found it."

Gabe had gone to Uno in Manassas, Virginia, by mistake. They had been waiting for Judy Ward and Doug Miller (pseudonym) to show up there. Finally realizing his mistake, he drove Jessica and Kalea to the restaurant in Woodbridge.

Jessica recalled of the first meeting, "Judy and Doug were sitting at the bar when we walked in. And so we sat down and Gabe started talking to them. And Kalea kept saying, 'Mommy, I'm hungry.' And I went looking for and found some peanuts, so we started eating peanuts."

When Gabe and his family first met Judy and Doug, Judy recalled, "They had nothing. They just barely had the clothes on their backs. And at the restaurant, we talked a lot about God and helping people. And he said there was another girl in the game that he had talked to, and she was just sixteen years old. And Gabe said he wanted to protect her because her parents were in the process of a divorce, and he got the impression that they didn't care about her. He drew out my compassion about this. And Gabe and his family needed a place to stay for a week."

Despite barely knowing Gabe, except on the

Internet, Judy and Doug agreed. The Morrises came over to Judy and Doug's nice suburban home in Dumfries. It was a house that Doug's mom was letting them live in.

Jessica recollected, "Doug offered to get a pizza to share, and we ate that while they talked. Since we only had the ten dollars, Gabe asked them if we could stay with them. And Judy said we could."

As it turned out, Gabe, Jessica and Kalea did stay at the house that Judy and Doug shared. Gabe, Jessica and Kalea were given a bedroom, and Judy and Doug took another room, which was not their usual bedroom. Jessica recalled, "We got their bedroom, which had, like, a king-sized bed, and they slept in a different room. Gabe may have stayed up that night. I don't remember. I was really tired and went to sleep.

"The next day Doug took us over to a sandwich shop and bought us some lunch. He was very nice and very kind. I remember at one point I told Judy, 'It's really hard to take charity,' and she just smiled."

The next day, Judy discovered something that really concerned her. She looked in her closet and there was a small blue bag. In the bag was a semi-automatic pistol. But then she remembered that Gabe supposedly worked for the air force on secret missions. She assumed he needed this weapon for his job. What she didn't seem to consider was, why was a secret operative so short of money?

Judy recalled, "My husband drove a truck, and

we didn't give Gabe or Jessica any money. My husband pays for our meals and putting gas in the car and things." Gabe and his family just basically hung out at their house, eating their food and not having any money to contribute.

Judy did say that at least Jessica helped out a little bit around the house. "She did cook. She was very, very quiet and didn't say much. One night my brother and my husband's best friend just showed up at that house, and she didn't eat until everybody else ate.

"Every time she talked, she was very tentative. About Gabe, everything he did, she justified as being God's work or whatever. I asked her one time when he wasn't around, did she ever doubt his actions or what he says, and she said no. She did say sometimes something seems off, but that was just her insecurities and lack of faith in him."

One of the more incredible lies Gabe told Judy and Doug was about the living arrangements that had occurred in Bandon, Oregon. Judy recalled, "He said that he had a house and he let his mom and her boyfriend stay there. They took care of it while he was out doing business. When he was not there, they would stay there. I got an impression of the place that it was remote, not within a city with a lot of lights, because he talked a lot about the sky. He didn't go into a lot of detail about the house."

As far as Gabe's early life, he told Judy that his mom had been a prostitute when he was young. Something that was totally untrue, of course. Gabe said they had been living on the streets, which was also untrue. And as far as being in Michigan, Gabe told Judy that he had gone there because he had a grandfather buried there.

A big concern for Jessica was that she noticed plaques on the walls of the house noting that Doug's mom worked for the police department in some capacity. It seemed to concern Gabe as well. He told Jessica, "Get ready to leave. Not immediately, but get ready."

By February 17, Judy recalled, "Gabe kept talking about Florida. My husband and I always go to Florida for a vacation, and Gabe was talking about going to Florida or getting an RV, or traveling all over the place visiting different people. Just hanging out and having a good time."

Judy didn't drink, but Gabe and her husband did. She said later, "My husband came back from work and brought some absinthe, some Southern Comfort and Captain Morgan. Gabe got very, very drunk. And he got sick. Jessie tasted some absinthe, and I tasted it, but we didn't drink."

The most amazing thing was, Judy saw Jessica, whom she called "Jessie," smoke marijuana with Gabe. And more than that, Gabe wanted to try salvia, which was legal in the state. He tried it and tripped out.

Judy added that around this time, her "sister came over, and she was a little late getting back after dropping a friend off somewhere else. And Gabe said, 'Let's drive around to the friend's house to see if she's there.' He had the gun with him. He had the ammo clips on his lap, and he got out of the car. He went over to a 7-Eleven and got an apple, and while he did that, he had me hold the clips of ammo." Judy didn't know if he took the gun with him into the convenience store or just kept it under the seat.

The initially charming Gabe was now overtaken by Gabe and his all-too-frequent rants. Judy said later, "I didn't start to get really scared until the weekend. That's when there were, like, two different sides to him. Like he just completely flipped to a different demeanor. He got more aggressive, more demanding. He was getting very restless, and that's when I started to get scared. But I didn't know where the fear was coming from.

"He was talking about all kinds of things. He was talking about hanging out with Snoop Dogg and Jay-Z, and I was like, 'Come on, I can't believe this.' And he brought up about how his mom tried to poison him. It was rat poison. And he said they stuck around for a month trying to reconcile. And there was an urgency in his voice. He led me to believe that he felt threatened, so he shot his mom and her boyfriend. I was led to believe he shot them just once.

"I was there, and Jessica and Kalea were there

when he said this. And he looked over at her and said, 'Didn't you see me shoot my mom and her boyfriend?' and she said that she heard, and then she saw the bodies later. But she never said she physically saw him shoot them."

Judy added that Gabe told her that his mom had hired someone to kill him or something like that. It was all very unclear. And that was part of the reason he had to shoot her. "His mom was supposedly doing it for money. Like one hundred thousand dollars or something. She was heading for the door, and he knew somebody else was behind the door, and he felt threatened. And that's when he shot her and the man." This was yet another of Gabe's continually evolving stories about the shootings.

Gabe was also becoming more and more persistent about having things his own way. Judy recalled, "He wanted me and Doug to go with him, and we were both being resistant. We couldn't just jump up and leave, and I wasn't leaving without Doug. But whenever they went anywhere, we were always with them. There was one time, I think it was Saturday, we went back to Uno's to eat and the place was crowded. We were sitting at the bar area and the bartender was backed up with dishes piled up, glasses piled up, and the waitress waiting for drinks. And Gabe got mad. He went and spoke with the manager and the manager got short with him. And

Gabe left the table. He left the restaurant. He got in his car and he left. He wasn't gone for very long, maybe ten minutes, and he came back and he said he had to go take out his aggression. He said he went over to the gym and he picked a fight with somebody. He didn't go into details beyond that."

It was all becoming very weird and scary for Judy by that point, but still she did not ask Gabe and his family to leave. And it may have been around this time that Gabe and Judy had sex. Judy thought that Jessica knew about this and she was either okay with it or was so browbeaten by Gabe that she didn't make any complaints. And apparently Doug did not know about this at all.

By Saturday, Gabe was very restless. Judy said later, "He always said that he was going to leave by Monday. And he always said I was going with him. He tried to convince me to go with him, with or without my husband. And I said 'No, I can't go without my husband.' I told him outright, 'I'm not going with you,' and he said, 'Yeah, you are!'

"He started packing on Saturday night. He and his wife started packing up my clothes. They kept saying we were going to leave now. 'We're going to leave now.' But they kept putting if off because I was resistant. He kept threatening me that he was leaving, and I had been sick. I had been sick for years. I recently had surgery last year and he knew about it. I wasn't doing very well physically. So he, and my husband, and his wife there for support, did a prayer, and I did feel better. He used that against me. And he said that if I didn't go with him, I would be sick again, that I would start hurting again, and I was scared.

"I was scared of the pain, and scared of him. Because at that point, he started threatening me. He never told me where we were [specifically] going. He always said we were going to Florida. The night before they had my clothes laid out, not in bags, but just laid out aside. Both of them did that. And he tried to get me to gather some items myself, and I never did. But I always had a to-go bag packed, that just had basic toiletries, toothbrush and stuff like that."

Apparently, Gabe told Doug a slightly different tale about the murders, and added that he had to kill his mother to protect his family. As to the reason why, Gabe said that his mother was "evil" and had been hired by the people who were trying to kill him and his family.

In this tale, Gabe said that his mother was part of the plan with Bob Kennelly to poison him with rat poison. And he said that he'd ingested a lot of rat poison, and that would have killed a "normal human being." However, he was able to heal himself because he was beloved by God.

One of Gabe's most outlandish claims to Doug was that there was a conspiracy by the government to set off fault lines in California and sink it into the ocean. Perhaps the reason why Doug did not turn Gabe in to the police was because he thought the man was just a raving lunatic and everything he said was either a lie or a delusion.

CHAPTER 21

On Monday morning, February 22, Judy recalled, "I think Gabe knew he was surrounded. He started freaking out. Because his urgency—it went from restlessness to urgency on Monday morning. That's when I got really, really scared because I had no idea what was going on. My mother-in-law called me and wanted me to get out of the home. I found out later she had gone to work and was talking about Gabe to a couple of her coworkers, and one of the coworkers asked what his name was. So my mother-in-law told the woman because he had used his real name. And you know what? This woman looked it up on the computer and a story came back about *America's Most Wanted*. And that's when my mother-in-law called it in to the police.

"Anyway, my mother-in-law called my cell phone and didn't get in touch with me right away. And Gabe came into the room and said she had been trying to call me and to call her back. So I called her back and she said her mother was in the hospital up in Fairfax and she needed me to take her car up to her. She was basically trying to get me out of the house, and I could tell by her voice that what she was saying wasn't true.

"Gabe was sitting right there. I got off the phone with her and then he said to call her back and to tell her I was going to take a shower first and then be there in thirty-five minutes. So I did call her back and told her that. Then Gabe said to call her back again and ask where the keys were to her car. So I did.

"Basically, Gabe was biding time, and she called back again somewhat later. And in the meantime I was telling him I was not going. And that's when he started putting my clothes in bags and Jessica started getting their stuff together and packing up Kalea's stuff. Right before we walked out the door, my mother-in-law called again. And right at that time, I don't know why, my brother walked in the door.

"I was standing at the top of the stairs. And my brother walked in and said, 'They have the roads blocked off to the entrance of the neighborhood.' And there was a SWAT team out there and snipers on the roofs. And that's when Gabe flipped out."

Around 10:30 A.M., Special Weapons and Tactical (SWAT) team members started blocking all routes in and out of Dominion Drive in the Prince William Estates neighborhood. Snow lined the roadways, and it was a very cool and shadowed morning under the trees.

The SWAT team was actually a part of the Capital Area Regional Fugitive Task Force (CARFTF) and they were suited up, heavily armed and ready for anything. They already knew all of the wild claims Gabriel Morris had been making to everyone, and he was clearly unbalanced. The worst fears were that they might now be headed into some kind of hostage situation or a shoot-out. This could be especially dangerous, since they knew Gabe had been a trained police officer. They didn't know what kinds of weapons he might have with him or if he was wearing body armor.

Judy recounted, "He didn't say anything. He just basically pushed us out the door and started giving orders. I was completely terrified. He found my dad's rifle, and I don't know if it even had any ammunition in it, but he wrapped it in a blanket and handed it to me. I don't know what he planned on doing with it. And then he took all the bags and took them out. He said I was riding with him. And he made my brother give him the keys to his SUV. He told my brother to drive his car." In fact, Gabe made Jessica and Kalea go in the Silver Ford Taurus with Judy's brother.

By that means, perhaps Gabe was hoping to get away with Judy while the others were detained. If so, he was sacrificing Jessica and Kalea at this point in time.

Judy recalled, "I was so scared. I just kept thinking, 'Somebody stop this! Please, somebody stop this!' Then we got to the intersection, and that's when the police pulled behind us. They had their lights on, and pulled us over and stopped us. And Gabe actually stopped."

At around noon, as the Ford Taurus and Ford Explorer made their way from the driveway onto Dominion Drive, the SWAT team members suddenly broke cover and swooped in. Jessica, Kalea and Chris were detained first. Gabe and Judy made it a little farther, onto Curtis Drive, when they were suddenly blocked by squad cars.

As the *Inside NoVa* weekly newspaper related, *The roar of cars and trucks on nearby Interstate 95, which runs adjacent to the neighborhood, drowned out commands shouted from a police bullhorn used to coax Morris from the car. From 150 yards away, police could be heard telling Morris to get out of the car with his hands up.*

Despite their worst fears, Gabe surrendered without incident, even though he was in possession of a loaded .45 pistol and a rifle in the vehicle. Jessica surrendered as well without incident.

Judy recalled, "Gabe saw the police car lights and he said, 'Oh, well.' I'm not sure exactly how he phrased it, but he said, 'They're pulling us over.' And I said, 'I'm really, really scared.' And he said, 'Just do what they say.' And then that was it. He cooperated one hundred percent and it was over."

* * *

The U.S. Marshals Service (USMS) soon came out with a short statement about the arrests, and they also related how many law enforcement agencies had been looking for Gabe, Jessica and Kalea. These included the USMS, FBI, U.S. Marshals Oregon Fugitive Task Force, Washington County Sheriff's Office, Portland Police Bureau, Oregon State Police, Multnomah County Probation and Parole, Clackamas County, Coos County Sheriff's Office and even the Oregon National Guard.

Of course, Bill and Rita Pope were the two people waiting most anxiously for an apprehension of Gabe, Jessica and Kalea. On that Monday morning, they got a phone call from the Bingham County Sheriff's Office. Rita said later, "Bill phoned me immediately at work. He was in tears, and he said, 'They're okay!' During the past two weeks, I had every worst-case scenario running through my mind. I couldn't stop thinking of the horrible things that might have happened."

But the worst things didn't happen to Jessica or Kalea. In fact, the Popes were informed that Kalea was now with police officers, eating popcorn and "having a great time." Prince William County Police Department (PWCPD) 1st sergeant Kim Chinn later said, "We've got her at the station and we've had her coloring and giving her snacks."

Around that same time, a reporter for the *Blackfoot Morning News* contacted the Popes. Bill Pope said that they were anxiously awaiting word that they could go and see their daughter and get their granddaughter. Bill added, "I do know because of the spirit and nature of my daughter that I'm sure she wasn't involved in it. He probably threatened her and told her he would kill her if she didn't stay right with him."

Bill was wrong in this assessment, but it may have been a type of brainwashing on Gabe's part that had made Jessica go along with the whole cross-country scenario. By February 2010, she was fully under his spell.

Rita Pope told the reporter that she had pleaded with her daughter not to go to Oregon in an attempt to patch up her marriage with Gabe in 2009. Rita said that Jessica knew before going that Gabe had put them deep in debt. Rita added, "But I don't think she really knew how bad it was until she got out there. For years, she was the only one working to support the family."

The Popes were determined to go to Virginia in person and collect their granddaughter. They made plans to drive down to Salt Lake City, Utah, and catch the red-eye to Washington, D.C. Rita told an Idaho reporter, "I just can't wait to get there and hold my little granddaughter."

CHAPTER 22

Gabe was taken to an interview room in the PWCPD. Despite the fact that he sat in a straight-backed chair for the next four hours, he never complained or whined like some suspects did. And though he did not look outwardly agitated, his voice betrayed an inner turmoil.

The two investigators, one with the last name of Coady and the other with Troutner, were not confrontational in style. They tended to let Gabe answer questions in any length that he wanted. Coady started out by asking how Gabe was at the moment. Despite the circumstances, he answered, "Just fine." Then he added, "I'm breathing, alive."

Coady replied, "You can't beat that."

To which, Gabe said, "Well, it's a matter of time, I suppose." Which indicated he thought he might be heading toward the death penalty.

Coady said, "Well, it's a matter of time for all of us."

Gabe responded, "Right. You know, I'm not gonna

make this difficult for you. You have questions—just shoot 'em and I'll tell you the truth. I'm not gonna play games with you. I'm not gonna try and be intelligent. You guys got a job and I'm not gonna frustrate it. If I'm in your custody, that's what should be."

Coady said there were two sides to every coin. He wanted to hear what Gabe had to say about all of this. "We're not gonna get a dome light out or beat you with rubber hoses. That's not what we do."

Troutner added, "You're in custody. We gotta take care of some business first." So then Coady read Gabe his Miranda rights, and Gabe said he understood them and wanted to keep talking, anyway.

Coady then said, "What it sounds to us is you've had a bad time of it. You've had some pretty strange things happen in your life recently."

Gabe stated, "Yeah, for sure. It's been a strange life altogether, to be honest with you. But what can you do?"

Troutner added, "I know that Judy has a lot of respect for you, 'cause she really feels that you helped her out [with her medical condition]. And Doug said they don't really understand how. All she knows is that she physically feels better."

Gabe responded, "She will always be that way. She'll never go back to the way she was before."

Troutner said, "Yeah, I think she believes that too. I was talking to Doug and he said, 'You know, I don't understand it. I don't, but it worked.' It meant a lot to Judy too, because she'd been in chronic pain for so long. And then just to have it go *poof*—that's pretty amazing."

Gabe replied it would be nice if everything could be that way.

So Troutner added, "It has been a long trip, hasn't it?" He might have meant from Oregon to Virginia. But Gabe took him to mean about his life. Gabe said, "It's thirty-three years so far."

Coady said, "I think probably the last three weeks have probably been the hardest, though, wouldn't they?"

Gabe's answer completely surprised them. He said, "No."

Coady replied, *"No?"*

Gabe continued, "No. I mean, you know, you live every day and you're grateful for each one. And the experiences you have at each point and each turn teach you something new about yourself, and the people around you, and the world you live in. Sometimes it rains and sometimes it's sunny."

Coady said, "More often than not, there's a reason for a man's actions."

Gabe agreed that was true, and added, "I can tell you anything you want to know. I'm not gonna lie to you."

Troutner spoke up and said, "We heard second-hand that you were concerned about getting sick and—"

Gabe broke in with, "We all get sick. I mean, people freak out and say, 'I don't wanna get sick from this. I don't wanna get sick from that.' We're all going to die from getting sick from something. But, I mean, shit, you can be sick and then be fine the next day and—"

Troutner jumped in and said, "Your family was getting sick."

Gabe saw where he was going with this. He replied, "Oh, the poison." And then he added something very odd: "Well, I'm not worried about that sickness, because we don't have it anymore."

Troutner was surprised by this comment as well, because the supposed motive for the killings was because Bob Kennelly and possibly even Robin were poisoning Gabe's family. At least, that is what Gabe had been telling Jessica.

Troutner said, "Um, you did what you had to do to protect your family. You got 'em out of the situation. You got 'em away from what was making them sick. Like any father would be expected to do."

Coady added, "You're gonna do whatever you have to do to protect your kids, right?"

Gabe responded, "I'll tell you what I did. Where to start? You tell me."

Troutner replied, "We understand you had a rough childhood. I'm just telling you what your friends told us."

Gabe said, "Okay, my dad took me out in the ocean when I was about four years old. He dropped me into it and came back to the beach. I was aware that he had done that. And I passed out and blacked out and woke up in the water. So either I'm nuts or I remember that happening. But I don't really feel like I'm crazy. I mean, I've been to psychiatrists and they say I'm a little intelligent. Dad dropped me off in the ocean and I walked back to shore, and Mom and Dad looked shocked that I came out, and I'm happy."

And then Gabe accused his half brother of beating him and sexually abusing him as a child—the same Jesse who had always taken his side and tried to protect him.

Gabe said, "I remember when I was, like, six, he got the local black girl and forced me to have sex with her. Him and all his little friends. And, like, Mom, she says she loves me, but beats me with the wooden spoon and stuff. And I mean I'm not angry or bitter. I love them. I mean, when I describe my mother, she's, like, the only reason I made it through my childhood somewhat decent. Though, I suppose, in these circumstances, that's somewhat questionable."

And then Gabe went on a rant, without hardly drawing a breath. "Even as a young child, I learned to close my eyes and ask for help, and that's why I'm alive." Gabe seemed to be indicating that he asked for help from God. "That's how I continue, and that's how I grow. That's how I learn things and can bless the people around me.

"I know that Mom made more than just an attempt, and then she took off. And I think he's dead (his father), and a sister I had never met called me and said she had his ashes and wanted me to be involved with that. But I told her no. I don't want anything to do with it. I've never loved him, never knew him. It's hard to talk about it.

"When I was nineteen, I looked up and I realized I was making decisions with my life based on weaknesses versus faith. At nineteen, I decided I was done with weaknesses and fears. But I did love everybody. I didn't want to hate anyone. And so, quite honestly, I turned to God and I asked him if this whole Jesus story and spirituality was true. And I got a resounding yes.

"So it wasn't, like, 'You're holy. You need to save the world.' It was, like, 'I love you, man. Come to me.' Very humbly. And then I tried to forgive my dad. I made contact with him. He said, 'Why don't you come out to Oregon and spend some time with me?'" (Apparently, Danny Morris lived in Oregon at that point.) "You know, he hadn't changed a lot. It's hard to try and forgive someone who's done stuff to you. And I let him go out of my life. He ain't gonna change. I even invited him to my (Author's note: Gabe mentioned some kind of event), and my mother had a reception at her place.

"I know some special things. I went over to Australia on a mission. I learned some special things over there from beautiful people. Polynesians, Samoans, Aborigines."

Then his mind quickly went back to his mom. "She ended up being in a relationship with an individual named James Anstey. And she had a heinous relationship with him." This was an odd comment. Gabe had spoken previously of James as the good father he never had. But now he seemed to be lashing out at everyone who had been close to him.

Gabe went on to accuse James of all sorts of illegal activities, which were not true, and talked about the divorce. Then Gabe ranted about his mom supposedly giving children medications from a hospital, and it wasn't clear if he was talking about himself and Jesse as children. This quickly changed into the subject of Bob Kennelly.

Gabe said, "Boy, the hell that guy gave to her life. She didn't have a clue. I'm pretty clued in. I try to pay real close attention. And we (Gabe, Jessica and Kalea) go over there and try to make a life with him. We try to make Mom happy. We try to bring energies and the knowledge that we have and healing, and love, consideration, prayers and music.

"They got medical marijuana up there in Oregon, and they got a future and can just relax. Get off those crazy meds that are making you crazy. Mom is goin' nuts. And I start overhearing conversations about how they want to hurt us, because I don't sleep very much. I stay up. And I felt that something was wrong and I had to pay attention to what people were saying. And I caught Robert putting rat poison in food that night. So I purposefully drank in this food because I wanted him to see it wasn't gonna affect us, because I was pretty certain Jessica and Kalea had gotten some.

"So I shared it with them, slept close to them, prayed for them and took it (the poison) out of them. I experienced it myself for me to die. I mean, he made a solid threat on our life. And it was a situation where I had an advantage and took it. And I have been a police officer before.

"I have seen rape cases. I've seen beating cases. And I heard him (Bob) talking about a building with a nice little room for himself, which my mom never knew. I can put that on the table. Okay, I have to spend the rest of my life in prison so that my daughter can believe in her father. She saw me do these things. And I know she's got a memory, because I had a memory from the age of four. And that's what the world wants to do to individuals who can do these types of things.

"I'm happy, okay. I mean, have I had a hard day? No. The world's having a hard day. And when I'm sitting next to a cellmate and I talk to him and I discuss with him his life, I will love him just as much as I've loved my daughter, as I love my mom, as I love anyone else in the world. And we'll see what happens because He's the reason I'm here. So are you two. So I mean, there ain't no complications. I ain't gonna tell you a different story."

CHAPTER 23

Gabe continued, "If you go through my past and you talk to people I've known, you go to Sydney, Australia, and talk to a number of families over there, they're gonna tell you the same thing. But we don't make paper out of it. You know what I'm saying? I don't put a medal on my chest. I mean, that's not what it's about.

"Like Michael Jackson, you know, doing crazy things. So, man, that's it! That's all there is to it. My motive? Protection of my family, because I'm not gonna wait for a judge to put some guy . . ." His mind went off on another angle. "Some guy, I believe in Bingham County, Idaho, raped his pregnant stepdaughter and been sent to some other county." Gabe seemed to indicate that the person who raped her got off without any conviction.

Troutner said those kinds of things were frustrating to a police officer.

Gabe alleged that Bob Kennelly was about to rape Kalea. And then he said, "I'm not gonna let

Kalea ever believe that at one point her dad would ever let anything like that happen to her. So if I have to die, if I have to go to jail, and have to spend the rest of my life in prison, I will do that for her, because she's the most important thing I've ever had in my life. No matter who takes care of her, she'll always know that she was loved."

Troutner said, "Well, she's a beautiful, happy little girl."

Gabe continued, "She'll always be. She'll probably teach the individuals that get to take care of her a whole hell of a lot more than they'll ever teach her." Then he laughed.

Troutner said, "Yeah, some souls just shine and affect people around them for their whole life. I can certainly understand why you made such a positive impression on Doug and Judy. I mean, you're very well spoken. You're obviously very intelligent. You have a sort of calm demeanor that just sorta brings my blood pressure down and—"

Gabe did not let him finish. Instead, he said, "He's an amazing Creator, gentlemen, and that's the way He is. He is no angry individual who hates us all. You feel confident. You feel like everything is going to be just fine, and you feel like you wish that your kids would feel that way when they sit next to you. That everything is going to be all right."

Coady interrupted Gabe and said, "I think Detective Troutner and I, we're not adversarial kinda guys. We're more into conversations. We're not here to be the bad guys."

Gabe agreed and replied, "I didn't even believe that for a second. I truly believe you guys are here working to provide something for yourselves, for your own ambitions, for family. I mean, you're doing a good job. There's a lot of people out there, when I first started my career in law enforcement—I had a heart for seeing injustices. Shit, I've seen 'em my whole life. I think I poked my first dead body when I was seven. Oh, my gosh, it's horrible! I didn't even know what it was. I mean, you see that stuff and you realize we need the business of preventing it. We're in the business of cleaning up after fucking addicts. Sorry for my language."

Troutner expounded on this code of conduct. "Um, you're called to do this, because you want to help. He thinks you can help, so He calls you to this protection like a preacher or something. You do this service at your own peril, because you have to see these things. You do have to interact with that part of society. I mean, you put yourself at risk. . . ."

Gabe interjected, "I think every man should be one. I think they should reach a certain age and they should realize that they're the only ones that have the ability to use their strengths and their manipulations to take advantage of anybody." Then Gabe's following line of reasoning didn't make a whole lot of sense. "And there should be a community where people, if they want to do that, they're invited to leave. And if they voice it and they speak it and they show interest, then they're told to leave. And if they act on it, they're punished and not welcome back."

Gabe went on, "Because, I mean, shit, you touch my little girl, you're probably gonna touch someone else's little girl, and, shit, man, I read psychological books. I've sat down with psychiatrists for, like, twenty million hours talking to them. They're the ones who go down to the state prisons and talk to people and ask, 'Why did you do this and why did you do that?'"

Troutner said, "That's the thing, you know, especially the ones that touch kids—they don't ever stop."

Gabe agreed and added, "I am not God's sword here on Earth to save the universe. I'm someone who pays attention to what He wants, and He says, 'I'm not going to let anything happen to [your] girl.'" Apparently, God was talking to Gabe by saying, "'So get to work, son.'"

Once again, Gabe quickly changed gears. "If someone around me is sick, and they do believe me, it will work. If someone wants to hurt anybody that I'm called to protect, I'm going to invite them not to do it. I'm going to say, 'You best not do it.' I'm going to scheme against someone. 'Hey, man, I feel your heart. I see what you want. Is that what you want? You like little girls? You like women? Show me what you got in your head.'"

Then as if he was talking to that person, Gabe said, "'Let's have a couple of drinks here. Let's have ten. Because I don't mind ten shots of gin. I can make it through that, no problem.'"

Coady wanted to know if Gabe had confronted Bob Kennelly about something in this regard. Gabe said, "Yeah. He said, 'I like porn.' And when he got really, really drunk, and when he got really, really high, he talked about it. He mentioned how he did like looking at smaller women. He talked about how over in Russia, they know their place. And, you know, he's sitting out there and bouncing around like all's good. He had a wife that mysteriously died. Come on, now, she had cancer from what?"

Troutner pushed Gabe on this. "So he's confirming what you're suspecting?"

Gabe said, "Yes, but who do I tell? Not someone who's going to give me eight months."

Troutner added, "So you weren't going to wait for it to happen."

Gabe replied, "No, it's not that. I'm not going to act until he makes a move, until I caught him putting poison in the food, until I catch him being physically active toward me."

And then as if talking to Bob, Gabe said, "'Okay, you're with my mother. I love her. You're a king, man. You're obviously a tough fella.'" And then that abruptly stopped, and Gabe said, "Okay, so here goes. Because the biggest charge against me is probably going to be homicide. Maybe two."

Coady jumped in and said, "So, how'd that night happen?"

All Gabe did was sigh.

Troutner took his turn. "You said he [Bob] made a move. But you had a position, an advantage?"

Gabe responded, "Yes, I wanted to record his admission. And I didn't have a recording device. But I had the ability for Jessie to hear it. So she could overhear it and be a solid witness. And usually he kept a firearm with him. He had a concealed-weapons permit. He showed me more than one firearm he had in his home. And I knew that he thought that I was a threat, because I had showed him physically that he was not a threat to me. So oftentimes when men's egos get checked . . ." Gabe's thought ran out.

"I had overheard both my mom and him talking about taking advantage of us. They discussed it, and considering I have a four-year-old girl, I was going to talk to him and make him admit it. I had Jessie sleeping with Kalea in bed, and then one of them would be asleep. And so I approached him and told them to take me very seriously. I said, 'Please understand I'm here.' He reached. He didn't have a gun, but he reached. He reached back. I think he reached for what wasn't there. But if you gentlemen, who are in a law enforcement position, and you're talking to someone who thinks they're gonna get you, and they reach, you've been trained to respond. And I did."

Coady asked, "So you had a gun with you at the time?"

"Yes, I did."

Troutner wondered, "Was it your gun or one of his guns?"

"It was one of his guns. It was the HK. So, I mean, the rounds that were there were the rounds that were used. He made a move after I asked him not to."

Troutner asked, "Were you standing in front of him?"

Gabe said, "No, I was not. I was on the balcony. If you had the drawing, it would make sense."

Coady said he would grab a piece of paper for Gabe to draw on. Meanwhile, Gabe told Troutner, "You've got an upstairs and there's downstairs a little plaza."

Coady gave Gabe some paper and possibly a pencil. Then he asked Gabe, "You're not gonna give us any trouble, are you?"

Gabe responded, "Oh, gosh, hell no. I mean you know that."

"Okay, give me your handcuffs."

The handcuffs were removed and Gabe began drawing. "The house—there's, like, a doorway right here. You've got a stairway that starts up here. You've got the hallway, and you've got a bedroom here, and you've got a bedroom there. Kitchen here. Doorway there."

Gabe then said, "They walked down through the front door. And they started talking. They're together and I come out and say, 'Take me seriously! Have a seat!' And he came up that quick. He made a real quick move. Done."

Troutner asked, "Could they see you were holdin' a gun at that point? Do you think that's why he reached?"

Gabe answered, "No. I mean, he made a move. And I don't know my mom. I've never known her. I don't know anything. I don't know what she's got." (Author's note: Perhaps Gabe meant a weapon in her possession.) "I don't know how capable . . . All I know is she's making plans to hurt us and feed me rat poison. So he makes a move, and they're both dead."

CHAPTER 24

Troutner asked, "You shot 'em?"

Gabe said he did. So Troutner asked, "Do you remember how many times?"

Gabe said that he didn't know.

Troutner added, "In that situation, a cop doesn't ever remember. You know. They just shoot until the threat goes away."

Gabe replied, "My thought was, shit, make it not hurt for my mom. So hit, move down and make it not hurt. Enough shots to make 'em stop."

Coady asked where Bob and Robin had been standing, and Gabe showed him on the diagram he had made.

Troutner said, "Do you remember where you shot them when you came downstairs?" Gabe drew on the diagram and said, "Robert Kennelly was right here. And Mom was there."

Asked how Kennelly's last name was spelled, Gabe said, "Hell, I don't know."

This drew a rejoinder from Troutner. "You didn't know that guy at all, did you?"

Gabe replied, "Not very well."

Asked if his wife and daughter woke up at the sound of gunfire, Gabe said that they had. "And at that time, I wasn't hoping that anything would happen. I had some feeling, because there was a murderous intent already. My intent was to sit down and get them recorded, and get them to say a lot, and have a witness and make them stop. I had a little mic thing. And I had planned on having Jessica listen in. But the recorder wasn't on, and, like, all of this wasn't planned. Like, we were planning on coming back and talkin' to Bob and Mom. And there you go."

Coady said that Bob and Robin, obviously, had been shot, "and you need to get your family out of there, because you don't want them involved in all of this. So, what happens next?"

"Okay, we go and get the car. See, now, gentlemen, this is where we start getting into motives and 'why you do this' and 'why you do that.' I know there is no one else, except for a handful of people, who love their children as much as I love Kalea. And if you guys are Christian and you go to church, you can think I'm nuts. But guess what? So is He. I'm not coming in here and saying, 'I'm Jesus and I can cut people's heads off.' No, that ain't it. Motive for why you do what you do—well, does Kalea need to be in the possession of people who are gonna give her prescription meds to shut her the fuck up when she's supposed to? I said no. That ain't appropriate. That ain't even legal.

"So I gotta get Jessie and Kalea out of there, and let's find somewhere better than with the two of them. Whatever happens to me, I don't care. So, come on, gentlemen, if you're a woman, do you think you'd be a little bit intimidated by me? I mean, if you're small and have a kid. Yeah, it's going to be terrifying. And they might all say I'm a really nice guy, but at the same time it's scary.

"I mean, I've trained in martial arts since I was five or six years old, and I've done it intensely on my own with a master, with teachers, with people I've known. I've learned healing. I've learned praying. I've learned meditation. I've read books on anatomy and physiology. I've read books on botany. I've read books on just about everything there is out there so that I can better understand the world we live in. And what I've seen is an entire group of humanity steal and rob and take everything from everybody and then charge people a hundred dollars for just a fraction, when it's all out there and you put your hands on a woman who's been in enormous pain through pancreatitis for ten years going on.

"Kalea isn't going to have another human being in her life that can do that. So at least what I want to do is, I want to find someone that experiences this and have it happen to them. And then, maybe there are a few other people out there that Kalea . . ." Gabe then mumbled some unintelligible words.

"It's hard to find anybody who will even let someone put their hands on you and heal you. They don't even want it. They want to be sick. They want their meds. The want their calm-down factor.

"You know, they want their security. They would rather have security, even though their whole household is miserable. Solutions to problems can't be charged. You can't make money on a solution. And I can't get paid. Right? If a doctor could do this, he'd be a jillionaire. He'd do it for Magic Johnson. He'd do it for someone else and someone else, and then he'd get paid."

Perhaps to keep him talking, Troutner said, "I see what you're saying."

Gabe was very irritated that he hadn't been paid for his "healing powers." He said, "This ain't a paying job! I mean, I'm not going to say a lot more than what I've said, because you guys got it."

The detectives didn't want him to stop there, however. Troutner asked, "What happened to the HK?" They were referencing Bob's semiautomatic handgun.

Gabe either lied or he truly didn't remember. He answered, "It's gone. I don't know. I seriously don't know. I forget. I think I threw it out the window somewhere. And, honestly, I drink. That's part of it. People want to say, like, I'm an alcoholic. Some guys are alcoholics. I've met those and they beat women and they're pretty nasty. Some people drink and there's a different reason why they drink."

Troutner said, "You drink, like, to take the edge off?"

Gabe replied, "No. I drink to sometimes just shut me the fuck up so I can be faithful and just listen and stop getting my intellect and my ego and my dumbassedness and my forward planning and my . . . all my actions—why I sit there and ignore everyone around me—just to shut up!"

Coady asked, "Do you remember what vehicle you took?"

"I think it was a Dodge. Bob had a truck. White. I can tell you where it is, if you haven't found it."

Even though the detectives knew it had been found, Coady asked Gabe where it was, anyway, possibly to see if he would tell the truth.

Gabe answered, "It's in Coquille. Near the front of the Eschlers' home."

"A friend of yours?"

"I wouldn't say a 'friend.' A past acquaintance. I mean, people knew me when I first joined the church when I was nineteen. And Fred was the one who baptized me." Gabe left out a lot here, considering the fact that he had dated the Eschlers' daughter for years.

Gabe continued, "So I went to their home and I told them I was in trouble, and I said, 'I need a vehicle. I need a firearm. I need some money.' And then Fred gave it to me."

Troutner asked, "He have a gun?"

Gabe said that he did.

"Is that the Beretta?"

"Yeah, but I also had an HK with me."

"Well, we're not trying to get Fred in trouble. We're just trying to keep track of guns."

"Yeah, so I got the Beretta from Fred. I got the car. I got some money."

"Did you trade him?"

Gabe said that he hadn't done that.

"You didn't give the HK, like a trade?"

"No, I did not. I did throw the HK out the window. I do know that. I just can't remember when or how. I remember I was looking for it. And thinking, 'Man, why the hell did I throw it out the window?'"

The detectives wanted to know about Gabe's route after they left Coquille. Gabe answered, "We took a ride down to San Diego. We went to Oceanside. We stayed at a hotel down there. The gun—I mean, it's not going to be found, I guarantee you."

Of course, it already had been found.

Coady said, "Well, that's my concern. I don't want a kid to find it alongside the road."

Gabe replied, "No, he won't. I took the pieces apart. I'm pretty sure I did that." Gabe was either lying or he truly believed he had done that. "I don't have anything to hide. I'm serious. I'm not going to lie about where the gun is. I'm certain I took the cylinder out. No kid is going to find it and shoot somebody."

Troutner asked what Gabe's plan had been when he, Jessica, Kalea, Judy and Judy's brother were leaving, when they got caught. Gabe actually laughed and said, "I knew it was coming. But the safest way to do it was street style."

Troutner asked, "Yeah, but why'd you take everyone with you, if you knew you were going to get caught?"

"Because you don't want to get a door kicked down and guys coming at you and surprising you. You stopped two vehicles, right? I was not with my wife and daughter. I'm with Judy, and Judy's a little bit more brave and courageous and just got healed, so she has faith. I know what to do in these situations at a vehicle stop. You know that you're in public. So there are people watching. If you shoot wrong, if you go into a house . . . well, a vehicle stop is the safest way to get picked up."

Troutner said, "And you know you're not going to get shot, because there are witnesses?"

Gabe said, "No, no, no. It's just that I wanted everyone to get picked up safe."

Troutner asked, "Did you know we were out there?"

Gabe said that he did, and he added, "I knew a few of you were. It was pretty easy. I mean, the white Explorer down the road and then there was that vehicle coming down a back street. And then I saw a fella in another little black one, but I wasn't running because I was afraid."

Troutner said, "Well, they said you were very co-operative."

"Yeah, and I didn't want to give anybody any trouble, unless they want to hurt someone. My daughter has finally found a place and she visualized it. She's been in the experience really strong, and it's warmed everybody's hearts. She's had a personal experience. I went up to the top of the stairs, and she was there, and she looked down on me and said, 'I love you, Daddy.' It was, like, a really, really intelligent way of looking right at me.

"So it was like telling everyone, 'Everything is going great. We're gonna go on a trip down to Florida to have a vacation. It's all gonna be good.' We were going to have a good time. And I knew that Judy's brother was a real sweet guy and he wasn't going to get anything out of me. And with Jessie, I was telling her, 'Don't be foolish.'"

Troutner wanted to know when Judy and Doug figured out that he and Jessica were on the run. Gabe said, "They didn't. No, nobody ever thinks I'm wanted. They want a story. They want to think I work for the government. They want that, so I go along. Sometimes I do tell people different things to get them to feel relaxed and comfortable. They ask, 'Why do you seem to know how to shoot?' 'Oh, I worked for the military.' All right. Fine. Whatever you want to hear. Whatever makes you believe that your ego doesn't want to shoot me in the head because I'm a cop, and you can't shoot that well. Now, let's just say I worked for the military a long time ago. Who cares? I'm doing it because Tony (a person Gabe knew) comes back from Iraq and he's really enjoying this ability. And I'm a fine shooter. And I haven't been in the military, right? So him and his buddies want to talk to me about maybe having an accident on a training environment, to prove me wrong, or stuff like that. So, 'Hey, guys, I've had training like you.' Don't trip out. I'm not like some hillbilly that learned how to do it better than you. I'm just better. 'All right! I've got good training.' You know? Ego. It loves to get out there. So people hear you're in the military and that's intimidating. I mean, it's better than saying, 'I'm the Son of God. I'm Jesus.' And I'm not." By this point, Gabe was barely making any sense at all.

And then Gabe was off and running again. "That's the whole point. People want to say, 'Oh, you know, this guy, he wants to hurt people.' I don't want to hurt anybody. All I want to say is the truth, which is very difficult nowadays. Because you have to have a bowl of truth to talk about the truth, and half the time the proof . . . Well, the proof is just what you can find and what a lawyer is paid to find, to find his side of the story. So either I'm crazy or I know what I'm doing. I'm not going to sit here and plead my case and say I'm innocent, because I know the shit is out there. I'm guilty of what I've done, guilty as charged of what I've done, and much more. I mean, you can go through my past. I lifted a gun when I was five. So, yes, that kind of stuff does happen, and we live in a world where you cannot go and heal a fella in a hospital who's got cancer. You cannot go and go and do anything without someone thinking you're nuts.

"I would like to find an environment where my

daughter could grow up learning these things, because they're beautiful things. Where she can be safe. Unfortunately, here, I don't know where to find that. So I have to leave it in His hands, and I gotta deal with what I've done. Fair enough. I trust Him. He's the one who taught me how to do this stuff. So if He says, it's what to do, then that's it. I mean, there ain't no more motive. There ain't no more secrets.

"You guys probably have the stuff about what I've done or had around me. There are no people I know like me. There's a few I've seen in other countries. I mean there's some Polynesians. I've seen people who can do this." (Author's note: Gabe was probably alluding to his healing abilities.) "I've seen it in movies. But, quite honestly, gentlemen, I've never met another human being who can do the stuff I do. Believe it, or don't believe it. I mean, I love you, and I wish you would believe me. I wish you could go into the night, and get on your knees and ask Jesus, God, in His name and say, 'Hey, man, was this fella telling me the truth? I know we gotta do what we gotta do. We got a job, but, shit, man, what about my life? What about my kids? What about the people who are suffering? What about the next time I have a family member who goes down to the hospital and has cancer? Is that what I want to pay my money for and get into debt for? Or would I really like to know what it felt like for God to say, "Hey, why don't you come on over."'"

All Troutner could think to say to this diatribe was "I'm Catholic. I believe in miracles."

Gabe replied, "Amen." Then he was off and running again. "Keep preaching that, and hope that no one attacks you and you gotta be in this situation—"

Troutner interrupted and said about the shooting, "I'm like you. The training kicks in. We're trained and trained and trained. And the muscle memory kicks in."

Gabe veered off once more. "You know, in Salt Lake City, there's a fella that started pulling a gun—the guy that took me down was an off-duty police officer, but he had a sidearm. I didn't have a gun, and somebody starts going AWOL, and goes killing. Man, guess what? I'm running at him, not from him. So I just don't have a badge on me. I don't know. It's up to Him, really. I don't want to spend the taxpayers' money to argue over whether I didn't get some public attorney to come here and be stressed out because this case is way more fuckin' than they know what to do with. And the lawyer thinks this guy (meaning Gabe) is a crazy SOB."

Coady agreed, "Our lives would be a lot easier if more people felt that way."

"Yeah, life would be a lot easier if more people took responsibility."

All of them took a coffee break, and Coady said, "I'm tired."

Gabe piped up and responded, "I'll bet. You've got a lot of work to do."

They then all talked about the bad economy. Troutner joked to Coady that in thirty years he'd have about twenty-seven dollars in equity in his house.

CHAPTER 25

After the break, Gabe was in for more questioning. About his long-distance trip, a detective said, "Well, at least you got to see some of the country in the last few weeks."

Gabe replied, "I've seen a lot of the country. That's the point. You get out there and you look at people in their faces and you stop watching TV, and you realize that people out there are a whole lot different than ones on television."

Troutner added, "Especially the ones not on the Coast. I grew up in Washington State. And I know all about the Northwest's kind of liberal vibe."

Gabe added, "A lot of people are hungry. A lot of people are starving. A lot of people are hurting. A lot of people can't find a job, no matter how hard they try."

Coady said, "I'd like to go see your neck of the woods (Oregon) someday."

Gabe responded, "Go see the Coast while it's still there."

Coady asked, "Is it going to fall into the ocean?"

Gabe laughed. "Well, eventually it will."

Coady then asked if Gabe had been up to Seattle recently. He answered, "Yeah. Real recent. As a matter of fact, I took Jessica and Kalea up there before this all went down."

"Did you jump over and see any of the Olympic stuff up there?" Coady was referencing Canada.

"No, we went to [the] Pike Market, where they throw the fish and stuff. Just a road trip. You know, let Jessica see a better world. I mean, I kinda know what's coming."

Coady asked, "Oh, yeah?"

"Yeah, seeing things, but not always real clear on how things are going to come out. You sense things. Our egos get us into big trouble. Make us look like fools in front of each other. Now that we've got that out of the way, let's realize that we're different, but we can get along fairly well."

Coady said, "There was a time in the world where two guys could have a disagreement, duke it out and then go to the bar and have a beer together."

Gabe replied, "That's right. And now there's a time where two guys have a disagreement, they have a beer and they shoot each other."

"Exactly, and we deal with that a bunch."

Gabe added, "The world should say, 'There's plenty of food to go around. There's plenty of love. There's plenty of everything.' I don't see why you can drive downtown, where you have a lot of people going hungry, and they're throwing food away."

Troutner once again said he grew up in the Seattle area, and wanted to know why Gabe and his family had gone up there just before the shootings. Gabe said, "There's no ulterior motive. I'm sure there's some suspicions on that. You know, like maybe we had contacts." And then he angled off again, "But God knows everything, and so did Nostradamus a long time ago. I don't really think he was a prophet. I think he probably robbed a prophet and stole his writings and started making money off it.

"You know, John, sitting on the island, was shown a whole hell of a lot. And I'm going to tell you the rest of the story. So you all know what's going to happen, but you're going to die before it does." Gabe was alluding to the Book of Revelation. "I mean, you ain't got M. Night Shyamalan making a movie right now, so I'll just show it to you. Well, it's like fiery wheels spinning. And it's like someone's telling me this stuff. But his name ain't Fahad, and he ain't no Arab, and it ain't no Asian guy. It is a loving Creator, who would really love His children to know what they're gonna do in themselves, not what He's going to do to them. And it's all a bunch of children who don't want to know. Now, most people are going to say, 'This guy's a lunatic,' unless they meet me and sit down and have a chat. I'm kinda nutty, but, you know, I've seen nutty, and that ain't it. All three of us have seen it, and you know you're not looking at it. As a matter of fact, you probably know someone that lives in your neighborhood and they're a hell of a lot nuttier than me. Probably eight people in this department, and we don't need to confirm that."

Troutner laughed and said, "Yeah, I can touch that."

Gabe continued, "At least, we can have a laugh, because that's the truth. So, how does anybody know anything? How did anybody learn anything? How does someone learn how to make a car? How does someone learn to have the balls to stand up and say, 'My gosh, this slavery's getting' a little too old? Let's march right to D.C. and talk about this shit right in the open.'

"How do people get the inspiration? They get to a level of desperation when things get to be too much. Guess what? When you rub the lamp, the genie does show up. You know we can argue and say that the Catholic Church is true, this church is true, that church is true. Any human being that drops to their knees in humility and cries out for some help and some knowledge is gonna get it. And what they do with it is up to them. If they want to sell it and dance up on a stage and sing it and make their money, they can. Then that's their reward. A lot of people like yourselves use your talents, and I fairly think this occupation could pay you a whole hell of a lot more for what you're doing. And give you better medical insurance, but you do it because you've got the heart to serve. And I bet you anything, you guys have been inspired on cases plenty of times."

Coady agreed with that, and Gabe went on.

"Sometimes something catches your eyes. And you go, 'Oh, my gosh, I wouldn't have noticed that at all.' But then you go on. We all have lives. We all have bills to pay. We—"

Coady may have had enough of this rambling and asked, "So, how'd you get out here from Oregon?"

Gabe said, "Drove. You want to get a map? I'll tell you the route."

Coady replied, "What were some of the highlights? What did you see on the way?"

Gabe whistled and replied, "We stopped in a place and it was like an Indian relic. And we dropped in there and had a really awesome conversation with a gal that was trying to buy the place. And we felt what people were feeling out there. I mean, I know you guys feel what your wife is feeling sometimes. You walk in the door and you already know what she's feeling before you start talking."

Gabe would not stick to the subject of what route they had taken to Virginia. Instead, he said, "There's a reason ninety percent of our brain isn't working. Most people aren't quite ready when you're even using twenty-one percent of it. And if someone develops that talent, they usually get them in the lab and create a nice form and say, 'Hey, we're going to create pure energy.' And then they make a big-ass bomb with it and blow up two towns. Built with really cool people, I'm sure. So listen, I'm no terrorist. I have a plan. I have no bombs. I have nothing I'm going to drop on anyone. We can do a lie detector test on that."

Coady said, "I don't think either one of us would accuse you of something like that."

"I know. My trip was to go to New Mexico and show Jessica and Kalea a little bit of the country-side. We stopped at a couple of churches, met some people and attended a service." Interestingly, Jessica would not mention this later. "Went to a restaurant and listened to people's stories. Saw a guy asking for a ride on the side of a street, cold fella waiting for the bus or something. And I said, 'Hey, man, let me give you a ride. Where you going? Tell me about the town. How's the economy here?' And I gave the guy a White Castle burger. It was like thirty-nine cents. And, my gosh, he thought I was the Savior. I don't think there's prob-ably a human being in town who couldn't have spent fifty cents on at least one bum for a White Castle burger. I mean, where was that guy going to go and get any kind of job? You can't go to a store and beg for help, because people will just turn up their noses and they won't help.

"You can't go to your cousin's, because your cousin's got the same problem. So, what do you do? You can't go to the countryside and farm. So you're stuck and nobody is out there caring. And you know what? I see Melissa Etheridge telling us we need to spend eight dollars a month to feed our doggies and kitties. But what about that dude right there? I see people giving charity funds for Haiti. I mean, they're God's children. But Tom down at the White Castle, he just needs to get some gas money to get a job in a better state."

To all of this, the detective just kept saying, "Mmm-hmmm," to keep Gabe talking.

"Jesus often said when he was here, 'Man, this isn't my job this time around. But, boy, I'll tell you what. There's something waiting on the other side that isn't happy with the way you treat each other and women, especially women.' And that's the world we live in. It's going to get worse. We have an economy right now where there are three organizations powering us—gas, food and electricity. And in law enforcement, you guys are doing an excellent job. I swear you're overworked, man. The tide coming in at you is just going to get worse. Because you've got a whole lot of lions who ain't got enough food for their kids. So they're just going to be jacking each other.

"What happens, hypothetically speaking, is China pulls off trade and says, 'We don't make shit for you anymore. We're not going to supply your plastic, your peanuts. We ain't gonna make your shirts. We ain't gonna make your shoes. We ain't gonna make nothin' for you.' Who's going to make it for us? Mexico? I mean, we've got plenty of them over here doing our jobs, anyway. Have we got a populace that is going to be willing to get paid three-fifty an hour to do that?

"Which means you guys aren't going to have cell phones, because the public doesn't give much of a damn about you. And you're not going to have the technology. You're not going to have what you need. And so, hypothetically speaking, there doesn't need to be terrorist acts to cause trouble here.

"It's just people being fed up. So don't be telling me you should be buying stuff made in America. You can't buy it. Guess where I shop, gentlemen. The clothes I've got, the shoes I've got—Walmart. They're Chinese. The president doesn't say it's getting better. The governors aren't saying it's getting better, except for Schwarzenegger, who's going to legalize marijuana and he's hoping that's gonna boom the economy. But that's a joke. So it isn't going to get better.

"People want more and more stuff and want to do less and less and less. I mean, you've seen this civilization. That's why we go to history. I don't have to sit down here and say, 'I'm a prophet of God.' I've read my history books. I mean, this is exactly the climate in almost every major civilization when things started to go seriously downhill. So this isn't a conversation of what I'm guilty of. This is a conversation between three men about what's coming and it's predictable. I mean, an intelligent human being could predict it.

"The big one is coming. But it isn't God punishing His children. Like people want to believe He's super angry. Is He angry? Yes, yes, you would be angry if something happened to your children too. And you would lose control, or humble yourself for the rest of your life. One or the other. I would strongly suggest you pick the first one. You'll feel a hell of a lot better about yourself about it. I guarantee you."

And now Gabe got to a point where he couldn't even string together a coherent sentence. "If I get to live, I'll bet you anything . . . I'll meet a new friend. I don't care how violent or ugly they are. I mean, Dad threw me in the ocean, man, let's dance. Who cares if that guy don't love Jesus? He gives me permission to say okay. But that is reserved for His . . . whatever. I mean, my plan is to love everybody. I love you two guys. If we met under different circumstances, you would all be real happy you met me. If I met you in a bar, I'd buy you ten shots. I've been in your seat. I used to pull people over and tell them that their car matches the description of stolen circus monkeys. I saw the damn tail on the back."

Troutner laughed at that comment.

Coady said, "You spent time as a cop. And you know what it's like to wear the uniform. I'm just wondering if the night Robert and your mom walked in the house, that this confrontation happened— if there was a police officer walking in with them, would that have happened the same way, or do you think it would've been different?"

Gabe said, "It depends on what cop walked in with 'em."

Coady stated, "Well, just hypothetically speaking, what would have happened?"

"I think if a cop walked in and Bob reached for the gun, and made me make the same decision, I'd be safe from all this crap because the cop would have shot him. I'd thank goodness, because now I can hang with my daughter and have a life, or different life, or whatever. But you know, that didn't happen."

Then Gabe laughed and said, "Unless Robert Kennelly is a cop. Boy, that'd be crazy, wouldn't it?"

Troutner said to Gabe, "Okay, when we pulled you guys over, in part of the car, we found a nine-millimeter casing. The gun we found was a Beretta nine-millimeter. So, obviously, a round had been expended at some point."

Gabe said, "Oh, gosh. Out in the desert. I wanted to make sure the gun worked." (Author's note: Gabe's admission was at variance with Jessica's saying that he shot at an embankment near a home in Ohio.)

"What state was that in?"

Gabe replied, "I can't remember. But you know, I'm a bright fellow, and if I think it's massively important to take a good look at something and memorize it, like anatomy or physiology, because I need to understand those things, or better understand the world, I pay a lot more attention." And then Gabe asked, "Has anybody else been damaged, hurt? No. And if they had, I would tell you."

Troutner said, "So there's not going to be any more shell casings showing up? Because you know they've got the national computer database. So, how many times did you shoot it out there?"

Gabe said, "Maybe two."

"This is not going to show up at a robbery scene?"

"No, no, no, no, no."

Coady asked, "So your adventure through the country has been crime free?" Coady and Troutner already knew about the two robberies.

Gabe shaded his answer. "Harmless. I've hurt

nobody. Nobody has been hurt with the gun. I've done no damage. I've done nothing to anybody, except tell them I love them."

Coady said, "Where'd you get your money? That's expensive traveling around."

Gabe replied, "Begging. Jessica was very humble and I was too. I'd go over and say, 'Hey, bud, I'm hurting for gas and I'm trying to get a job, heading south.' Usually to truckers. You know, guys that have been traveling and probably have secrets of their own. You look them right in the eye and you'll probably see what they're seeing. And they say, 'Yeah, I got some money for you.' Not a lot. Spend enough time at the gas station and ask enough people to get gas, and off you go."

Then Gabe said, "Specific questions? Shoot it. Go straight to the point. You guys got questions or anything else out there that you want to know. I'm gonna tell you."

Coady asked, "When you guys left that night in Oregon, who drove?" Coady already knew that Jessica had driven away from the Eschlers' home.

However, Gabe lied to him, straight-faced, and said, "I drove."

"Um, does Jessica even know the people who gave you the car?"

"No, not really."

"She had never been there before?"

"No, not to that house. Those people were at our wedding, like seven or eight years ago."

Troutner asked, "If we hadn't caught up with

you today, where do you think you would have ended up in the next few days?"

Gabe replied, "I really knew you were catching up, so I don't know."

Troutner said, "Something going on down South?"

And Coady added, "Family or something in Florida?"

Gabe answered, "No. You know what? We talked about possibly going on a road trip with Doug, and said, 'Hey, where would you like to go?' And that was hypothetical. We even thought about staying here. I thought about finding a place for Jessica and Kalea, and seriously was thinking about turning myself in, finding an environment where I could walk straight into a police department, hands on the table, and say, 'Gentlemen, my name is Gabriel Christian Morris. Let's talk about what I've done.'

"And I'd tell them, 'You probably want to put some cuffs on me and put me in one of these rooms and let's have a chat.' You know, I almost did that in San Diego. But I didn't feel comfortable that Jessica—well, Jessica does what I tell her to do, because I'm intimidating. I mean, if you've got a guy who just shot two people, and he told you to get in a car, you're going to get into the car. That type of woman is going to get into a car, especially if you've got a four-year-old girl. You're terrified— wouldn't you be? So that's the case with her.

"Because when you hear that girl's story, man, she's an honest girl. Who is ever talking to her, she'll tell them everything. She's as clear about things as I am. And I truly believe that Kalea is more than most parents can handle. People put their kids in day care, and they're not there intently listening to what they say. So Kalea is going to end up in day care or with some parents who give her Ritalin because she is so much. That girl is insanely bright, insanely fast, insanely quick on the take. Very aware of what's going on around her. And she listens. And I meant that ain't LSD or smoking some weed. That's a girl praying to God, and guess what, man? You've got . . . you've got spiritual something in there—"

Coady interrupted and said, "Speaking of kids, there's going to be a CPS worker talk to you. Just who can call for Kalea and that sort of thing."

Hearing about Child Protective Services, Gabe said that was fine.

Troutner added, "Our priority's been her this whole time. They're coming up with a safety plan for her, and she's going to be taken care of."

Gabe said, "You guys are fantastic. I would really like, no joke, and this ain't no bullshit. . . . It's probably going to sound crazy comin' from the main suspect, but the gentleman who made that stop on me, and commanded me back, I mean he was fan-fucking-tastic. He did not treat me roughly. He knew I was complying. He paid real attention. He was conscientious. While he was giving me the command, he had control of a lot of edgy dudes. He was calming people down while giving me directions, had dogs barking, had me on the ground, had me completely under control, was talking to me, talking to you guys. That guy was a pro."

Coady answered, "There are a lot of good people here."

Gabe wistfully said, "I wish I could have gotten a job here ten years ago."

All Troutner had to say to that was "Hmm." Then Troutner added, "You know there's no allegations or suspicion of you guys doing anything wrong with the child. But you're both in custody, so we have to come up with a safety plan. We already talked to your wife and she said it was okay if her parents came and picked up the child, for the time being. She'll be with someone that you guys trust and everything."

To this, Gabe said, "If Jessica feels that's the solution, then that's the solution."

After that, Gabe was led away to a jail cell. For Coady and Troutner, it must have been one of the most memorable interviews they had ever conducted.

CHAPTER 26

Around that same time, Judy Ward was being interviewed by Investigator Bill Fugate. Fugate was an OSP detective and he told Judy, "We're getting a lot of details here and just want to let you know that we're just trying to get a better light from talking to you and your boyfriend."

Judy corrected him and said that Doug was her husband. They just had different last names. Bill acknowledged that and added, "We're just trying to piece this all together. You're here as a witness, not a suspect, and you're free to leave whenever you want."

The first thing Fugate wanted to know was how Judy first came in contact with Gabriel Morris. She told him that she'd known of Gabe since September 2009, when they first "met" on the game Perfect World. They, of course, hadn't met in real life, only on the Internet. She said she had checked her log on that; the last time they had been on the computer to each other was on January 26, 2010.

She explained, "It was in a game and I sent him two e-mails, one the first week and one a couple of days after he didn't log in, after January twenty-sixth. It was, like, 'Where'd you go? What happened?' And he replied on the day before Valentine's Day, so that made it February thirteenth."

Fugate asked, "Why did he say he was coming to Virginia?"

Judy answered, "He just said he was visiting people he knew on the game."

Fugate asked, "Was it your belief he came here because he was attracted to you and hoping for a relationship?"

Judy replied, "I wasn't looking for a relationship with him. After thinking about it, after putting the pieces together—we had a relationship in the game. We'd talk in the game, and we had a relationship in the game, and you can actually get married in the game. But we never did. We did spend a lot of time in the game doing stuff, and he got to know me and what I thought. Yeah, there was an attraction."

Fugate said, "He knew you were vulnerable to him?"

"Yeah, I think he just knew I was vulnerable and would allow it."

Fugate added, "Was it pretty soon after they arrived here? It's like he really tried to stay close to you, waiting for an opportunity."

Judy replied, "I didn't feel that he was pressuring me into anything. I never felt that, up until the last two days. I feel sorry for Jessica because he affected me this much in just one week, and he's been with her for years. And I think she's scared. Like he has a way of using his beliefs and your vulnerabilities. It gets to you, and I didn't see that until Monday, and I started piecing it together. I got used by him."

Fugate asked, "On the week that they were living there, did Jessica pick up on his attraction to you? Was that causing a problem with her?"

Judy responded, "She knew, but she didn't say anything. It didn't seem like it bothered her. She just went her way."

Fugate asked if Jessica would just stay in the other part of the house when Judy and Gabe were together. She answered, "Yeah, yeah. She was either downstairs cooking or was with Kalea or doing whatever. But she knew we spent time alone. Most of the time we spent alone was just talking. And it was mostly him trying to tell me that I could be like him. I kept telling him that I couldn't, because he is such an extrovert and I'm not. He's just wild and animated."

Fugate asked, "Was it causing a problem with you and your husband, or anything like that, because—"

Judy interrupted him and replied, "Gabe was always, always, always around me. So I never got a chance to talk with my husband in private, hardly at all. And even then, Gabe was only steps away."

"Was it because he was attracted to you?"

"I guess, yeah."

"And you had a relationship?"

"Yes."

Fugate wanted to know if Gabe ever used his real name and not his "game name." Judy said that he had. "Around the time he told us about killing his mom, he said that his name was Gabriel Christian Morris."

Fugate wondered if Judy or Doug ever searched Gabe's name on the computer. She said they had not done so and added, "I don't know if Gabe ever searched his own name. He used the blue tower computer. And there was Internet access on there."

Fugate asked if either Gabe or Jessica ever used phones at her house. She said she never saw them do so. Asked about wallets or purses, Judy said she never saw Gabe with a wallet or Jessica with a purse.

Judy spoke about a sixteen-year-old girl whom Gabe knew online. Judy said this girl lived in the Central time zone. Then Fugate asked how many times Gabe talked about killing his mom. Judy said it had only been one time.

Judy then added, "Jessica was right there and Kalea was right there too. Jessie said that she heard it (the gunshots). He interrupted her and said that she had seen the bodies. She went, 'Yes, that's right.' She just changed from saying that she heard to agreeing with him, like 'Yeah, I saw.'"

"Okay. When she said she heard it, what do you assume she meant by 'I heard it'?"

"I assumed that she meant she heard the gun,

the gunshot, or shots, but she just heard it. And right after that, he interrupted her, like, in an aggressive manner, like she said something wrong. She never did talk very much, and when she did, it was always to agree with him."

"Tell me about the conversation where he said he shot her and then shot him."

Judy said, "The whole time he was talking about it, he wasn't saying it, like being serious. Like sitting down and saying this is what I did. It was like storytelling. Like fiction or fantasy. So I never believed him. Then I think he just changed the subject. And with Jessie, she always seemed like she was scared. And there were tears she was trying to hide. And I think he was trying to convince her that her mom was evil."

Fugate wanted to know if looking back now, Judy could see how manipulative and off center Gabe was.

Judy replied, "Looking back now, nothing makes sense. Him wanting a place to stay, that does make sense."

Fugate wondered if Judy thought it was odd that no one in Gabe's family had a cell phone. He said, "In America, every thirteen- or fourteen-year-old has a cell phone."

Judy said, "Hindsight is the best sight."

"So looking back, you can honestly say something's up here. Do you think, looking back now, do you think Jessica was aware why they were on the run?"

"Right."

"So you think she was following him when he told her—"

"I think she was just following him. I think she was scared and has been scared for years, however long they've been together. I think that she loves him and she wants something that he won't give her—which is loving her. He even told me, he can't give her what she wants. He can't give her a kind of loving relationship that she wants."

CHAPTER 27

All of the events in Virginia, of course, were very important to Detective Daniel Looney, the lead investigator on the case for CCSO. He related later, "I got a call from a detective from the Prince William Police Department in Virginia. Once Gabriel Morris was arrested, I went back to Virginia and helped in the search and seizure concerning the vehicles. In the trunk of Fred Eschler's Ford Taurus, I found a shoulder holster, a nine-millimeter Beretta, binoculars, five loaded magazines for the Beretta and shotgun shells. The front license plate of the Taurus had been removed and placed in the trunk. There was also a license plate stolen off a vehicle from California in the trunk.

"Inside the vehicle was a phone book of the Detroit, Michigan, area and a map with some routes drawn upon it. These markings in red showed from Santa Fe, New Mexico, to Colorado Springs and Denver, Colorado. Then two routes were marked in red, one being from there to Omaha, Nebraska, and the other one to Kansas City, Missouri. St. Louis, Missouri, was circled in red." Gabe and his family had not gone that way. Instead, they had cut across Texas and Oklahoma.

"There was a route with blue ink to Indianapolis and Fort Wayne, Indiana, and then Detroit. From there, [there] was a route to Pittsburgh, Pennsylvania, and Washington, D.C. Dumfries, Virginia, was circled in red."

While in Virginia during the search-and-seizure operation, Looney found a note in the Taurus. It was a message from Fred Eschler: *The holder of this note has permission to drive my car. Fred C. Eschler. 2/8/10.* A toll road receipt was found for February 14, 2010, for the Ohio Turnpike. And Looney also found a container of salvia, a plant that can cause hallucinations for a short period of time.

The Popes originally weren't sure which airport they would fly to on the eastern seaboard. Eventually they arrived in Dulles International Airport, near Washington, D.C., on the morning of February 23. From there, they headed to the Garfield police station in Woodbridge, thinking that Jessica and Kalea were being held there. A reporter, who happened to be there at the time, noted that Rita Pope said, "We need to see our daughter. We're her parents and we've just flown from Idaho." Rita's hands were visibly shaking as she said this.

The Popes were told to go to Prince William–

Gabriel (Gabe) Morris went on the run with his wife Jessica and his daughter Kalea. Gabe was a murder suspect; Jessica was wanted as a material witness to murder. *(Coos County Sheriff's Office)*

Gabe Morris and his half-brother, Jesse, grew up in Southern California near San Diego. *(Author's photos)*

When Gabe Morris was fifteen years old, he left his father's custody
and moved in with his mom in Coquille, Oregon. *(Author's photos)*

In 2005, Gabe became a deputy in the Bingham County, Idaho Sheriff's Office. *(Coos County DA's Office)*

Gabe's patrols took him into farmland, ranches at the edge of the Indian reservation, and these lava badlands. *(Author's photo)*

After leaving the sheriff's office and enduring various business failures, Gabe moved his family to Bandon, Oregon. *(Author's photo)*

They went to live with his mom and Bob Kennelly.
(Coquille Valley Sentinel)

A Coos County Sheriff's Office deputy went out to Bob Kennelly's property to tell him that his pickup was illegally parked in downtown Coquille. *(Author's photo)*

State's Exhibit #13

Bob Kennelly's property included a main house, barn and sheds in an area known as Flower Hill. *(Coos County DA's Office)*

Manassas regional jail; but when they arrived, they were told by a jail employee that there was no visitation on Tuesdays. The Popes were distraught, after having come so far, but another employee intervened when this person found out they had flown all the way from Idaho. After showing their identifications, the Popes were allowed to see their daughter. Bill Pope said later, "She is not looking good, and she doesn't want to talk about anything involving Gabriel, unless an attorney is present."

Bill added that it looked as if Jessica had lost thirty pounds since he'd seen her last. He was convinced that she had been forced to go along with whatever Gabe told her to do. Bill told a reporter, "He is a very cruel person. He probably told her that 'if you try to make a run for it, I'll kill you and Kalea,' or 'I'll kill you, Kalea and your parents.'"

The same reporter noted that Rita Pope burst into tears when she first saw Kalea running around, laughing and playing with officers. And Rita kept crying when she learned the officers had bought Kalea a Happy Meal from a local McDonald's. Rita said, "Yesterday we didn't know if we would ever see her alive again."

Another person vastly relieved by the outcome was Coos County DA Paul Frasier. He knew very well this whole scenario could have had a much more tragic outcome. Frasier told reporters, "Mr. and Mrs. Morris will be held in custody there, on the warrants previously issued. When they will be returned to Coos County is not known, if they decide to fight extradition."

Frasier and four Coos County detectives caught flights to Virginia. Just like the Popes, there was no straight shot directly to the area from Coos County. They had to make their way to Portland first and then a long flight cross-country to the East Coast.

All of this was, of course, big news in the Bandon, Oregon, area. On February 22, *The World* had the headline COPS CATCH MORRIS IN VA. The next day's edition had the headline COUPLE WILL REMAIN IN VA. The article got to the fact that both Gabe and Jessica would be able to fight extradition back to Oregon. This could slow down the process of getting them back there for a considerable length of time.

Just how long it could take was addressed by DA Frasier. He said that it could take weeks or even months if the Morrises fought extradition. Then Frasier added, "Everyone here is relieved that we've got them in custody. And the biggest thing is, nobody got hurt."

As far as how Kalea was doing, a reporter spoke with Sergeant Kim Chinn of the Prince William County Police Department. Chinn said, "She's being entertained by police officers and eating snacks. She's cute as a button."

A short time later, the newspaper got to the fact that DA Frasier originally didn't know that Fred Eschler's first phone call to him on February 9 about terrorists and dead bodies somehow had a link to a double murder in Coos County. The headline was DA DIDN'T CONNECT 2 CASES.

The reporter related that DA Frasier and Fred Eschler had known each other for years. The article revealed that both men had known each other since 1993, and both went to the same LDS church in the area. Not only that, Frasier's son Robert had dated Eschler's daughter Elizabeth in the late 1990s. Robert, eighteen, and Elizabeth, seventeen, both died in a car crash in 1999.

As far as Fred's original call to the DA's office about terrorists, Frasier commented, "It was kind of hard to swallow." It wasn't until the bodies of Bob Kennelly and Robin Anstey were found, and evidence started pointing toward Robin's son, Gabriel Morris, that Frasier linked Fred Eschler's phone call to the crime scene.

Some in the community wondered if Frasier should or even could prosecute the case, since there was this situation with the Eschlers. Frasier let it be known that he didn't see any conflict of interest. In the past, he often had been involved in trials with people he knew, since the Coos County populace was not large. In fact, Frasier said that he had even prosecuted one of his wife's coworkers in a previous trial.

Frasier stated, "This case is nowhere near that level of contact. I do not believe my impartiality is going to be affected in any way in this case." And as far as Gabriel Morris went, Frasier had not seen him in more than ten years, when Gabe was young and attended the same LDS church that he did.

Even though Jessica Morris had no charges filed against her, she was still being detained in a Virginia jail by the first days of March 2010. A spokesperson for the jail said that this did happen sometimes when a person was a material witness to a crime. One obvious reason was that Jessica had shown she'd been willing to flee a state. One thing Jessica already said she would not do was fight extradition to Oregon.

That was not the case as far as Gabe went. He let it be known that he would challenge extradition to Oregon. DA Frasier then took steps to request a governor's warrant. He said that this could be a complicated process that a defendant could challenge as it moved forward. In his twenty-five years of practice, Frasier had only dealt with this kind of thing once before.

In this request, the governor of Oregon would have to ask the governor of Virginia to have Gabriel Morris returned to Oregon to face charges on two counts of aggravated murder.

Jessica's future became more problematic after March 1 when she was back in Coos County. She had a six-minute hearing in which DA Frasier said he would be convening a grand jury and intended to indict her for aiding and abetting her husband in the crime. Frasier related, "She provided aid to her husband to avoid detection following the deaths of Robin Anstey and Robert Kennelly." Frasier stated in Judge Richard Barron's courtroom, "She helped Gabriel Morris get away."

During the hearing, Jessica sat quietly in a jail-issued orange jumpsuit and listened to the proceedings as she brushed away tears. She wore glasses and seemed to be concentrating on every word that was spoken. It was obvious to those in the courtroom that she had lost a lot of weight.

On the premise that Jessica Morris might be indicted by the grand jury, Judge Barron temporarily assigned public defender John Meynink to be her attorney. Jessica's bond was set at $1 million.

At a press conference later, Frasier said, "I've got to keep her here. She has no ties to this community at this point. I need some substantial security to make sure she shows up if she were able to post bail."

Even though the Popes were working to be granted custody of Kalea, she was still being held by CPS in Virginia. The Popes wanted to get her out of that environment as soon as possible and back to Idaho.

The grand jury testimony may have been kept secret, but just who would be testifying to them was not. The list included police officers connected to the case, the doctors who had done the autopsies, friends of Gabriel and Jessica Morris and even Doug Miller's mom in Virginia. She was not flown all the way out to Oregon, but rather was on a live video feed from her home state.

When it was over, the grand jurors agreed that Gabriel Morris should face the two charges of aggravated murder. They also agreed that Jessica should face a charge of hindering prosecution. If the charges against her went forward and she was found guilty, she could spend five years in prison.

It only took a few more days for Frasier to make a dramatic decision concerning Jessica Morris. He let it be known that if she testified against her husband in a trial, he would be willing to cut a deal with her. Even if she was just a material witness, she could be ordered by the court to stay in jail until the trial. Frasier said, "If she decides to be a cooperative witness, we might be able to work something out." In other words, if she was cooperative, the deal could entail her being released from jail.

DA Frasier began studying just what aspects of marital immunity applied to this case. One thing covered would be statements that Gabe made to Jessica. She could not testify to those. But she could testify as to all the things that happened before the crime, during the crime and after it occurred.

Reporters wanted to know if the medical marijuana grown on Bob Kennelly's property had anything to do with the shootings. Frasier said, "There is a lot of speculation about that, but I can't tell you anything yet."

And there was another new development by March 5. Kalea had been released by CPS in Virginia to the care of Bill and Rita Pope. They took the young girl with them back to Idaho. Just how long it would be before Jessica could be reunited with her remained very much in question.

It took less than two weeks for Jessica Morris to come to a decision about what she would do. Through her lawyer, she let DA Frasier know that she would testify against Gabe in exchange for the plea deal that Frasier had offered her.

On March 17, Jessica and her attorney, Carole Hamilton, sat down with DA Frasier, Detective Dan Looney and John Riddle, an investigator with the Oregon State Police. In order for a plea deal to go forward, Jessica had to answer all of their questions truthfully.

DA Frasier explained to her, "We're going to put you under oath to tell the truth. So if you'd raise your right hand, 'Do you solemnly swear or promise that the statement you're about to give in this matter will be the truth, the whole truth and nothing but the truth, so help you God, understanding it's under the pains and penalty of perjury?'"

Jessica said that she would.

Detective Sergeant Looney began by asking if Jessica remembered him. She said that she did and commented about the sixteen-hour plane rides back to Coos County, Oregon. Looney then related that he and the others were going to ask a lot of questions, and Jessica said it was good they were doing it that way rather than her just trying to do a narrative of what had happened.

The early part of the interview covered the events of February 8 and then the Morrises going over to the Eschlers' home. Jessica added, "Fred baptized Gabe, and he was really good friends with them. They had a daughter who died in a car accident, and Gabe was really good friends with her. One of the Eschlers' kids, we had gone to their son's wedding reception in Idaho." Then Jessica got back to telling what happened at the Eschlers' house and the trip to Southern California.

The detectives asked her about the events there, and Looney wondered about Gabe getting money there. "Did the cash he gave you . . . Did that look like it came from a business or a bank?"

Jessica said, "There were one-dollar bills and [a] fifty. That was the biggest bill. It was mostly ones."

"Did he rob somewhere?"

"I believe so."

Then the questioning concerned the trip from Southern California to Arizona. Jessica spoke about being with some of her friends there, the robbery in Arizona and details about the route to Virginia.

Looney told Jessica, "I'm going to start asking you for more details. And I know some of it's going to be quite painful. But I need to know everything."

And Frasier added, "We know a lot of stuff because we talked to a lot of people, and we're kinda testing whether you're giving us the whole story, so you need to be completely honest with us."

Now the detectives got Jessica to speak about all of the events of the week before the murders, the actual shooting and then being at the Eschlers'. The questions and answers were much more detailed than the initial questioning. At one point, Looney asked about the events of February 8, "So, why didn't you guys just go up the driveway and talk to Bob and Robin?"

Jessica stated, "Well, Gabe said we shouldn't do that. I didn't feel like we should do it either. We didn't know what Bob would do. By this time, Gabe knew what he had done to us. He wasn't sure what he would do. He knew that Robin knew it too." Jessica was referencing the supposed rat poisoning. "We felt like Bob was hurting us, and she knew, but she didn't care because she was with a man. We just wanted to get our stuff."

"So, in your mind, you wanted to get your stuff."

"And talk to them. Gabe was going to see about us possibly staying there again. Maybe even living over at Robin's house."

There were a lot more details about February 8, and then the questioning turned toward Gabe's affair with a woman in Idaho. Looney said, "Was that the girlfriend he was living with for a while?"

Jessica's naivete must have stunned him. She said, "Um, I don't think they actually lived together."

Looney asked, "Where did she work for him?"

"As an American Family Insurance agent."

Riddle asked, "What did he steal?"

Jessica answered, "I don't remember what she claimed. We were talking to my dad, and he said that she was trying—well, he had been contacted with regard to it or something."

Apparently, this issue about Brenda and the stealing came up again when Gabe, Jessica and Kalea were on the road, heading up to Seattle, in early February. Jessica said there had been a call about it on their cell phone. She added, "Gabe told me to just throw the cell phone out the window of the car."

Getting back to the aftermath of the murders, Looney said, "Did you ask Gabe later what happened?"

Jessica said, "I asked him on the way to Roseburg. I was in shock. I couldn't believe it. He said that they had come in the house. He sat down to talk to them and Robin got up and started making as if she was going to leave. And that's all he said."

"How [did] her trying to leave turn into a shooting?"

"I asked him why, and he said it needed to happen."

"And why did it need to happen?"

"I didn't ask."

"What did he explain?"

"I didn't ask."

"Had he mentioned doing this, that he was going to do this, or that he thought about it?"

"No."

"Did he mention that his mom needed to pay, or anything like that?"

"No. He loved her very much. So do I."

CHAPTER 28

The questioning got back to the details of the cross-country trip to Virginia. Looney asked, "Did you guys ever get into an argument about what had happened?"

Jessica said they had not.

Looney asked, "Did you ever confront him?"

"No. After he said that it had to happen, I didn't talk about it anymore."

"So, how do you think it all went down up there?"

"I think, when they came in, Gabe was in the kitchen or something and they sat down to talk. And at some point, Gabe brought the gun out or something. I don't know if Bob charged him or said something. And then Gabe's mom got up to leave and Bob followed her, and—"

Frasier interrupted and said, "I think she needs to know how it happened, because I've got some questions in my mind about what's going on here. I think we need to perhaps have a more heart-to-heart discussion here. I think we've been skirting around the issues and we need to get down to brass tacks. And if you guys want me to take the lead, I'll do it."

Both Riddle and Looney said for Frasier to go ahead.

He began, "Jessica, the physical evidence shows that your husband was standing outside the door of your bedroom. He was standing on top of that balcony. The evidence shows that your mother-in-law and her boyfriend came in the door and they had barely gotten inside the door when he opened fire on them. He shot at them. There was that big plant there by the door, and we got bullet holes through the leaves of that plant. It looks like he went down the balcony and fired a series of shots. He then went out to the bottom of the stairway, and actually he admitted to the police in Virginia that he shot Mr. Kennelly while he was lying on the ground. Shot him in the chest, and then shot his mother. The mother was killed by a bullet wound to the head. You said you heard Robin say something. But the head shot would have killed her. So there's discrepancies about what we're hearing, in which you recall what happened, and what the physical evidence is telling us."

All Jessica had to say to these revelations was "Okay."

Frasier continued, "Another thing that kinda jumps out at me, and these guys can come back and talk about it later, it seemed like you were minimizing his marijuana use and drinking. We know about the medical marijuana card. And we know about the grow."

Frasier turned to Looney and asked, "Didn't we find some marijuana plants in the Castle Room?"

Looney replied, "Not in that room, but Gabe had been smoking marijuana like a madman."

Hamilton jumped in and asked, "In the Castle Room?"

Frasier said that was correct.

Jessica started to say, "I don't think he smoked—"

Frasier cut her off. "If he's spending all day in there, he's smoking dope around your kid."

Looney added, "There was dope all over that room."

Jessica said, "I didn't know he smoked in front of Kalea."

Frasier continued, "Well, the paraphernalia certainly was in there. She's in the room. She's exposed to it. I guess what it boils down to is, did you know before it happened? Did you know that Gabe was going to kill these people?"

Jessica emphatically stated, "No."

Looney declared, "Because I can tell you, he ambushed them. There was no discussion with them. There was not a word said."

Jessica still couldn't believe it. She replied, "He said that he had sat down with them."

Looney responded, "Nope. Impossible. They still had their coats on."

Riddle added, "They barely had time to set their

things down that they brought into the house with them."

Looney continued, "And they set it down and it was never touched again. I can prove almost everything, because of stuff we found. Those shots came from that balcony, except for a couple of them. And the last shot would have been in your mother-in-law's head, outside."

Frasier interjected, "She woulda dropped like a rock right there. I'm going to play devil's advocate here—I'm a defense attorney for Gabriel. I'm going to point a finger at you, trying to make you look like the bad guy, on at least part of this. So you came to the conclusion that Robert Kennelly was putting rat poison in your food and dishes. Did you ever see him do that?"

"No."

"And you prepared the food, right?"

"Yes."

"How would he have had the opportunity to do that?"

"I left for work when everyone was asleep. About the time they would go to sleep, I was gone."

Frasier asked, "When you were preparing food, did you see anything to cause you to believe it had been tampered with or anything?"

Jessica replied, "A couple of times, I saw some residue in the pans, but I thought it was just that I hadn't cleaned them very well."

"Okay. Did you ever go to a doctor yourself, or

take Kalea to the doctor, or have any tests run to say that you were poisoned?"

"We didn't have insurance. We had to let it go. We didn't have enough money for it."

"Did you go to the police about it?"

"No."

"You see what I'm saying?"

Riddle jumped in and added, "Did you get on the computer and check out the symptoms of rat poisoning?"

"No, I didn't."

Riddle added, "I mean, your husband's spending hours and hours on the computer. It stands to reason that you could have punched in the symptoms of rat poisoning and have the World Wide Web help you out."

Jessica responded, "We didn't get a chance to. The only time we were by a computer after that was back at Grandma's house."

Frasier said, "Who brought up the idea that you'd been poisoned?"

"Him."

"Okay, the other thing that's confusing is, if you know or believe that Robert is poisoning you, why go back to talk to him?"

Jessica said, "Because I felt like Gabe could talk to them, and because his mom was in danger and that she needed to be taken away from that situation because she needed to be helped."

"Did you believe Robin was in on the poisoning?"

"I don't know when I came to the conclusion, but she knew about it, but didn't do anything about it. And that she knew he was poisoning her as well."

Frasier continued, "So you know this could get turned around and the one who gets a finger pointed at is you. You and Gabe figure that Robert is poisoning you, and you guys went back for retribution. I could see a defense attorney representing Gabe, pointing the finger right at you."

"I can see what you're saying."

"All right. So there's that, [which] you need to think about a little bit. The other thing is, did Gabe ever in your presence tell anybody that he'd killed his mother?"

"Yes. He told Judy."

"What did he say when he was talking to Judy?"

"He said that he had killed his mom and her boyfriend, and he looked at me and asked if I knew that. And I said, 'Yes.'"

"Okay. So you know that's what we've been skirting around here. You know that Gabe killed those two folks and you were driving away and so forth."

Jessica agreed with that, so Frasier continued: "Another question that's gonna pop up is it's obvious from what you've said today, and what we already know, that there were multiple occasions where you could have walked away from Gabe. Driven away with Kalea, gone straight to the police and told 'em what the hell happened—pardon my French—but you didn't do it. So the question is, why didn't you run from this guy?"

Jessica paused for a moment. Then she said, "I love him. I wanted Kalea to have her dad."

"Did you really think that Kalea could have her dad after he killed those two people?"

"Gabe said it was possible."

Riddle jumped in and said, "Explain that."

So Jessica stated, "He said we could get different names or something and that we'd never use our names again."

Frasier asked, "What was Gabe's relationship with Judy?"

Jessica replied, "On the game, I don't know. He talked highly of her, said that she had a lot of character. That she stuck up for him in situations where other people didn't. And when we got there, Judy was very sick. She has like an eating disorder, stomach pains or something, that just makes her not want to eat. If she eats, she hurts, and if she doesn't eat, she hurts. So she just chooses not to eat. And that's why she's so skinny. And Gabe wanted her to be better and he healed her. With Doug's help."

Now Frasier really rocked Jessica's world. He asked, "Did you know Gabe was sleeping with her?"

Jessica replied, "No. He would invite her to come and sleep. . . . It was a king bed, and so I would sleep here and Kalea was in the middle. Judy would sleep on the other side, and he would sleep at the bottom of the bed. But that he actually slept with her, I did not know that."

"Okay. Well, we know he had sex with her, and Judy says you knew about that."

All Jessica said was "No."

Thinking about this more, however, Jessica added, "There were several times when he would be upstairs in the room with her, and I went up to get a toy for Kalea or the hairbrush or something. And just a couple of times, he would follow me back downstairs and say, 'Why are you coming up here? Are you trying to spy on me or something?' And I told him, no, that I was just getting a hairbrush or toy or whatever. Did Judy really say that?"

"Yes, she did, when we interviewed her in Virginia. We've got her on video telling us that there was a sexual relationship between her and Gabriel."

"No, I didn't know."

CHAPTER 29

Frasier wanted to know why Gabe was so insistent that Judy and Doug go with them when they were going to leave Virginia.

Jessica said, "Because he knew he could trust them and they had a different car and money. And so we wouldn't have to worry about money. I wouldn't have to beg anymore."

Frasier asked, "Well, what do you think would have happened to Doug and Judy, once Gabe had the car and money?"

"Nothing. They were going to come with us."

"Do you really think they were going to come with you?"

"I really did."

"You don't think Gabe would have killed them for their identification?"

"No."

"Okay, well, that's another thing I'm throwing out there so you're aware of it."

Looney added, "The problem is, there's a good

chance that's exactly what he was going to do.
What's the difference? He's already killed two
people."

Jessica was still insistent. "They were coming to
help us."

Frasier replied, "Yeah, but the reason they were
coming to help you was because Gabe talked them
into it. Right?"

"Yes."

"Okay, I guess I'm trying to get across to you,
whether you believe me or not, Gabe sold a bill of
goods to you since the beginning. That girlfriend
or whatever, in Pocatello, it's real clear it was a
sexual relationship. We know about that. He convinced you otherwise. We know about the divorce
proceedings that were started and, apparently,
abandoned. That's why we're having this talk, because, you know, I'm not trying to be a jerk, but it
seems like we have to ask lots of pointed questions
to get the information we know you know. And it
could be that it's just your personality. Or it could
be like you say, you love the guy and you're holding out hope that you guys can be together again.
And I think Carole's talked to you about that."

Jessica agreed that she had.

Frasier continued his outreach to Jessica: "I think
your mom and dad have talked to you about that
too. Probably ad nauseam. So I think what you
need to do is think about how you want to conduct
your life from here on out. Because, quite frankly,
Gabriel Morris isn't going to be part of it anymore—
not if I have anything to say about it. And you need

to be aware, as the case progresses, that he's going to turn on you. And I think Carole can verify that would be a common tactic that is used to make you look like the worst person there is."

Hamilton did agree with that.

Frasier added, "I mentioned the divorce, because I was made aware that there had been a divorce filed. So, is there something you wanted to tell us about that?"

"I don't want to tell you, but if you want me to, then—"

Frasier said, "Well, yeah. Tell us who filed it and why."

Jessica stated, "Gabe, like I told Carole, went down to Las Vegas to help a fellow coworker that he had been training with. She was an American Family Insurance agent as well. So in November 2008, he asked both of his employees if they would go with him and one said no and one said yes. And the one who said yes was Brenda. And so they went down to Vegas and they were there a few days. She had an open house and he wanted to be there for it and help her with it. And he came back and he was always strange after that. I don't know if that's when their relationship began. But that's when he started talking about getting a divorce. He said he would still be a provider, and give us money to live on, but he didn't want to be married anymore.

"I didn't want to fill out the papers. So he went and got them and brought them back and left them with me so that I could fill them out. And I didn't want to. I fought it. And so I didn't fill them out for a long time. And then I finally did, like in February 2009 or something. And he had been gone, off and on, since November. He would just leave and not come back for a while.

"I remember I took a picture at Christmas and he was just pouty in the picture, like he wasn't excited to be there. I mean, Kalea was sitting right next to him, but he was sitting there, pouting. And he went and saw Brenda and her family after that. So he had me fill out the papers and I finally did, and we went over and turned them in. I cried the whole time. Kalea sat on the bench behind us, and the lady behind the counter—I can just remember her face. She saw me crying and got really mad at Gabe. You could see it in her face. And he started laughing and joking and stuff.

"He told me later in April or May 2009 that I had forgotten to fill out something, like a really simple thing. And then he didn't pursue it after that."

Jessica was in for another surprise, as far as Gabe was concerned. Frasier said, "I don't know the exact status of the paperwork. I know it's still pending."

"Oh, really!" she exclaimed. "I was told that if it doesn't happen in six months, it just drops off or something."

Frasier stated, "I don't know what your plans are. I'm not putting any pressure on you. It's still there. That's an avenue available to you. I don't know if you want to go through with it or not. Maybe your dad or somebody could go down and look at the paperwork and see what needs to be finished, if that's what you want to do."

A break was taken for the evening, and the next day the same people assembled for another round of the interview. Jessica started out by saying, "In jail last night, I just started thinking about things. And they're not in any order—just completely random. The first place Gabe came back with money when we went to Southern California was by Balboa Park and a hospital. The second place was in Arizona. When he got back in the car, he said that he thought the people there thought he was a Hispanic guy. I think it was a hair place, but I don't know for sure.

"And about his alcohol use, he bought the bottle of gin at Edgefield (in Oregon, when they went to the Silverton/Portland area). And he always had one in the car. And down in Southern California, he didn't have an ID."

Frasier wanted to know if Bob and Robin smoked marijuana. Jessica said that Robin didn't like it, and she never saw Bob smoke any. The whole thing to grow marijuana was supposedly for selling to clinics. Jessica added, "But Gabe wanted to smoke it."

As far as the Bingham County Sheriff's Office went, Jessica was in for another surprise. She said, "He was going to be a policeman in Anchorage, Alaska. And he had been let go from the sheriff's office because of his shoulder injury." Frasier wanted to know whether the sheriff's office told her that or if Gabe had. Jessica said that Gabe had.

Frasier explained, "Well, just to let you know, we've heard that he quit the sheriff's office for a couple of different reasons. One was that he quit because he didn't get a promotion to detective. Another was that he didn't like how somebody was giving him directions, and he went to the sheriff and told him, 'I don't like how this is being done.' And the sheriff basically told him to buck it up and follow what the person was telling him."

CHAPTER 30

Jessica now continued her random thoughts. She said, "When we were in the car, he started talking about how Bob had talked to him about wanting to kill people. And Bob said he had done it over a million times in his mind, but didn't have enough guts to do it."

According to Gabe, this had happened in the room that John Lindegren had built on the property. Frasier said, "I live here in Coquille. I know Big John."

Jessica retorted, "Okay. I guess everybody knows everybody here." And then Jessica reiterated that she hadn't heard the initial gunshots, but Kalea must have. Kalea had started screaming and woke up Jessica.

Jessica got into the situation about Gabe and the ROTC. And once again, she didn't know about the other stories Gabe had told different people concerning that. Jessica said, "He told me he got a pilot's license and—"

Frasier interrupted her and asked, "Did he show you any paperwork that he'd gotten a pilot's license?"

"No, but I knew he did. You can contact the ROTC. They can tell you. He did get it. Colonel Ringer told me." (Author's note: Colonel Ringer was most likely a fictitious name Gabe had come up with.)

Frasier said, "We're hearing a different story."

Once again, in surprise, Jessica said, "Oh, really!"

"We're hearing that he didn't get a pilot's slot and that's why he didn't go in the air force."

"Really? Because I remember when he found out that he'd gotten it, we were at my sister's wedding. And he'd just gotten his pilot's slot."

"Well, see, that's another discrepancy we're finding out."

Jessica must have been reeling at this point. It was obvious that Gabe had told her one lie after another. She said, "So the ROTC said that he didn't get it at all?"

Frasier replied, "The information we were given was that he didn't get a pilot's slot, and he got mad and that's why he didn't go into the air force."

Looney added, "So he quit ROTC. They were going to give him a slot as something else, something else on the ground. It wasn't a pilot."

Frasier then said, "You mentioned that when he was working at American Family Insurance, in the second month, he got a life insurance policy on you and Kalea?"

Jessica said that he also bought a policy that

covered himself in case of death. Frasier wanted to know if Gabe had taken out a life insurance policy on anyone else. She said that she didn't know.

Frasier asked how Gabe had obtained a certain firearm when he was with the BCSO. Jessica said, "They [the sheriff's office] gave him a rifle that was in the trunk of his car all the time. But he bought a gun at Sam's in Pocatello. A handgun."

Frasier said, "Mr. [James] Anstey says he gave Gabe three hundred dollars to buy a gun he could have to work for the sheriff's office. Do you know anything about that?"

Jessica said that she didn't.

Looney queried, "We sorta talked about it yesterday. What was Gabe's whole idea on coming back to the house on the eighth? I mean, I don't understand it. He was sneaking around up there. That seems odd to me. Why didn't you just drive up the driveway, if he was wanting to talk to them?"

Jessica answered, "It was just because Bob had done the whole poisoning thing. We weren't sure how far he would carry it. Gabe just wanted to be in the house and be able to talk to them on his terms."

"Did Gabe tell you something about Bob being a pedophile?"

"No."

"Okay, so Gabe wanted to talk to them on his own terms. How did he say his own terms were going to be?"

"Just that he wanted to be in the house and ready for them to come in, so that Bob couldn't grab a gun or something like that. So that he could be protected."

"When Gabe was doing these things, was he including you in his decision making?"

"Sometimes."

"I mean, did he talk to you about everything, or did he surprise you all the time?"

"He gets inspired a lot and he does it. He doesn't talk to me about it. He just does it. Whatever he thinks to do or feels to do, he does it."

Looney wanted to know if this meant she was surprised by a lot of Gabe's decisions. She said, "Yeah, like when we arrived at McMenamins restaurant in Washington. I was completely shocked. I had no idea—"

Frasier interjected, "What I think Dan is getting at, if you look at what you've told us, Gabe is telling you that Bob's putting rat poison in the food, or something along that line. You guys leave and then Gabe says, 'We need to go back.'"

Jessica replied, "That was a joint decision."

"Yeah, but you come back, and if you look at how you came back—you parked down the road. And then Gabe sneaks up, looking around. Then he calls you on a walkie-talkie. You get the car up there and you're hiding behind the garage, and he's in the woods scoping out the house. You see what I'm saying? He goes in there and arms himself with one of Bob's guns. He brings you guys into the house, and he's waiting for them to come in. It doesn't take a genius to figure out Gabe planned it. He came back to kill his mom and Bob, and all of his actions that day show that this was a preplanned event. You see what I'm saying?"

"Yes."

"Yesterday you told us you didn't know he was going to do it. But you look at all the plans that he's doing and it's real clear that he planned on killing his mom and her boyfriend. So we just want to make it abundantly clear you did not know what was planned."

Jessica said, "I did not know."

"And you didn't help plan it out or anything like that?"

"No, I did not."

Jessica's attorney spoke up and said, "Can I interject something?"

Frasier said that she could.

Hamilton said, "I've asked Jessica something several times and I think it might be important she have an answer to this. I asked, even if Bob were giving them rat poison, did she think that justified shooting them?" The attorney turned to Jessica and said, "And your answer was?"

Jessica replied, "No."

Moving on, Looney asked if Gabe had told her that he'd purposefully eaten rat poison and healed himself. Jessica said yes. Then Looney asked if that surprised her. She said that it didn't. When asked why it didn't surprise her, she replied, "Because he is blessed in the ability to be able to heal people. He's a priesthood holder in the Church and he healed Judy through the power of God."

Looney wanted to know if she believed all of this because she had seen it, or because Gabe had told her those things. Jessica answered, "Throughout our marriage, whenever I was sick or Kalea was, he's given a blessing and we healed. We started feeling better immediately, especially Kalea. When a little one gets a cold and can't tell you what's wrong and just looks at you with her eyes, and you know that they're talking to you, but they have nothing that they can say, because they don't know how to talk yet, he was able to give her a blessing and heal her."

Frasier, who was a Mormon, was not going to let this explanation stand. He said, "This brings up a side issue. It may be something you need to think about. Being a member of the Church myself, and knowing things that you know, and knowing that you've been on a mission, like I've been on a mission—you have to know that under the doctrine of the Church, that for a person to be able to do this, you have to be a worthy individual to do that. And you're telling me that Gabe was not abiding by the Word of Wisdom in terms of his drinking alcohol, smoking marijuana, and then he goes and kills two people. And then he heals Judy? I mean, the problem I'm having here, which I'm trying to gauge, is how could you feel he could do that when the doctrine of the Church would indicate that that is not a possibility?"

Jessica answered, "With regard to Judy, priesthood holders give blessings in the name of Jesus Christ. And he did it in the name of the Holy Ghost."

"But you have to know that is contrary to Church doctrine, don't you?"

Jessica paused and then responded, "I would say, yeah."

Moving on, Frasier asked if Jessica was scared of Gabe when she and Kalea left with him after the shootings. Jessica said, "I was scared. I don't know if it was of him. I don't know if it was the shock. I was just scared."

So Frasier asked if Jessica was scared that Gabe was going to hurt her or Kalea. She said that she wasn't.

"Okay, and I think you told me this yesterday, that you stayed with Gabe through this whole thing after the shooting, went all over the U.S., because you loved him and wanted to stay with him. Is that right?"

Jessica answered, "And I believe in him." Then she corrected herself, she said, "Believed." It was past tense now.

Frasier said that he wanted to make sure that she had not been forced to go along with Gabe across the United States. She said that never had been the case.

Changing tracks, Frasier got into the fact that Gabe had lost a lot of weight in 2010. Jessica said that it was because he was hardly eating anything. Frasier retorted that Gabe might have been doing methamphetamine. People who abused that drug often looked and acted the way Gabe did. Frasier said they had pressured speech, could not sit still and lost a lot of weight. Jessica said she did not think Gabe did meth, but she knew he drank a lot of alcohol and smoked a lot of marijuana.

Frasier wondered why Bob Kennelly's wallet was never discovered. Jessica said that Gabe took the cash out of the wallet and stuffed it in his pants pocket. She thought he might have tossed the wallet out the window of the car when he had tossed out Kennelly's gun accidentally. Gabe had been very drunk at the time.

Frasier also wanted to know why Gabe left the Popes' pickup truck at Bob Kennelly's house. Jessica said that it had been having problems and Bob's truck was more reliable. And as far as the shooting went, Frasier asked, "How much time do you think passed from the time you heard the last shot till Gabe's telling you, 'We gotta get out of here'?"

Jessica replied, "I don't know for sure. Under a minute, I would say."

"And when you came downstairs, Gabe was already in the truck?"

"He was outside. Initially I couldn't find our shoes upstairs. I was looking everywhere and I was scared."

Looney asked, "Did Gabe tell you there were terrorists out there?"

"No."

"Did he make any other excuse other than he shot his mom and Bob?"

"No."

"So he never told you that the whole trip?"

"No, until at Judy's when he said that to her. But he didn't come out and say, 'I just shot them.' He didn't say that [in the car]."

Frasier asked, "He just said, 'It had to be done'?"

"Yes."

Finally, after two grueling days, the interview was over. Jessica was led back to her jail cell. Unlike with Gabe, a process began in the DA's office for her release. Gabe was not going anywhere.

CHAPTER 31

On March 22, 2010, Jessica and her lawyer were back in Judge Richard Barron's courtroom. Jessica was shackled and dressed in the orange jumpsuit again. Her attorney, Carole Hamilton, sat beside her.

As the proceedings went on, Jessica answered questions in a soft voice and often sniffled. During the hearing, Frasier pointed out that Jessica had been the one who drove the car away from the Eschlers' home, with Gabe and Kalea in the backseat. He added, "She even told investigators she wasn't forced to help her husband, nor was she afraid for her life or that of the child."

Nonetheless, Frasier was now allowing Jessica to be released from jail and she would only have to be on probation. She could not leave the state of Oregon while on probation, but she would be allowed to have custody of Kalea at some point in the future. All of this was dependent upon her actually testifying against Gabe at trial.

Frasier added that if new evidence was found that Jessica had more to do with the murders of Bob Kennelly and Robin Anstey than was known at the time by investigators, he had the right to charge her, according to that new evidence. Frasier said, "We are still free to prosecute her for the murders, if that is the case."

After the court hearing, Frasier told one reporter, "She [Jessica] needs to get her head screwed on. She has some things she needs to work on." In light of all that had happened, she had plenty to work on.

While Gabe was waiting to see how his extradition hearings would be going, he made a collect phone call from the Prince William County Jail to half brother Jesse McCoy. Jesse later said, "Instead of me blatantly asking him, 'Did you kill our mother?' I said, 'Gabe, do you need my help?' I was still hoping the little kid I once knew was hurting, was scared. I got nothing. He said, 'I don't know why the fuck I'm here!'

"I said, 'You're there because they think you murdered our mother. Do you know that Mom is dead?' He just went right to something else. I don't know this guy he is now. He has become a master liar."

Around that same time, DA Frasier let it be known that he wouldn't be charging Fred and Laura Eschler with any crimes, even though they had provided Gabe and his family with a gun, ammo, car and other items. The reason Frasier chose not to do so was "because they said they didn't know what Morris had done." The evidence seemed to back up this contention.

Some in the community, however, wondered about the fact that Frasier and the Eschlers had known each other for years, and how much of a factor that was in Frasier's decision. To lay to rest any of these suspicions, Frasier asked officials at the Oregon Department of Justice (DOJ) to look into the case.

On April 3, 2010, Frasier had his answer. Sean Riddell, the chief counsel for the DOJ, said, "Based upon the information provided, we concur with your assessment that there is insufficient evidence to support a prosecution of either Mr. or Mrs. Eschler for supplying listed items to Mr. Morris."

This ruling also removed any roadblocks for DA Frasier to move ahead as the prosecutor on the case. And a few weeks later, the case was definitely moving forward. In early May, Gabriel Morris was back in Coos County, Oregon. He was immediately taken from Virginia to the Coos County Jail in Coquille, where he waited arraignment before Judge Martin Stone.

The actual arraignment for Gabe Morris was somewhat unusual. He appeared at the hearing via a video link from the Coos County Jail library. As Judge Stone asked Gabe a few questions, Gabe sat quietly and answered them all in a polite tone. In fact, Gabe ended each sentence with the words "Your Honor."

Judge Stone appointed Peter Fahy, of Corvallis, to represent Gabe. Part of the reason was the fact that Fahy had represented other clients charged with murder. Fahy let the judge know that he would be seeking co-counsel in the case. He would be contacting Michael Barker, of Corvallis, Oregon. The reason was because Barker often dealt with death penalty cases. Bail was set at $5 million and then Gabe was escorted back to his jail cell.

Through it all, Gabe had sat as if he didn't have a care in the world. Just why that was would soon be delved into by both psychologists and psychiatrists for the defense and for the prosecution.

CHAPTER 32

Early on in the proceedings, one of the things the defense wanted to determine was whether Gabriel Morris was competent to stand trial. If he could not understand what was taking place in a courtroom, what the functions of the various people were, such as a judge and jurors, and could not help his counsel, he would be found not competent and a trial could not commence.

To ascertain just where Gabe stood on these issues, one psychiatrist and one psychologist were brought forward by the defense to look into Gabe's present mental state. A psychiatrist was brought on board by the prosecution.

The first man called in was Dr. Loren Mallory. He was a psychologist with a subspecialty in neuropsychology. Mallory had a B.A. from Point Loma Nazarene University, in San Diego, with a major in psychology and a minor in computer science. He went on to Fuller Theological Seminary, in Pasadena,

California, where he obtained a master's degree in psychology and a master's degree in theology. Eventually he obtained a Ph.D. in clinical psychology.

Mallory also had a lot of hands-on experience by 2010, which included stints at Pasadena Community Counseling Clinic and the Stop Abusive Family Environments (SAFE) program. He did a lot of forensic psychology work within the court system. In 1991, he got his license to practice in the state of Oregon and had been doing so mainly at the Willamette Valley Family Center in Oregon City ever since.

In a later court hearing, Mallory explained about the difference between a forensic psychologist versus a psychiatrist. He said, "A psychiatrist is a doctor trained in much more of a medical background. They understand all of the medical diseases and medications of an issue. I'm trained in psychological testing, evaluation, diagnostics, as well as therapy. What really sets neuropsychologists apart is the depth of testing and psychometrics. In other words, the measurement of behavior."

Even before meeting with Gabe, Mallory was given a lot of written material about the case. Mallory reviewed police records from Oregon and Virginia, Gabe's interview in Virginia to investigators, as well as the interviews of Judy Ward, Doug Miller and Jessica Morris.

Mallory's first face-to-face meeting with Gabe had to do with the "aid and assist" question. In other words, could Gabe aid and assist his counsel in his defense? From talking to Gabe, Mallory thought that Gabe had a "good base of knowledge about how the court system worked. He is intelligent and can reason things through."

Where the neuropsychologist found troubling issues about Gabe concerned what Mallory began to believe was a delusional disorder. In fact, by now, Gabe was no longer saying that he killed his mother and Bob Kennelly, as he had stated in Virginia. He was saying that a shadowy assailant had. Mallory intended to find out if this was part of a delusion, amnesia or just plain lying.

Gabe told Mallory that "the investigators allege that I killed my mother and her boyfriend." Gabe now said that he hadn't done that at all, but rather that he was innocent and "an intruder broke into the home and killed them." That was the reason that he, Jessica and Kalea had fled across the United States. Gabe told Mallory that he worked for the government in some kind of clandestine role. It had been some rogue government agents who had killed his mother and Bob Kennelly.

Mallory questioned him at length about whether he really had worked for the government. Eventually Gabe said he had made up stories about that. And then he told Mallory the "real" reason he supposedly had made up those stories. Gabe said, "God has been talking to me my whole life. He's always talked to me, given me dreams and feelings. God got me through abuse and neglect as a child. By high school, I realized God was leading me. So I cover it up by saying I work for the government.

No one would believe that God has blessed me and tells me what to do."

Gabe was unclear to Mallory as to whether he actually heard God's voice or not. He did clearly indicate that God communicated with him in spiritual ways. Gabe then went on a long and convoluted rant about the ways God communicated with him. Mallory noted that by letting Gabe just ramble on, "He became more pressured, disorganized and delusional."

Gabe finally admitted that sometimes he did hear an outside voice, which he assumed was God's voice talking to him. But mainly he just "knew" God's thoughts and feelings that God shared with him. And then he explained that he didn't actually need to hear God's voice, "Because if He has to holler at you, you are already in trouble."

Gabe denied having any history of mental-health issues or counseling, other than briefly seeing a counselor when his parents divorced when he was ten years old. Gabe did believe that mental-health issues and counseling were "real stuff and is irrefutable." But then he added, "I have studied the mind and I didn't find anything that would suggest that God was leading me toward mental-health problems. The opposite! This is science. You can prove it!"

Mallory noted that Gabe understood all of the basic points of the charges against him: what a defense attorney did, what a prosecutor did, what a judge and a jury did. He also understood about plea deals. As far as Gabe was concerned, what

Mallory had difficulties with was that "Mr. Morris does appear to suffer from delusional beliefs. Those who suffer from delusional disorders believe their delusional material, even when confronted with obvious and logical alternative information."

Mallory noted that people with delusional beliefs tended to rely on those beliefs and make irrational decisions, even in court matters. Mallory wrote that it would be difficult for Morris's defense attorneys to reason with him. Gabe's defense attorneys already attested that Gabe did not believe he was in any danger of being found guilty. God would not allow that to happen according to Gabe.

Gabe believed that God was still guiding him and would save him, no matter what. Gabe even told Mallory, "The jury will know what God wants them to know." Mallory said later in a court hearing, "I was worried that he might not make good decisions to help out his attorneys. From the beginning, he denied suffering from any mental illness. He never showed any interest in looking at the evidence against him."

Mallory wrote at the end of his report: *In short, Mr. Morris is at high risk of judging and acting on his delusional belief system, rather than on accurate information.* Therefore, Dr. Loren Mallory did not believe Gabe could adequately aid and assist his counsel.

The second doctor in the mix was Dr. Jerry Larsen, who was a psychiatrist. He had graduated from the University of Oregon, been to medical school and eventually had been given a fellowship in psychiatry that was only granted to sixteen candidates each year in the United States. Later he returned to the University of Oregon Health Sciences Center and became the director for emergency psychiatric care. By 2010, he saw eight individual clients per week and looked into at least two forensic cases per week. He had also written part of a previous *Diagnostic and Statistical Manual of Mental Disorders* (*DSM*) about alcohol and substance abuse.

Like Dr. Mallory, Larsen's task was to look into the "aid and assist" issue. Dr. Larsen visited with Gabe in jail and also talked to the jail staff about him. Larsen interviewed Gabe about his family history, later life and full range of his life in general.

As Larsen interviewed him, it was apparent that Gabe understood the legal process and understood what a judge, prosecutor and defense lawyer did. And yet with so much evidence against him, Gabe told Larsen that he believed the police had not done their job and had not looked for another suspect in the case. He was convinced another man had killed his mom and Bob Kennelly. Gabe absolutely thought he was going to be able to get on the stand and convince a jury that this was so. He said he could explain why he had given a false confession in Virginia. And God would direct him, as he was now being directed by God in jail. He was sure he would be acquitted and allowed to go home.

Gabe went even further than that. He believed he was now in jail as part of God's plan for him. He was there to help other people who were in the Coos County Jail. Gabe said he consistently got messages from God. These were not necessarily voices, but they were messages. These messages were essentially to protect him in jail. One thing Gabe was very adamant about was that he was not mentally ill. At one point, he refused to see a defense investigator because this investigator did not understand his relationship with God. And at another point, he wanted new attorneys because he believed they did not understand his special relationship with God as well.

Larsen noted later, "He was absolutely opposed to the fact that his attorneys might raise the issue of mental illness as a defense. It was odd, however, because he did it in a concise, calm manner. He didn't lose his temper, get angry or become agitated." Dr. Larsen had grave doubts that Gabriel Morris could aid and assist his attorneys.

The third mental-health specialist to interview Gabe was Dr. Michael Sasser. He was a psychiatrist and an undergraduate at the University of Oregon in biology. He later went to medical school at the University of Oregon, where he got a degree. Sasser eventually became director of the mental-health clinic in Medford, Oregon, and had a private practice as well. Dr. Sasser did about forty forensic evaluations a year for court cases.

Like the other two doctors, he was asked to look

into the competency issue for Gabe. Sasser read the transcripts and looked at the videos of the interrogation of Gabe in Virginia. He also looked at those types of materials concerning Jessica Morris. Then he got documents on the psychological testing that Larsen and Mallory already had done.

In his first face-to-face meeting with Gabe, Dr. Sasser went through his background and asked about his religious beliefs. In this area, Sasser later said, "I thought his ideas might be zealous, but not delusional. He spoke about having a special relationship with God and about some premonitions. He denied auditory hallucinations of God's voice actually talking to him. Once in Australia, he got a sense that he needed to go out to a certain area because God was leading him there. He went there and converted that family, but that is not inconsistent with the faith."

Dr. Sasser also got into Gabe's use of alcohol and marijuana. Gabe talked about dabbling with it in high school; but he admitted that just before the shootings, he was smoking four or five pipe bowls per day.

As far as aiding and assisting his attorneys, Dr. Sasser recorded that Gabe expressed a rapport with his attorneys in the case. Unlike the other two doctors who examined Gabe, Dr. Sasser determined that Gabe understood the workings of the court system and was competent to stand trial.

* * *

Whether there would actually be a jury trial, however, started to be questionable by May 2010. DA Frasier let Gabe's attorneys know that if Gabe pleaded guilty to the charges against him, he would take the death penalty off the table. Frasier would then argue to have Gabe sentenced to life without parole, while the defense could argue for a more lenient sentence. And the defense could present a mental-health case as part of sentencing.

It was a struggle to make Gabe admit to anything that he had done, since to some degree he still believed in the shadowy figure who supposedly had killed his mom and Bob Kennelly. His lawyers worked long and hard on this issue, and Gabe had come to trust them. Bit by bit, they got him to move toward this avenue, which, at least, would spare him the death penalty.

CHAPTER 33

The issue now became whether Gabriel Morris was too mentally ill at the time of the murders to understand the illegality of what he had done. The same mental-health professionals who had seen Gabe before on the "aid and assist" issue would interview him once again.

Dr. Mallory noted that Gabe was interviewed in the Coos County Jail in a small room with thick windows, a table and three plastic chairs. Gabe was dressed in jail garb and was "cooperative and appropriate. His motor movements were normal, and he was calm. He spoke in a clear and easily understood voice, and his volume was low, but easily heard."

Talking with Gabe about his personal history, Mallory noted that Gabe had been born in the San Diego area and lived there until the age of fifteen. Gabe got into all of the family dynamics: the rift between his mother and Danny, and his mother suddenly leaving.

Gabe told Mallory, "I had an awful and shitty childhood. I was abandoned by my mother." Gabe got into all of the alleged abuse at the hands of his father, but he added, "I felt some pity for my dad. I could see he was in a lot of pain."

Gabe then described moving up to Oregon to live with his mother and John Lindgren, his missionary days and going to BYU. After that, he started talking about his marriage to Jessica. Once again, he called her a "wonderful person," but he admitted that there had been problems in the marriage. He added, "I gave up being an airplane pilot for her. There wasn't any physical or verbal violence in the marriage, but we had our disagreements."

And although Gabe knew that in the Mormon culture it was important to have children, he now stated, "I told her several months into the marriage I didn't want children. I wanted to be a pilot with the air force. She became very sad, crying a lot, depressed, gaining weight—all because of wanting children. But I told her what I was about."

Gabe talked about his work history and it was all over the map. He said he had been a cook, a clerk at different stores, art framer, waiter, mechanic, psychological technician, personal trainer, manager of a gym, insurance agent and even bartender. He did not say where this had occurred, although it may have occurred in Las Vegas when he was living there. When asked specifics about these jobs, Gabe was very unclear as to when they had happened or just exactly what his duties had been in each. When asked why he hadn't worked for eighteen months before being arrested, he had no answer.

Even though Gabe was calm for the most part, he became more animated when subjects had religious overtones. At those times, Mallory noted that Gabe became more pressured in his speech and spoke "like a preacher." When given structured questions, Gabe had appropriate answers. When he was allowed to go on at length, his sentences became more incoherent and illogical.

As far as being in jail, Gabe said that he was in good health, slept well, didn't have suicidal thoughts or homicidal thoughts. Then he added one odd comment, "My life fascinates me. I've always been interested in reading books on history, culture, psychology and physics. I'm still able to enjoy these things."

Mallory explained later in a court hearing the importance he put on testing. "The process tends to be oriented to specific questions at first, and then more open questions, where a person can say things beyond yes and no."

In the Reynolds Intellectual Assessment Scales (RIAS) test, often referred to as an IQ test, Gabe scored as slightly above average. And in the Kaufman Functional Academic Skills Test (K-FAST), he scored in the 87 percentile.

It was with the Psychological Assessment Inventory (PAI) test that he started showing problems.

The answers indicated a defensive-response style and a denial of psychological problems. "His pattern of responses suggests that he tends to present himself in a consistently favorable light, and as being relatively free of common shortcomings to which most individuals will admit." He failed to recognize the areas where it was obvious he did have problems. These included suspiciousness, impact of traumatic events and distrust.

On the Positive Impression Management (PIM) test, he had a markedly high indication of paranoia. There were thought patterns of persecution as well. And this test was important in another regard. It tended to rule out malingering, where an inmate tried to fool a psychologist into believing he was mentally ill so that he couldn't be held accountable for his alleged crime. Gabe kept insisting he was *not* mentally ill.

Normally, Dr. Mallory did not do a Rorschach inkblot test, but with Gabe he did. Mallory noted that Gabe seemed to suffer from bouts of depression, even though he would not admit to these: "He tends to misperceive events and to form mistaken impressions of people and what their actions signify." Mallory said this was significant and often caused Gabe to make poor decisions in his life. And also important: "He shows less interest in other people than ordinarily would be expected."

Mallory pointed out that individuals with persecutorial beliefs will often believe that someone close to them is somehow involved. These individuals were likely to incorporate someone close to them into the delusions, rather than incorporating strangers. In many instances, this was more dangerous than believing some stranger was responsible. Since they were in close contact with a family member or friend, there were more chances of lashing out at them in a violent manner.

Mallory looked into the fact that Jessica had started to believe Gabe's delusions about being poisoned. This went into the realm of folie à deux, meaning a shared paranoid disorder. An individual with this disorder becomes so connected to a delusional person's disorders, he or she becomes delusional too. Usually, the second person in the folie à deux has low self-esteem and follows along with the stronger personality of the original delusional person. Gabe was the dominant person in this marriage, and Jessica went along with what he said—no matter how outlandish it might be.

Mallory looked at information to see if Gabe fell into the category of having an antisocial personality disorder. To fall into that category, a person needed to have conduct disorders before the age of eighteen, little or no regard for other people's feelings, and a lack of remorse and into conning others to get what he wanted. With that, there would be a history of psychopathy, violence and, most likely, trouble with the law. There had been none of that with Gabe through most of his life. Those around him had spoken of a kind, caring individual who went out of his way to help others. Even while on the run, he gave a man, who was waiting at a cold bus stop, a ride to a hamburger place. It was an act of kindness. He was able to function on various levels, but not when it came to the predominant theme of his delusion, according to Mallory.

The leading test on psychopathy had been developed by Robert Hare and was used by Mallory. Essentially, it was a checklist on an individual to see if he fell into the category of having an antisocial disorder. By means of this test, Mallory deemed that Gabe did not suffer from antisocial psychopathy.

And from what Mallory already knew about Gabe, he began to suspect that Gabe suffered from a "delusional disorder." The *DSM-IV* related: *The essential feature of a delusional disorder is the presence of one or more non-bizarre delusions that persist for at least one month.*

Mallory later explained what a non-bizarre delusion was. He said, "What they mean by that is that the delusions come from normal life. Bizarre delusions are like 'The green aliens are chasing me with a ray gun.' That leans toward schizophrenia." A non-bizarre delusion would be "My neighbor is trying to poison me." In other words, it is almost plausible, but not based upon any facts.

Mallory noted that Gabe had very odd beliefs about religion. Much of the time, he truly believed he was a prophet, and he even told Michael Stockford, the LDS branch president, that he was Jesus Christ. Gabe believed he had special healing powers and got messages directly from God. There were a few times when he actually heard God's voice, as if someone was speaking to him. This crossed the line into hallucinations.

The second major theme Mallory found with Gabe was grandiosity. In essence, no matter what an individual is interested in, he has a need to be better at it than anyone else. Or, at least, to make himself believe he is better than anyone else in that field. In Gabe's case, he came to believe he was bigger, better and more skilled than others. He came to believe he was in the Special Forces and on black ops missions. As Mallory noted, "It became real for him. This is not like a liar who knows better."

Mallory later explained in a court hearing, "This really comes from a broken ego inside—a very broken, very disturbed and very scared individual. It gets turned into the opposite of what it is and gets projected outward. Gabriel told stories of being almost drowned as a child and learned to breathe underwater. He told of running through the forest blindfolded." In part, Gabe may have felt that he never measured up to his older half brother, Jesse. To compensate for this, he told tales where he had led a much more adventurous and exciting life than had actually occurred.

"There was remarkably good functioning in other areas of his life, and that continued up until the last few months of his life before the murders. I believe he had these delusional beliefs for years, and they increased over time. In the last months before the murders, his life was falling apart.

"He believed the world was going to come to an end. Everything was mixed up in his mind. He was in a long-standing mentally ill delusional state. It was escalating and spinning out of control. He was very paranoid about his mother's boyfriend poisoning him and his family. And the paranoia moved on to his mom poisoning them as well. All that paranoia, all that agitation, put him at a point where something was ready to blow, and something tragic was ready to happen."

Mallory noted that delusional disorders generally developed in males in their twenties or early thirties. As far as Gabe went, Mallory said that he had been struggling with these things, but keeping them inside, while presenting a "better exterior presentation." And then Mallory added, "What I really noticed with the people who had known him a long time was the remarkable change they saw in him from what he used to be."

Mallory read reports that came from the Virginia investigators. In one report, Doug Miller had told the investigators that Gabe had told him that the federal government was planning to explode dynamite on a California fault line to make it sink into the ocean. And in another report, Gabe thought something catastrophic was going to happen in Coos County, Oregon. He had been sent there by God to give warning to those around him.

For his diagnosis, in the all-important Axis I category, Mallory said that Gabe suffered from a "delusional disorder with religious and grandiose content. His ability to understand his situation and the decisions required of him to a reasonable degree of rational understanding is compromised." If a jury believed this as well, they would have to send him to a mental hospital rather than to prison.

CHAPTER 34

Like Dr. Mallory, Dr. Larsen's task now was to try and determine if Gabe had not been able to understand and control his actions at the time of the shootings. Dr. Larsen interviewed Gabe several times in jail. Larsen later said that every interview with Gabe was "appropriate and engaging. He was cooperative and at times even joking. He remembered questions from previous evaluations. He seemed calm and at peace in jail, which is very unusual."

As Larsen looked at Gabe's family history, it became obvious there were several difficulties in his life, going back to his earliest years. Larsen noted that Gabe had extremely low self-esteem in his interactions with people. There was a need for him to feel good about himself. Therefore, he aggrandized his accomplishments. He talked in a way that would draw people's attention. He felt that if he was an accomplished individual, people would respect him. He told stories that made him seem greater than he really was.

Larsen believed all these stories created by Gabe were to try and compensate for his low self-esteem. As time went on, the stories got out of control. He was working for the government on black ops missions; he could run through the forest blindfolded at night; he could predict the future. On top of that, Gabe became more and more paranoid, especially about Bob Kennelly. This went from believing Bob had murdered his first two wives, to Bob trying to poison him and his family with rat poison.

Larsen noted that it was extremely unusual to have such a long record, as stated by others, about the mental illness occurring over years of time. With Gabe, one person after another who knew him spoke of his progressively deteriorating mental state. And in the fourth interview with Larsen, Gabe was very emotional when talking about being sexually abused by his father. Even one of Gabe's maternal aunts said that Gabe's father would not allow him to wear underpants. And Gabe's grandmother wondered if she had spotted anal bleeding when Gabe was a boy.

There was one aspect of his findings that Dr. Larsen was adamant about. In a later court hearing, he said, "One thing we know, you have to develop a relationship with the person being interviewed. You have to act in such a way that the person will be open and direct with you. We look for what happened in the developmental history of the individual. Let the person talk about how he felt about this or that. If you don't do that with a person who is delusional, they are not going to tell you. You won't get at that problem.

"The last thing is, you have to really be careful if you're dealing with someone who is delusional and psychotic. You cannot disagree with the delusion. If you do that, you're not going to get data and you may get incorporated into the delusion. And that could present a dangerous situation." In other words, if the patient believed that Dr. Larsen did not believe in his delusion, then the doctor could become an enemy, just as Bob Kennelly had been in Gabe's mind.

Gabe told Dr. Larsen about his father and mother and that she was present when Danny Morris tried to drown him in the ocean. Gabe said they both had looks of surprise and consternation when he walked out of the water and onto the beach. According to Gabe, they could not believe that he had survived such an ordeal.

Later on in an interview, Gabe said that his mother was naive and he felt abandoned by her when she left for Oregon. Gabe also thought she was not good at picking relationships with men. He thought she was sexually promiscuous. Then his delusions seemed to take over again, and he told Larsen that his mother in her antique shop in Bandon had been selling pornography and ripping off customers. Not one shred of evidence pointed to anything like that.

Gabe talked about his use of alcohol and drugs, but he did not say he was using a lot in Oregon in 2009 and 2010. This was at variance with what many other people reported, especially his half brother. There were other areas where he either did not tell the truth, or simply did not know what the truth really was. Gabe told Larsen he had quit ROTC because his wife was depressed. And the supposed reason he had left the Bingham County Sheriff's Office was because they were corrupt.

Interestingly, as Gabe opened up more and more to Dr. Larsen, he said that he had visualized his mother's death weeks before it happened. He did not say in what manner she would die, or if someone else was responsible for her death.

Larsen tested Gabe to see if he had disassociative amnesia, especially where the actual shootings took place. Larsen's conclusion was that Gabe might have had it, even though it was rare for it to occur weeks after an event.

As to his ultimate diagnosis, Dr. Larsen wrote, *Mr. Morris suffers from a delusional disorder that has significant religious content. This disorder rendered him as to not appreciate what he was doing, and therefore not able to control his behavior to the tenets of the law.*

CHAPTER 35

Dr. Michael Sasser also evaluated Gabe as to whether he suffered from a debilitating mental-health problem at the time he murdered his mom and Bob Kennelly. Sasser said in a later court hearing that there was some information that Gabe would not share with him, and this mostly centered around his time in Las Vegas. Gabe even asked Sasser, "Are you a Mormon investigator?" He seemed to be concerned about all of the alleged sinning he had done in Las Vegas.

Sasser replied that he was not a Mormon investigator, and he was trying to get information about what had happened around the time of the shootings. When Sasser told Gabe that, Sasser noted, "He accepted that and was responsive to my questions."

Since Dr. Sasser knew about the rat-poisoning issue from Larsen's and Mallory's reports, and Gabe was not sharing that information with him, Sasser asked him about it. Sasser noted later that

Gabe said it was not a major issue. "He said his wife, mother and daughter got ill and he found some rat poison and wondered if Bob had put it in their food. His wife went to see a health care provider and got some antibiotics. He did not say that the rat poison issue was something that really motivated his behavior."

When Dr. Sasser asked him about the killings, Gabe denied being the shooter. Gabe came up with answers about a shadowy figure in the house who had done the shooting. So Dr. Sasser asked him, "Well, if you had been watching the house all day, where did the shooter come from?" Sasser noted later in a court hearing, "I think he was surprised that anyone asked him that question. He would not give me an answer."

Dr. Sasser asked Gabe about going to the Eschler house after the murders, and Gabe told him that it was just a "fabricated story to get what [Gabe] wanted." Sasser noted later, "He didn't qualify it with God was talking to him and they wouldn't understand, so he made up the story about black ops."

Dr. Sasser's diagnosis was different than Mallory's and Larsen's. Sasser stated that Gabe did not suffer from a delusional disorder, but rather from personality disorders, which were not in the Axis I category. Unless they were in that category, they were not enough to show that he was incapable of understanding or conforming his actions at the time of the murders.

* * *

Through her lawyers, Jessica Morris had already agreed to testify against Gabe at trial. In a pretrial hearing, DA Frasier had many questions put to Jessica Morris. One of them was about whether she believed they were being poisoned with rat poison. Frasier asked her, "When you were in the kitchen in Bob Kennelly's home, preparing food, did you see anything that would make you think it was tampered with?"

Jessica responded, "Sometimes I saw residue in the pan. At first, I thought it was just because I hadn't cleaned it."

Frasier then wanted to know if she believed that Kennelly was poisoning them, why did they go back to the place on February 8, 2010?

Jessica said, "Because we felt like Gabe could talk to them, and because Mom was in danger. She needed to be taken away from that situation."

"Did you believe Robin was in on the poisoning?"

"I don't know when I came to that conclusion, but I came to believe she knew about it and didn't do anything about it."

Frasier asked about Gabe's belief that Bob had murdered his first two wives and gotten away with it. Jessica said, "Everybody knows everybody around here. And some thought Bob had harmed his wives. Bob had joked with Big John (Lindegren) that in that room (the marijuana-growing room) that nobody could hear any screams." Of course, Jessica had heard this story from Gabe, and assumed it had really taken place.

One of Jessica's own delusions had been that

during the time Gabe was separated from her and with Brenda, she believed that he was on secret missions for the government. She now said, "He was sent somewhere by the government to assassinate people." She had believed this story rather than have to admit to herself that Gabe was sexually involved with some other woman. As her own father, Bill Pope, had said, it was always easy for Gabe to pull the wool over Jessica's eyes.

As a trial approached, Gabe and his lawyers made a dramatic decision. In May 2011, Gabe decided to have a judge, not a jury, decide if he was guilty or not guilty, and then decide what his sentence should be if he was found guilty. It was also determined that his lawyers would be presenting an insanity defense.

In a document to this effect, Gabe agreed that he had a right to a jury trial and the right to have a jury decide what sentence should be imposed if he was found guilty. But then he also agreed to the following statement: *After being fully advised, and of my own free will, I wish to waive my right to a jury trial on all parts of this case, including of whether I am guilty or not guilty, and a determination of any sentence that may be imposed. I also wish to waive my right to see, hear and cross examine witnesses that otherwise would be necessary to prove the stipulation presented to the court this day.*

In other words, Gabe, through his lawyers, was stipulating to certain facts that had occurred.

When the judge heard the case, DA Frasier would present just what those stipulations were.

Judge Martin Stone, who would be deciding Gabe's fate, signed this document on May 4, 2011, and added that all parties were to present him with pretrial memos by July 29. A memo by the state saying they were no longer seeking the death penalty had to be to him by May 6.

Frasier lost no time in getting that memo to Judge Stone. It was titled "Notice by State of Intent to Not Seek the Death Penalty." And there were some important provisions in it: *The State reports that this notice is based upon the knowledge and information now in possession of the State. We reserve the right to withdraw this notice if the defendant withdraws his waiver of jury trial or withdraws his agreement to stipulate certain evidence.*

Frasier obviously had concerns that Gabe was going to try and get around what the prosecution saw as due justice by claiming a mental disease or defect defense. And one of Frasier's early memos to Judge Stone stated, *We point out that the defendant does not believe he is mentally ill. Initially he did not want his counsel to present this defense.*

All of that was true. Gabe was still insisting that he was not mentally ill nor had he ever been mentally ill. He was basically just going along with the defense his attorneys were going to present. Whether Gabe would get on the stand and testify remained to be seen. And if he did, Judge Stone could ask him questions directly.

In another memo, Frasier noted, *Obviously, the defendant by his killing his mother and her boyfriend has engaged in behavior that is disturbing. To many, the thought will be that a person has to be "crazy" to kill another, let alone his own mother.*

Then the prosecutor pointed out that mental disease was not something where a test, such as a blood test, could make an exact diagnosis. The psychiatrist or psychologist had to rely a lot upon the person being diagnosed. If that person lied to the mental-health professional interviewing him, it skewed the results. Frasier continued to maintain that Gabe was not delusional, but rather just a pathological liar. In fact, Frasier wrote, *The defendant's credibility is almost non-existent. He will lie at any opportunity. The defendant's guilt is beyond any doubt. The only hope this defendant has of ever walking the face of the earth as a free man is to be placed someplace, like a mental hospital, where he could be discharged in short order or from which he could more easily escape.*

Frasier even turned the fact that Gabe had not shot anyone during his robberies as evidence against him. He related that Gabe did not do so because he *could be in control* of his actions. A purely insane person would not care whether he shot someone during a robbery. The district attorney maintained that Gabe did not do so because he knew it would only make his flight from justice more risky.

And even though Gabe had talked to a lot of

people about his relationship with God, Frasier said that was not a motive in why he had killed his mom and Bob Kennelly. Frasier said that religious fanatics killed people all the time in the name of God, but they were not deemed to be legally insane. The DA contended that the only reason Gabe killed his mother and Bob Kennelly was because he was angry at them and did have something to gain financially by not having to pay back Bob Kennelly any money that had been loaned.

CHAPTER 36

On August 9, 2011, the court session began in Judge Martin Stone's courtroom in Coquille as to whether Gabe would be found guilty. If he was, then what kind of sentence would be pronounced? There was no jury—only Judge Stone would decide Gabe's fate.

DA Paul Frasier began his opening arguments, relating the timeline of all the events and pointing out the circumstantial evidence that he alleged showed that Gabriel Morris was the sole killer of Robert Kennelly and Robin Anstey. Frasier's opening statement was fairly short and so was that of defense attorney Peter Fahy. They were both going to let the witnesses on direct and cross-examination tell the story in full for them.

DA Frasier called Detective Sergeant Daniel Looney to the stand, and Looney went through questions and answers concerning Deputy Slater finding the bodies of Robert Kennelly and Robin Anstey, the investigative work in the house and on the property, as well as the connection to the Eschlers. He also testified about Kennelly's pistol being found down in San Diego.

Looney testified, "We put out a 'To locate Gabriel, Jessica and Kalea Morris' bulletin to law enforcement agencies. We knew they had a silver Ford Taurus that belonged to Fred Eschler. We used the media and *America's Most Wanted* and also the Center for Missing and Exploited Children."

Sergeant Looney went on about the items he had found in the silver Ford Taurus in Virginia, including maps with routes marked in ink and a note from Fred Eschler. There had also been ammo clips found in the vehicle and hallucinogenic plant material.

As far as the Popes' red pickup truck found behind a small hill on Bob Kennelly's property, there was a bunch of marijuana residue in there and a glass marijuana pipe as well. On the property itself, there was a small marijuana grow in the garage area with twenty-six small plants.

Looney said, "The defendant had talked Robin and Robert into applying for permits to grow medical marijuana."

Defense lawyer Peter Fahy objected to this, saying, "Objection to who advised about this."

The objection was sustained.

So Frasier got into the fact that in Gabe's room was a receipt for construction materials that were related to the marijuana grow room. It was a receipt from a hardware/lumber company in Coos Bay.

Looney testified that bullets recovered from the bodies of Robert Kennelly and Robin Anstey matched to bullets that would have been fired from the gun found in San Diego, California. And it was known that Gabriel Morris had been in San Diego on that date because there had been surveillance video of him robbing a convenience store there.

A check of Bob's residence had been made to try and find the holster that went with Kennelly's HK .40-caliber handgun. Looney said the holster had been found underneath Gabe and Jessica's bed in Kennelly's residence.

Looney next spoke about the area where Gabe had done surveillance on the residence in the morning hours of February 8, 2010. Gabe had been in a tree line above the garage area, looking at the residence through binoculars. The Popes' pickup truck was hidden from view behind a hill. All of this came from Jessica's interview concerning what had happened on that day.

Sergeant Looney's testimony on direct took quite a while, as photos and other evidence items were introduced, one by one. On cross-examination, Michael Barker asked Looney just exactly what his role was with the team that was put together to investigate the crime scene.

Looney said, "As a case officer, we have a multi-agency team that gets together on major crimes, such as homicides. The case officer, which I was on this case, directs people to go out and do things. I try to keep up with everything that is going on with the case."

Barker walked Looney through the trail of the Morrises down to San Diego after the shootings and asked what he had found in the Popes' red pickup, which had been left behind the garage area. Looney replied, "If I remember correctly, there was a sleeping bag or two, a box with some pots and pans, a guitar and bowling shoes. Jessica's purse was in there as well."

"Anything in the purse, like money?"

"I don't remember."

Barker also questioned about a check made out to the Morrises from Lewis & Clark College and whether they could have cashed it for money, rather than just leaving it in Coos County. Looney said he didn't know. The implication Barker was trying to get at was that Gabe was so delusional that he didn't even take this money with him.

So then Barker asked if anything belonging to the Morrises had been found in Bob Kennelly's white pickup abandoned near the Eschlers' home. Looney said there hadn't been anything.

Barker asked, "You talked about thirteen shell casings that were found. Am I correct that the lab decided that all thirteen were fired from the HK-40?"

"I believe so, yes."

"You found a clip that belonged to the HK-40 at the scene in Oregon?"

"Yes."

"Did you ever find a second magazine?"

"No."

"So that weapon that was sent back to you from San Diego was sent back without a clip?"

"Correct."

"As far as you know, the weapon was not fireable after it left the crime scene."

"That is incorrect."

Perhaps Barker was trying to discover if Gabriel Morris could not have fired the gun at a robbery in San Diego if it was inoperable.

Since thirteen spent shell casings were found at the crime scene, Barker wanted to know if all thirteen bullets could be accounted for. Looney said that not all of them had been found. He said there was at least one bullet that probably went through Robin's head and was out in the brush somewhere. The number of bullets found came to ten, so that left three not discovered.

Barker asked if a laptop computer had been found in the Castle Room, the room in which Kalea slept. Looney had to look through his notes and stated that they found a Dell computer, but he wasn't sure now if that was a laptop computer. He looked farther into the notes and said, "Okay, here it is, an HP Pavilion laptop."

Moving on, Barker asked if Gabriel Morris had a wallet with him when he was arrested. Looney couldn't find that in his report, so Judge Stone broke in and asked if Looney could check on that later. Looney said that he could, and Judge Stone said to Barker, "I'll have him look for it sometime this week and you can recall him if you want."

Barker next questioned, "You said that a vehicle had gone up against a bank as it left the area. Your words—'It was dangerous and silly.'"

"Yes."

In this line of questioning, Barker might have been getting at that nothing Gabe was doing that day made any rational sense.

"Is it true there is no way you could know where Ms. Anstey was when she was first struck?"

"Not for sure, but I can make a good educated guess."

"I'll ask you what your guess is."

"Okay, based on the evidence at the scene, both the individuals had just come home, they walked in the door, and Robin Anstey was probably just ahead of Robert. She set her purse down on the couch with some grocery bags, and then the defendant started opening fire."

Apparently, Detective Sergeant Looney pointed at Gabe Morris at that point, and Barker objected to Morris being pointed at.

Judge Stone replied, "I'll sustain the objection."

Looney went on with his testimony. "I believe Robin was real close to the chair with the bullet hole in it, when first struck. Bob was in the same area. The one French door was probably still open and then the shooting started."

"So you have to assume Ms. Anstey moved out under her own power?"

"Oh, absolutely. She was getting the heck out of Dodge."

CHAPTER 37

DA Frasier, on redirect, asked several questions about Gabe trying to get .40-caliber ammunition from Fred Eschler, but Fred didn't have any. So he gave Gabe a 9mm Beretta.

Then Frasier asked, "Last week, did you take the HK-40 out and test-fire it?"

Looney replied, "I did. I wanted to find out about its characteristics. Semiautomatics—they toss casings depending on the brand of the gun. I was curious which way the shell casings were tossed from that gun. I found that they basically would go right past my shoulder."

Frasier said, "There were no shell casings found on the balcony?"

"Correct."

"Yet there were strong indications, based on trajectories that the shots were fired from the balcony?"

"Yes."

"So, how do you explain that there were no shell casings up there?"

"Basically, the shell casings would have hit the bathroom wall and bounced down to the lower floor. And the shell casings down on that floor were where they should have been. They're also metal, so they went bouncing off the Pergo floor."

After Sergeant Looney was through, DA Frasier wanted the stipulations that had been agreed upon by the prosecution and defense to be read into the record. These, in essence, were things that the prosecution had contended, and that Gabe Morris and his attorneys agreed were true.

Among the first things stated were that both sides agreed the crimes occurred in Coos County between February 8, 2010, and February 10, 2010. Robert Kennelly and Robin Anstey were killed during the same episode, shot to death, and this occurred at Robert Kennelly's home. It was agreed that Robin Anstey was the defendant's biological mother and was the girlfriend of Robert Kennelly.

The defense even agreed that Gabriel Morris, Jessica Morris and Kalea Morris quickly left the scene in a pickup truck that belonged to Robert Kennelly. They also agreed that Gabriel Morris took an HK-40 handgun that was owned by Robert Kennelly.

The defense agreed with the prosecution that the defendant drove with Jessica and Kalea to the home of Fred and Laura Eschler, where he procured a car, clothing, money, a 9mm Beretta handgun and ammo clips. The defense also agreed that the defendant drove with his family to San Diego after that, then to Arizona, and eventually to Dumfries, Virginia. It was there that they all stayed in the home of Judy Ward and her husband, Doug Miller, from February 15, 2010, to February 22, 2010.

The defense even stipulated, "On February 22, 2010, the defendant attempted to leave the residence of Ward and Miller. Miller was at work and Gabriel Morris was driving a vehicle belonging to the brother of Judy Ward. Ms. Ward was in the vehicle with Gabriel. Jessica and Kalea Morris were following the defendant in the Eschlers' vehicle. After a short distance, Jessica and Kalea were stopped by the police. Then Gabriel Morris was stopped by the police. Jessica and Gabriel Morris were taken into custody."

Defense counsel Peter Fahy agreed that all these stipulations were true and factual. What he did not stipulate to was the alleged "confession" by Gabriel Morris to the killings while he was in Virginia. So Frasier had the audio and video of that interview played for the judge; it took up about a ninety-minute period of time.

The autopsies were entered into evidence, showing the various gunshot wounds and possible angles from which they had been fired. Like the other evidence, all of this was a slow and meticulous process. An item would be presented to Judge Stone, he would ask the defense if there was any objection; and with few exceptions, there were no objections to the admission.

Frasier got the interview with Judy Ward and

Doug Miller entered into evidence, and then he rested his case. He had called very few witnesses. In essence, he let the physical evidence and Gabe's own words to investigators in Virginia make the case for him.

CHAPTER 38

On direct from Peter Fahy, Michael Woods told what a good employee Gabe had been at the BMW dealership and an "all-around nice guy." Woods also spoke of when Gabe came to see him in early 2010 and he could not believe the changes in Gabe. Gabe seemed a lot more stressed, spoke in a nonstop manner and drank alcohol and smoked marijuana. Woods said it was radically different than the Gabe he had known.

It was this aspect of seeing Gabe in 2010 that Frasier zeroed in on during cross-examination. Woods said that he had met Gabe at a nice hotel in Troutdale, Oregon, and spent two hours there with him. "Gabe was smoking pot and drinking beer. I knew he had served on a mission for the LDS Church, but I didn't comment on any of this to Gabe."

So Frasier asked what Woods thought of that

activity on Gabe's part. Woods replied, "I don't know. I was just taken aback. It was such a drastic change from the way I knew him before. A lot of time had passed and he had grown up and changed." Woods was going to go on, and then was at a loss for words.

Frasier wanted to know why Woods hadn't said anything to Gabe about smoking pot and drinking beers.

Woods replied, "I was basically listening to what he had to say. And just taking it all in."

"Were you disappointed in his behavior?"

"I don't know."

"The reason I ask, sometimes people who see them doing different things—"

Woods broke in and said, "I felt, wow, he's kind of out there. It's such a drastic change. I didn't know what was going on."

Woods went on to say that Gabe told him about being in Special Forces, a black ops group. Frasier noted that Woods had spoken with an investigator for the defense about this. Then Frasier asked, "You indicated to the investigator that you didn't see any holes in his story. Why not?"

Woods answered, "The stories were very well-told. I mean, I knew that he had been in the military. I know that he wanted to be a pilot, but that didn't work out. From him being so truthful before, I trusted some of what he was saying."

"So your only source about this was Gabe. There was no outside source saying that he switched out of the ROTC or anything like that?"

"No."

Frasier asked, "Did you think you had to do anything to help this young man?"

Woods said at the time that he didn't.

Frasier followed up by asking if Woods thought Gabe might hurt someone.

Woods answered in the negative to that question and one that concerned whether he thought Gabe was delusional. In fact, Woods added that at the time he only thought that Gabe was telling him "big stories." He did not think that Gabe was out of control or hallucinating.

But when Frasier asked if Woods thought that Gabe was mentally ill, there was a long pause. Finally Woods said, "I didn't know what to think."

Frasier followed up with whether Woods said to Gabe that he needed to see a mental-health counselor. Woods replied that he did not. He also replied negatively to other questions. He had not gone to the police about this or Gabe's other problems.

Frasier wanted to know if Woods had any contact with Gabe in the week before the shootings. Woods said that he had not.

Frasier added, "You cannot give us an indication what his mental state was on the day of the homicide?"

"No, I cannot."

Fahy had his chance again on redirect and asked if Woods had ever seen any signs of violent or aggressive behavior on Gabe's part. Woods answered, "No, just the opposite. He was easygoing. I don't think I ever saw him get angry at anybody."

* * *

Switching to Gabe's days as a missionary in Australia, Dr. Terrence Barry was next on the stand. On direct, he spoke of what a fine young man Gabe had been. Fahy asked him about these qualities and Dr. Barry said, "He was pleasant, always upbeat. He had a very positive outlook." And once again he stated that Gabe was an extraordinary young man among extraordinary young men.

Fahy wanted to know if Dr. Barry ever doubted Gabe's honesty. Barry replied, "Never."

"Did he present any problems in his missionary life?"

"None."

"Could you have foreseen something like what happened?"

"No."

DA Frasier wanted to know on cross how long it had taken Dr. Barry to make Gabe a senior companion on his mission. He may have been getting at the assumption that it took longer than the norm. Dr. Barry said that he didn't recall. So then Frasier asked if it was outside the normal period of time. Dr. Barry replied that he thought that was not the case. Frasier queried if Dr. Barry had ever given Gabe a leadership role at any time. Barry recalled that he had made Gabe a zone leader overseeing other missionaries.

Frasier then got to the point that Dr. Barry had

not seen Gabriel Morris since 2001. Frasier asked if there had been any reunions of missionaries and if Gabe had attended any of those. Barry didn't know if Gabe had or not.

Frasier wondered how many missionaries Dr. Barry had seen while he was in Australia. Barry thought the number was somewhere between three hundred and four hundred. So Frasier asked if any of those had fallen away from the teachings and tenets of the LDS Church. Barry responded that he was sure a few might have.

Frasier asked, "You indicated that it was a surprise for you to see the defendant in this position. Is that correct?"

"Yes."

"In the intervening time from when you last saw him, you had no idea what decisions he made or how he ended up in this position?"

"No. The only information that I had was that this episode occurred."

CHAPTER 39

On direct, Dr. Barry's wife, Matrina Evanoff Barry, was also very positive about the Gabriel Morris she had known in Australia. She said that he was very humble, positive and compassionate. She testified to the time when Gabe had been very sick and living in a tenement in Sydney. Matrina said that even then, Gabe was more concerned about his missionary companion than he was about himself.

Fahy asked if Mrs. Barry had kept in contact with Gabe over the years. She said she had not until she started writing letters to him in the previous month while he was incarcerated. Fahy then wondered about the tone of the letters, without getting into specifics.

Mrs. Barry said, "When he wrote to me, I saw Gabe the missionary. I saw Gabe the compassionate person. I saw Gabe concerned about other people and how he could help them, lift them up and encourage them. The thing I really, really saw was his prevalent attitude to give people hope. He wanted them to know that they had worth and value and they were a child of God."

On cross, Frasier got immediately to the letters from Gabe. "They sounded like the Gabe in Australia?"

"Right."

"You didn't see anything in the letters that led you to believe he was having issues?"

"No."

Looked at in one light, this response by Matrina Evanoff Barry seemed to back up Frasier's contention that Gabe did not appear to be mentally ill. Since Gabe was not taking medication or having therapy while in jail, this seemed to corroborate Frasier's contention that Gabe was not suffering from mental disease or a defect that had impaired his ability to reason at the time of the shootings. And since he now behaved himself while sitting at the defense table, Frasier contended that Gabe didn't need medication or therapy because he had never suffered from a delusional disorder. In a very strange way, it was hurting Gabe's cause to be so civil at the defense table, because he was not acting out while in the courtroom. He just sat there quietly, occasionally taking notes; but more often than not, he was just sitting passively and listening to what was being said.

* * *

Colonel Roger Maher, who ran the U.S. Air Force ROTC program on the Brigham Young University campus, was next on the stand. Maher said that Gabe was "bright, positive, optimistic and personable." Maher even spoke of the dinner he and his wife had over at Gabe's house with Jessica, and that it had been a very pleasant evening. On direct, Maher said that Gabe gave as a reason for leaving the ROTC program: "'I have to protect my mother.' Out of respect for Gabriel, I didn't pursue that."

On cross-examination, Colonel Maher agreed that Gabe got some money for being in the ROTC program. DA Frasier wanted to know what happened if a person who was in the U.S. Air Force ROTC program dropped out of it before completing the program. Maher replied, "They are obligated to repay the money." Asked if Gabe had repaid the money, Maher said he didn't know.

Frasier then asked about when could a person in the ROTC expect to be assigned a slot in the air force. Maher said it was after the second year. That was a year that Gabe did not attend in ROTC.

So Frasier asked, "Was he ever given an assignment such as going to pilot school?"

Maher replied, "We had a pretty good record at BYU for those who wanted to go to pilot school. Probably about a ninety-eight percent placement ratio. So if he had the desire and was physically qualified, and academically qualified, he would have had about a ninety-eight percent chance of going there."

"If he told other people that he was a pilot, was he telling the truth?"

"No, sir."

"Did he ever tell you why he had to protect his mother?"

"It was not part of the conversation."

"If he told other people he wanted out of the program because he didn't want Jessica to be a military wife, that would be different that what he told you?"

"Yes, sir."

"When was the last time you had any contact with the defendant?"

"Some years after Gabriel left the program at BYU, I received a phone call at home. He was in Idaho, looking for a letter of reference. He had applied for a position with the police force."

Maher added that he was pleased to recommend Gabe for the sheriff's deputy position. Maher was sure that Gabe would do well there in his duties.

Gabe's grandmother Lynn Walsh was very emotional during direct testimony by Fahy. She started with Gabe's early life and the trauma of the divorce between Gabe's father and mother, and Gabe's being taken by Danny Morris. She also told of what she thought was very disturbing behavior on Danny's part in regard to his son.

* * *

Lynn was even more emotional when questioned by DA Frasier during cross-examination, often crying as she answered his questions. Frasier began by asking, "You're very concerned for your grandson, aren't you?"

She said that she was; so he next asked, "In fact, you came to see me in my office about what to do about this, didn't you?" She replied that she had.

Frasier continued by referencing how Lynn had said that at the time Gabe joined the ROTC in Utah, he was an honest person. Then Frasier asked if she had heard personally from Gabe that he'd actually obtained a pilot's position in the air force. She responded that she hadn't, but Jessica often called her during that period to say what was happening with Gabe.

Frasier next asked her about what she knew of Gabe's time as a police officer in Idaho. Lynn answered, "He called me when he was accepted. I told him I was concerned about it, but he told me not to worry. He told me he thought he could help people there and that was his objective."

"Did he tell you why he left the sheriff's office?"

Lynn said that he had not.

"Were you aware of Gabriel and Jessica separating?"

"Yes."

"Did Gabriel tell you why?"

"I didn't talk to him during that period."

"Why not?"

"Because he didn't contact me, and I didn't know where he was."

Moving on to when Gabriel came to see her weeks before the shootings, Frasier wanted to know if he'd actually gone there with his wife and child.

Lynn said that he had, and that Gabe, Jessica and Kalea had spent five days at her house. She added that she was upset about the state Gabe was in. "I cried and prayed and I worried."

Frasier asked if she thought that Gabe might hurt someone. She replied that she didn't think that.

"Did you attempt to get ahold of a police officer to express your concern?"

"No."

"Did you try to get ahold of a mental-health counselor?"

"No."

Frasier wondered what Gabe had said about his supposed "final mission" that he had to complete overseas.

Lynn said that Gabe insisted he was going to China to finish some kind of secret mission. "He had to go there to get some information on people that other people needed to know about."

Frasier looked at a report from when Lynn had been questioned by an investigator. Frasier then said, "I'm looking at the defense investigator's report, and you told her, 'He said he was in investigative work. He said I wouldn't understand it, but it went way, way back.'"

Lynn responded, "I told her what Gabe told me."

Frasier asked, "What would you like to see happen to Gabriel Morris?"

Lynn replied, "I would like to see Gabriel restored to good health, to be the person he really is."

"What do you think should happen to him, if, in fact, he killed your daughter?"

That possibility was so overwhelming that Lynn responded, "I can't believe he killed my daughter. Gabriel Morris would not kill my daughter."

Frasier could have continued on this track, since all the evidence and Gabe's alleged confession pointed to him having killed his mother, Lynn's daughter. Perhaps, though, Frasier could see how emotional Lynn already was, and moved on.

Instead, he asked, "You've been corresponding with the defendant ever since he was incarcerated, right?" She said that was so.

"In his letters that he writes to you, can you describe, please, the tone he uses with you?"

Lynn replied, "Gabriel and I have a loving, trusting, grandmother/grandson relationship."

"In the letters that you have received from the defendant, do you see any difference [in] what he says now than what you remember Gabriel being and saying several years ago?"

"Yes, I would say that Gabriel's letters do reflect a different mentality."

Frasier wanted to know in what way, so she said, "Some of it . . ." Then there was a long pause before she stated, "I don't know how to answer that."

"Does he seem to love you?"

Lynn answered yes.

"Does he express concern for others?"

Lynn said he did.

"Does he say the same type of things he said to you before this incident occurred?"

Lynn agreed that was correct.

"Well, what's the difference?"

There was another long pause before Lynn replied, "Probably, it's like a lapse. There's been a lapse in his life that he's not even aware of."

"Isn't it true you see the same old Gabe in the letters?"

Lynn responded, "I've seen progress in that way."

Redirect brought Fahy out to say, "Counsel asked you if you thought about calling the police. Previously, had you seen any violent behavior by Gabe?"

Lynn answered that she hadn't.

"Did you have any reason to believe he would hurt anybody, though he was acting irrationally?"

Lynn said that she didn't.

So Fahy asked if she did have concerns in that area, would she have contacted authorities?

Lynn replied, "Of course."

Fahy brought up the fact that she had told a defense investigator at some point that she had seen "Gabe start to crack."

Lynn added in testimony, "When he was in the

sheriff's office and insurance business, it was inconsistent with his personality. That's when he stopped communicating with me."

Fahy then asked, "And you said that he started to become the old Gabe after a year and a half of a stable environment in jail. Is that correct?"

Lynn said that was so.

"When you say you don't believe Gabe Morris killed your daughter, do you believe he would not be capable of doing that?"

His grandmother responded, "I do not believe he would be capable of doing that."

CHAPTER 40

On the stand, Jesse McCoy was very emotional and could barely hold back his tears. It was quite evident how much he still loved his little brother, even though he knew without a doubt that Gabe had killed their mom.

Fahy had Jesse go back through his life with Gabe, all the way from Gabe's birth through his early years and into adulthood. The testimony went clear up to Gabe being arrested in Virginia.

Then Fahy asked, "You're in a double bind here, Mr. McCoy. Did you love your mother very much?"

Jesse could hardly get the words out through his crying. He finally managed to say, "Yes."

"Do you still love Gabe?"

"Yes."

"What would you like to see happen to your brother?"

"I would want Gabriel to receive help. I want to see him get through this."

* * *

DA Frasier had a difficult task ahead of him. He had to elicit vital information from Gabe's half brother without antagonizing him or seeming to be badgering him. And the first question was particularly sensitive.

Frasier said, "Mr. McCoy, in some of the psychiatric reports we received on this case, I'm going to ask you about some allegations. Gabriel accused you of sexually abusing him. Is that true?"

Jesse said that it was not true.

Frasier continued with this thread. "Yesterday we listened to a recording of your brother, where he claimed he was forced by you to have sex when he was six years old with a black girl. Is that true?"

Jesse replied, "A six year old can't have sex. There might have been fondling involved, but Gabriel took it to an extreme. I can understand him saying that."

"Did you force him to have sex?"

"As much as a young person can force another to have sex." (Author's note: Jesse was only twelve years old at the time of the incident.) "I guess I might have provoked him to do that."

Frasier wanted to know if Jesse had denied this allegation to other people, and Jesse responded that he didn't think so.

Frasier continued, "Well, on September 9, 2010, you were interviewed by an investigator. She specifically related, 'I asked McCoy if he forced Gabriel to have sex with a female in the neighborhood.'

And you denied this and asked if Gabriel gave any other details. He alleged that you forced him to have sex with a black female while you watched."

Jesse responded to this by saying, "In the way she explained it to me, I didn't recall the incident happening. But the situation was seen differently by the two of us [Gabe and Jesse] and I explained that to her."

Moving on, Frasier wanted to know about what Gabe had told Jesse about supposedly being left in the ocean by his parents to drown. Jesse retold the story about the ocean that Gabe had claimed. He added, "I do not believe my mother would have ever let that happen."

The next issue concerned Gabe's drug use as a teenager, and Jesse said that he knew Gabe smoked marijuana in high school, but not to extremes. And Gabe did not drink alcohol or do hard drugs.

Frasier countered this by saying that Jesse told one investigator that he thought Gabe had tried LSD. Jesse agreed he had told the investigator that, but he had heard it secondhand, and had never witnessed Gabe actually doing that.

Frasier moved on to the time that Jesse and his wife, and Gabe and his wife, shared a house in Provo, Utah. Frasier asked what Gabe was doing in terms of marijuana use at that time. Jesse replied, "Nothing until the very, very end. It was about the time he felt anguish about going into the air force. There was some marijuana use, but nothing like in 2009 and 2010."

Frasier referred back to a report where Jesse

had told an investigator that Gabe would take an occasional drink in Provo, but "was using marijuana constantly."

Jesse replied, "I recall saying that toward the end there in that house, he would do that. And he would have a beer or two with me."

Frasier next wanted to know if Jessica Morris knew about any of this at the time, or if Gabe was hiding it from her. Jesse said that Gabe was hiding it from her. Frasier then asked how Gabe felt about doing that, and Jesse said, "He felt bad about it."

Following that line, Frasier looked into a report where Jesse had said to an investigator, "He justified it as, it would be better not to tell her and for her not to know." Jesse said he didn't recall those exact words, but he had said something along that line.

Frasier then said, "You knew that drinking and smoking marijuana was against the Mormon religion. Did you ask your brother why he was doing this?"

Jesse answered that he had not, and it was Jesse who asked Gabe to have a beer with him on occasion.

Once again, Frasier looked into an investigator's report. Jesse had told the investigator that he had asked Gabe how he could justify smoking marijuana with his Mormon faith.

Jesse replied that now he did not recall being asked that question. Jesse added that he [Jesse] never did care whether Gabe drank alcohol or smoked some marijuana because he [Jesse] did not believe in the tenets of the Mormon faith.

Frasier then wanted to know if Gabe ever told Jesse why he was smoking marijuana. Jesse said that he did, and Gabe's reason was "It makes me relax."

Frasier next got to a point where Jesse had told the investigator that Gabe was actually a huge proponent of marijuana use.

Jesse said that was so and added, "He believed that if everyone in the world smoked it, the world would be a better place."

Frasier went on with the report that Jesse had told the same investigator that Gabe would use marijuana to "self-medicate" and had done so for years. Jesse said that was incorrect, that Gabe had not smoked marijuana in the Provo house until the very end of the time he lived there.

In another part of the interview, Frasier noted that Jesse had told the investigator that Gabe claimed that he'd been offered a pilot's position in the air force, along with a good friend named Joshua. Gabe had also told Jesse that he turned the slot down because "God told me not to take it."

Jesse agreed that was basically true and Gabe had turned it down because he "didn't want to be a killer of human beings."

Frasier replied, "You tried to talk him into taking the slot, didn't you?"

Jesse agreed that he had and added, "I thought it was a good opportunity for him, and he was making a mistake by letting it go."

"That he could have had other positions other than a combat pilot?"

"Sure."

"Did he ever tell you that he was leaving the ROTC program because he didn't want Jessica to be a military wife?"

Jesse said that he did not recall any conversation like that.

Frasier then asked, "Do you feel you have to be his guardian?"

"I felt that way my whole life. But at this moment, I feel that 'guardian' is the wrong word. I feel hurt for him."

"Do you feel that it's your duty to help him?"

"I feel that my mother would have wanted me to help him."

Frasier wanted to know if Gabe had issues about his mother abandoning him when she left Danny Morris.

Jesse said, "In the very, very last phone call I got from him, yes, he talked about abandonment. He couldn't believe that Mom and I left him with Danny. He was very emotional on the phone call. This was just days before the shooting."

Frasier next asked about the way Gabe felt about Robert Kennelly and the living arrangement of his mother with Kennelly. Jesse said he didn't know how Gabe felt about it.

"Did the defendant ever express any concerns for the safety of your mother, because she was living with Mr. Kennelly?"

Jesse replied that he didn't, but he knew that Gabe did not like Kennelly.

"Did he ever tell you that he thought Mr. Kennelly was poisoning him?"

Jesse said that he didn't hear about this until Gabe spoke on the phone to him from Virginia. This was right after Gabe's arrest.

"Did he tell you that he thought Mr. Kennelly was going to sexually abuse Kalea?"

Jesse didn't remember any conversation like that.

Frasier wanted to know what Gabe had told him on the phone call just before the murders.

Jesse responded, "It was about what he was doing. He said things were okay and he had a big job coming up. Someone was going to fly out from overseas and he was going to meet this person in a hotel. There was going to be some good money in it, and things were looking good. He went on and on, just rambling. He also brought up how angry he was at the fact that Mom had abandoned him. I didn't even have a chance to talk about that because he went on to something else."

"Did you at any time see anything that the defendant's mental state posed a danger to Mr. Kennelly or your mother?"

Jesse said that he did not.

Fahy knew Jesse McCoy was a key witness, and he spent a long time on redirect. Fahy started out by asking, "On this whole issue of being sexually abused as kids, did you ever have any kind of sexual contact with Gabe?"

Jesse said that he did not.

"The first time you heard the story about his parents trying to drown him, that was when he started to go south in his mental state?"

Jesse agreed that was so.

At that point, Judge Stone chimed in and said, "I want to be sure I understand that. When did you first hear that story from him?"

Jesse replied, "I can't give you a specific date, but I'm sure it was after Utah and Idaho. It must have been in the Oregon time frame. Although it might have been when he was getting divorced from Jessica."

Fahy continued, "You have concerns for Gabe as your brother, but have you told this court anything except the absolute truth?"

"No."

"In other words, are you going to kind of fudge things to help your brother?"

Frasier objected, saying, "Your Honor, that is kind of [a] self-serving question."

Judge Stone sustained the objection.

Fahy tried again. "Well, is your love and lifetime attempts to help your brother clouding your ability to tell us exactly what happened?"

"Absolutely not."

"The stories he told you while he was in Las Vegas about stealing from the rich and giving to the poor, was there any evidence of that?"

Jesse said there was not.

"When you were on the phone to Gabe, you alluded to other issues. What issues were those?"

Jesse responded, "Sexual abuse from Danny and how mom and I didn't protect him. Some pretty graphic stuff."

Fahy wanted to know if Jesse ever got the idea that Gabe no longer loved his mother or was disappointed in her. Jesse said that Gabe was all over the place. And as far as Gabe becoming increasingly paranoid, Jesse testified that he absolutely was.

Fahy then asked if in the phone calls of the last few weeks before the shootings if Gabe was making any sense at all.

Jesse said that Gabe was not. "He just rambled on and on and changed topics very quickly."

Fahy wondered, "Was there any underlying fear and anxiety?"

Jesse answered, "Yes. It seemed very urgent."

At that point, Judge Stone spoke up and said, "Clarify one thing for me. You lived with him in Provo, Utah, from when to when?"

Jesse replied, "It would have been early 2002 to that later part of 2003 or early 2004."

"And your testimony is that he was not using marijuana in the home?"

"At the end, he was. The last few months that we lived there."

"And that was outside the presence of Jessica?"

Jesse answered, "As far as I know, yes."

CHAPTER 41

Witness David Grover was called to the stand to explain about what Gabe was like when he worked at Grover's restaurant the Kozy Kitchen in North Bend. Grover spoke of when Gabe had been an employee and what an exceptional young man he had been. Grover also spoke of Gabe's visit to him in early 2010 and how odd it was. Asked about how he felt when he heard about the double homicide, Grover replied, "I was absolutely shocked. It wasn't the Gabe I knew. It was beyond belief that it could happen."

On cross, Frasier wanted to know if Gabe had ever tended bar for him. Grover responded that he didn't think that Gabe had done so. And asked if Gabe drank alcohol, Grover said that he did not.

Frasier then asked why Gabe had come to see him in 2010. Grover replied, "I'm not really sure why he came to see me. He might just have been in town and wanted to say 'hi.'"

"So it was during this conversation that out of the blue he said that if you had any trouble, he could arrange someone to take care of it for you?"

"He said he could come in and pretend to be a dishwasher and he would help me deal with any problems I had."

Frasier asked if Gabe had told Grover that he was an investigator with the military.

Grover replied, "He said that he had been in the military and was now out. And he said he was in a small group of people who were doing their own missions. Something about a special operations team. He said while in the military, he had been given missions and had excelled at them. They just kept giving him more and more to do."

As far as the stories went in 2010, Grover said that they were convincing and he didn't see any holes in them. Grover believed them because Gabe had been so honest in the past.

Frasier asked if Gabe had said something about going to Seattle.

Grover answered, "He said, 'Why don't you give me your number. I have to go to Seattle now. When I get back, maybe we can get together and go out and have a glass of wine.'"

Since Gabe had adhered to strict Mormon principles about not drinking alcohol when he worked for Grover, Frasier asked, "Did that strike you as strange?"

Grover said, "Not necessarily. He didn't drink

before, but he was an adult now. The Gabe I knew was a very friendly person, and I took it as a nice gesture. Besides, I didn't know if he was still in the Mormon Church."

Frasier wondered if Grover thought Gabe was hallucinating at any time.

"Not hallucinating, but he was quieter than when I knew him before. He started out by being very friendly and cheerful, but then he got real quiet and serious."

"Did you see anything to make you think he was delusional?"

Grover responded that he didn't, but that he didn't understand Gabe's stories very well.

Frasier wanted to know if Grover thought that Gabe might be dangerous to people around him. Grover thought the comment from Gabe about taking care of people who might be giving him problems was odd. However, Grover never thought Gabe might be dangerous to Bob Kennelly or to his mother, Robin Anstey.

As far as the comment about Gabe might be dangerous to someone at Grover's restaurant, Frasier asked if Grover ever called the police about this.

Grover answered, "No, I mean I really didn't get into depth with him about this because the restaurant was busy. I talked to him about six minutes total. I took it [that] he might be going out and doing spy work. I just listened to him and took what he said for what it was. I mean, if someone was stealing from me, he might just come in as a dishwasher and watch. There wasn't anything about violence."

"So you didn't call anyone and say, 'Hey, you need to be careful around this guy'?"

Grover said that he had not done so.

"You asked him about his parents and he said what?"

"He said he didn't see them anymore. They were bad people."

"Did he tell you he was actually living with them at the time?"

Grover said that Gabe did not mention that.

"Did you have any reason to believe the defendant had been living in Coos County since September of the year before?"

Grover said no.

Fahy wanted to question Grover some more, and he said, "When counsel asked you if he was hallucinating, you kind of paused. There was an answer like 'No, but . . .' Can you explain that?"

Grover answered as many others had: "It just wasn't the Gabe I knew."

"You said that you didn't understand his story. Was he making sense to you?"

"It was hard to follow. It was disjointed."

Sandra Johns, the other restaurateur whom Gabe worked for, was next. She said she knew Gabe when she was a manager at the Rip Tide restaurant in Bandon. Sandra related that he was always pleasant, upbeat and cared about his customers. She added that when his mom and James Anstey came into the restaurant, Gabe always gave her a big hug.

When she first heard about the murders, Sandra said, "I was shocked. I didn't think it was the Gabe I knew. I looked it up on the Internet to see if the person mentioned had worked for us. I couldn't believe that it was the same person. It was completely out of character."

As with other witnesses, Frasier got Sandra to admit that she hadn't seen Gabe for years and had no idea what he'd been up to or what his lifestyle was like in those intervening years.

Frasier asked, "So you have no idea how he came to be in a position for which he finds himself today?"

"None at all."

Sandra Johns was not on the stand very long. She was followed by Isabelle Anstey Hayden. Isabelle was Gabe's stepsister and she spoke of how he had been so good to her when they were young. She repeated what she had said before, "He was the brother I never had."

She also recounted how much he had changed by 2009 and it was especially evident during the spaghetti dinner, where he had acted in such a strange manner.

* * *

During cross-examination, DA Frasier pointed out the remark about Gabe being crazy and asked if she had sought any mental-health counselors for him. Isabelle replied that she had not. Asked if she thought he was a danger to those around him, she said no. And when Frasier wanted to know if she had called any police agency or mental-health facility, she also said no.

Frasier asked if she knew Gabe had quit the ROTC, quit the sheriff's office in Idaho and wanted a divorce from Jessica at one point. Isabelle said that she did know all of those things. She even knew that he had moved in with another woman in Idaho and also spent time in Las Vegas, where he told others he had made money by gambling.

Frasier asked if she knew that when Gabe, Jessica and Kalea moved into Bob Kennelly's home in Oregon that Gabe was having financial problems. She answered that she didn't know that.

Frasier asked, "Do you know why they were staying with Robin and Robert?"

Isabelle replied, "I was under the impression there weren't any problems with them."

"Did the defendant ever tell you that he thought Robert Kennelly was poisoning his family?"

Isabelle said that he had not done so. Nor did he tell her anything about Robert Kennelly supposedly getting ready to abuse Kalea sexually.

Isabelle's answers were all "no" to questions of

whether Gabe had spoken of abandonment issues when he was young, spoken of Robert and Robin being "bad people" and if she knew what Gabe's mental state was in the two weeks from when she last saw him in January 2010 and up to the time of the murders.

Frasier then asked, "Is it true you do not want to see him go to prison?"

Isabelle began crying. Through her tears, she answered, "I would like to see him get help."

"What do you mean by him 'getting help'? There are two people dead here."

"I very much understand that."

"I will ask again, do you want to see him in prison?"

Isabelle cried, "I don't know!"

On a short redirect, Fahy asked if she loved Robin and was angry at Gabe for what he did. Isabelle replied, "Yes, I was very upset."

"Is it safe to say you have mixed emotions about this whole thing?"

"Yes, I do."

"Does it feel like you have suffered a double loss?"

"Definitely."

CHAPTER 42

Isabelle's husband, Robert Hayden, followed her on the stand. He spoke of liking Gabe when he first met him and what a great guy he had been. And then Robert noticed a huge change in Gabe during the latter part of 2009 and early 2010.

DA Frasier wanted to know if Gabe had ever told Robert that he had borrowed $25,000 from Bob Kennelly. Hayden said that Gabe did indicate that had occurred. Hayden added, "He was going to pay down some debts."

Frasier asked if Gabe had also talked about paying off someone who had shot a friend of his and that shooter was looking for him. Hayden agreed that conversation had occurred as well.

Hayden also testified that Gabe had told him that there were bad people looking for him in the Bandon area and some of them were looking for him because of a supposed murder in Las Vegas. Gabe was not very specific about this alleged murder. Gabe had also spoken about having two Beretta handguns to protect himself.

Hayden even testified, "During the spaghetti dinner, Gabe was losing control. I asked him if he ever worried about getting into trouble about these things he was talking about. He said that if he ever got into a situation with the police, he would not back down. He said, 'When they are firing their guns at me and have to reload, I have thirty-five round clips in my guns and won't have to reload.'"

Asked about what types of vehicles Gabe had been driving in December 2009 and January 2010, Hayden said that Gabe used a Mercedes E-Class sedan, a Prius, a small red pickup truck and Bob Kennelly's pickup truck.

Frasier wanted to know if Robert and his wife, Isabelle, were ever frightened for their safety around Gabe. Robert answered that they were. "I told my wife that I didn't want Gabe coming over anymore."

"Did you think about calling the police?"

"No, it was more of a family thing. It was the ranting about religion, and him trying to make us join him in something, that scared us. His mind was going a hundred miles an hour on this stuff."

Frasier noted that Robert and his wife were friendly with Robin Anstey. He asked if they ever worried for her safety around Gabe. Hayden said that they did not, nor were they worried about the safety of Bob Kennelly.

Even though Robert believed that Gabe had

mental issues, he testified that neither he nor his wife sought a mental counselor to see Gabe.

Frasier wanted to know why Robert believed Gabe's stories about being in the military.

Robert replied, "Because when I first met him, he seemed so calm, cool and relaxed. He'd been a police officer, and his mom had nothing but good things to say about him. I generally thought he was a great guy."

"So you had no reason to disbelieve he was telling you the truth?"

"Correct. But when he started telling me stories about the black ops, I thought some might be fabrications. And stuff like if I wanted one hundred twenty thousand dollars, I could get it in one day. Stuff like that, and things like getting orders for missions by a phone call."

On redirect, Fahy asked if there was any evidence that there had ever been a murder in Las Vegas. Hayden agreed there was no corroborating evidence. And as far as the $25,000 Gabe had borrowed from Robert Kennelly, Hayden said that he wasn't "going to stiff him. He was going to pay it back."

Fahy asked, "Was it obvious to you that you were watching someone having a mental crisis?"

Hayden answered, "In my opinion, yes."

* * *

Fahy brought Coos County deputy sheriff Richard Gill to the stand to testify as to what kind of inmate Gabe had been since he'd been incarcerated. This was important. When Judge Stone pronounced the sentence, he would have to factor in the "future dangerousness" of Gabriel Morris.

Deputy Gill said that Gabe had no discipline problems in the year and a half since he'd been in the Coos County Jail. Gill agreed with Fahy that sometimes he came into contact with antisocial individuals who were inmates. Gill agreed that as far as he knew, Gabe had never tried to manipulate him or other inmates. In fact, Gabe had been helpful to other inmates.

Gill said, "There was a young man incarcerated in the same cell block as Mr. Morris. This young man spoke very little English. He was an eighteen-year-old Hispanic man. Mr. Morris does speak some Spanish, and he would have conversations with the young man when they played cards. Mr. Morris's influence helped the young man to calm down. It made him adjust to jail life better. Mr. Morris kind of took him under his wing."

Fahy wanted to know if Gabe had ever referred to himself as a prophet.

Gill responded, "No. He has never referred to himself as something special. He had drawn parallels to himself and other scriptural characters who were incarcerated. But that's all."

Fahy asked what Gill thought of Gabe's personality.

Gill replied, "If we had met under different

circumstances, he probably would have been a close friend."

Frasier was skeptical about how well Gabe had adjusted to jail life. The DA said, "In fact, he's had issues with some inmates in jail, hasn't he?"

Gill answered, "In one of the kites [messages in jail], he gave us information about some other inmates who have been less than social to other inmates in the cell block. He complained particularly about one inmate."

Frasier asked if Gabe had been threatened by this person, and Gill said that he had been. Frasier wondered if Gabe had responded in a physical manner to this, and Gill said that he had not done so.

Frasier wanted to know if Gabe was receiving any medication while in jail. Gill responded that he wasn't aware of any. Nor was he aware of Gabe receiving any mental-health counseling.

On redirect, Fahy had Deputy Gill explain more about the "kites" Gabe had sent to the officers in the jail. Gill said, "The kites he sent, they were about these inmates acting out."

"Would you consider that to be snitching?"

Gill said, "I wouldn't try to get into his mind as to what his motivation was. I do know that the inmates he informed us about do have a reputation as being aggressive and antisocial toward everybody—inmates and staff."

"Has Mr. Morris asked for personal protection?"

"I have seen him working out in his cell. He is physically fit. I believe that he is more than capable of taking care of himself."

"Have you ever seen him speaking gibberish or acting crazy or delusional?"

"Never."

"He seemed to be pretty stable in the structured environment of jail?"

"Yes, sir."

CHAPTER 43

The Eschlers were, of course, important witnesses in the case. They had been visited by Gabriel Morris less than an hour after the murders had taken place. Fred Eschler recounted that Gabe had been his daughter's boyfriend. He had liked Gabe so much as a young man that he considered him to be a part of the family. Gabe went on camping trips with the whole family and dropped by, even when Esther Eschler was not home.

Fred recalled about the night of February 8, 2010: "There was a knock at the door at around nine. I was in the kitchen, sitting at the kitchen table. My wife and I were there talking. She went and answered the door, and I could tell by her greeting that it was someone she was excited to see.

"She invited Gabe, his wife and their daughter into the house, and they came into the kitchen. I started to be somewhat social and Gabe sort of stopped me and said he'd like to visit, but he didn't have the time.

"It wasn't really cold out, but it wasn't warm either. Their daughter didn't have any shoes on. In fact, they were all barefoot, which was strange. Gabe was dressed in a T-shirt and light pair of pants.

"Gabe said that he was in trouble and it basically had to do with him working with the police department undercover. Things had gone terribly wrong and people were after him and his family. These people had murdered his mom and her boyfriend.

"He said he needed to report to a large facility in San Diego so that he could be protected. He asked if either my wife or I could drive him down to San Diego, or if we had a vehicle we could loan him. I said that we couldn't drive him down there, but I had a vehicle that he could use.

"He also asked if I had some kind of weapon, and I asked him what he wanted. I had a nine-millimeter Beretta semiautomatic and I loaned that to him. I saw for one brief moment that he may have had a Glock handgun. It didn't appear to have a clip in it.

"I asked him if he needed any money, and he said he needed twenty dollars. I gave him forty or sixty. My wife fixed him a bag of food. We didn't have shoes small enough for his daughter, so we gave an extra pair of long socks that she could wear. And we gave him some clothes that were warmer than what he and Jessica had. He and his family were at the house maybe a half hour. He was very urgent, and he wasn't so much scared as agitated and concerned."

Fahy said, "Some people in the community were

faulting you for giving him what he asked for. Is that correct?"

Fred said that it was.

Fahy asked, "All things being equal, and not knowing the circumstances of what really happened, would you give Gabe those things all over again?"

Fred answered, "Yes, I would. When Gabe brought his little daughter with him, and she was distressed, and she stayed by her mom the whole time—with the story that Gabe told me, I had no reason not to believe what he told. Based on [the] Gabe Morris I knew, I had no reason not to believe him."

Before DA Frasier asked one question on cross-examination, he heaved a big sigh. He knew Fred Eschler and his family very well. Frasier began by saying, "I have in a police report a quote from you— 'Gabe has always been a bullshitter. He's always been pretty slick with words.' Is that correct?"

Fred answered, "If I didn't say it, I believe it. He's always been good with words."

"What do you mean by him being a bullshitter?"

Fred replied, "Kind of like me, a good story-teller. If you can tell a good story, that is interesting to listen to, people will listen. I'm not talking about lying. He just has a very amiable disposition. It wasn't exaggeration so much, but just a way of putting you at ease."

Frasier wondered if Gabe had a way of talking people into things they might not normally do.

Fred said that Gabe hadn't been that way with him. "He was just comfortable to talk to."

Frasier then asked how Gabe was behaving when he came over on the night of February 8, 2010. Fred responded, "When he came into the kitchen, I thought he was in control of what he was doing. He seemed to be pretty in control of the situation. He knew what he wanted and asked for what he wanted."

"Did everyone come into the kitchen?"

Fred answered, "He was a couple of steps in, and his wife and daughter were in the doorway. When we first talked, everyone was in the kitchen vicinity and could hear the conversation. Afterward, my wife and his wife went out to the car to clean some of the things out of there to get it ready."

"On that night, he did tell you he was doing some antiterrorist work?"

Fred agreed that was so.

"And he told you he had killed somebody?"

"Yes, that he had killed one of the attackers."

"Did you ask him any questions about what was going on?"

Fred answered that he hadn't.

Frasier looked at a report and then said, "Well, I see here the investigator wrote, 'Fred said, "Every time I asked a question, Gabe said, the less I knew, the better.'"

Fred replied, "Yes, I guess I asked him a few questions, and then he kept saying it was better for me not to know."

Frasier queried if the vehicle Fred gave to Gabe had a child seat, since Kalea was only four years old at the time. Fred said that if the car didn't have one, then there was one probably somewhere around the house. Asked if he offered one to Gabe, Fred responded that Gabe didn't want one. Gabe said he would be in the backseat with Kalea.

When the questions went to guns, Fred said that initially Gabe didn't ask for one. He was more interested in getting .40-caliber ammunition. Fred added, "I offered him a 410/45 and asked him if he wanted it. Or the nine-millimeter. He chose the nine-millimeter. I believe I gave him five clips for the gun. Gabe and I loaded those."

Frasier asked, "In your presence, did the little girl start talking about her grandma?"

Fred responded, "She was pretty quiet the whole time. As we were standing at the door, and they were getting ready to leave, she made a reference to her grandmother. And Gabe told her, 'Let's not talk about Grandma.'"

"Getting back to the defendant telling you that he had killed someone, did he indicate how much time had passed from the incident to him showing up at your house?"

Fred replied, "Actually, I never thought about how long in the past that had been."

"Can you describe what you saw when they drove away?"

"His wife was sitting in the front of the car, and she was driving. Gabe got into the backseat with his daughter, and he told me they were going to lie on the backseat so that they would be out of view. I assumed the people that were looking for him were looking for three people. With just his wife at the wheel, it would be the only thing that people could see."

Frasier looked at a report again and said, "You told an investigator that Gabe conned some people out of money when he was on his mission. Is that correct?"

Fred disagreed with that statement and said, "'Conned' is your word. Usually, when you go on a mission, somebody pays a monthly amount. That goes to the church, and the church dispenses what they call an allowance. It's for the young man or woman on a mission to live within the allowance. Gabe was writing people saying that if each of them sent him ten dollars, he would be able to buy a new pair of shoes. That was inappropriate for him to do. He should have talked to his mission president and got things settled that way."

Before Fred Eschler stepped down from the stand, he asked the judge if he could clarify one thing that he said. Judge Stone said that he could. So Fred explained, "The bullshitter statement— there are some people who can enter a room and not know people, and go up and feel comfortable with them. And they start talking immediately. Not necessarily seriously, but start talking about the weather, how are you doing, that kind of thing. And they seem to relate to people easily. That's what I meant about Gabe. I wanted to make sure that it wasn't interpreted as 'He's trying to take something out of your back pocket.'"

* * *

John Lindegren was next and testified that Gabe had a very close relationship with his mother, and John liked Gabe when the defendant was a young man. John said that he knew Gabe smoked marijuana in high school, but it wasn't to a great degree. Then John said, "When Gabe started dating Esther, he took his faith seriously. To my knowledge, he didn't do any drugs after that.

"It was a real blow when I heard that Gabe had killed his mother and her boyfriend. I was working out at the gym when I heard about it. It knocked me down. I told the investigator, who talked to me, 'Gabe wouldn't even be one in a million as to who was on my suspect list.'"

Perhaps to give his second some court experience, Frasier did not cross-examine Lindegren. Instead, Assistant District Attorney Chartray did. ADA Chartray asked if John knew that Gabe smoked marijuana in high school, and John replied that he did. John agreed that Gabe quit doing that when he began dating Esther Eschler. John also agreed that he hadn't had any contact with Gabe since Gabe was a nineteen-year-old, except for when John went out to Bob Kennelly's house for an estimate on drywall work.

John admitted that he had no idea of the decisions made in Gabe's life before the murders. Chartray then looked at a report and asked if John remembered telling an investigator that Gabe had stopped by his shop just a few days before the murder.

John responded, "No, sir, I don't remember that."

Chartray continued, "You don't remember saying he seemed like the Gabe of old?"

John replied, "I don't even know what investigator wrote that. He might have misunderstood me."

This led to another question about investigators and whether John recalled talking to one from the Department of Justice. It concerned the day that he had gone out to Kennelly's house and seen Gabe there. In this report, the investigator wrote down that John said, *"Gabe and Bob were not getting along."*

Once again, John said no, he didn't remember talking to anyone from the DOJ.

Chartray asked, "Well, did you observe that they were not getting along?"

John answered, "They weren't talking much to each other. It was a pretty odd deal. Just the body language. It was uncomfortable."

"Do you remember telling the DOJ investigator that Mr. Morris was looking to buy a gun?"

"No."

"Out at Mr. Kennelly's place, Gabriel Morris never mentioned hallucinating or anything like that?"

"Not a bit."

On redirect by Fahy, John said that he never saw anything that would have made him fear for Bob Kennelly's safety.

Before John Lindegren stepped down, Judge Stone asked him, "Tell me, when you went out to Mr. Kennelly's place to make that bid?"

John said, "It was ten or so days before the shooting."

"Was anyone else there besides Mr. Kennelly and Mr. Morris?"

"Robin was there."

"Were you inside the house or outside the house?"

"I was in the barn, and she came out there."

CHAPTER 44

David Bastian was next. He spoke of being in Australia on a mission in 1999 and meeting Gabe there. As the others had, Bastian said how honest Gabe had been and what a joy to be around.

Bastian spoke of Gabe and his family at church in January 2010, and then about them coming over to his house for dinner later that evening. It was during this visit that Bastian had real concerns about Gabe's mental health. It was such a concern that Bastian could barely sleep that night.

For his part, Frasier wanted to know if David had asked Gabe what he was doing for work when he and his family came over to Bastian's home in 2010. David was under the impression that Gabe told him that he was starting a new job with some insurance company. As far as the government work he had supposedly been doing, David said that Gabe was not specific. Gabe did say that it was secret and had to be kept that way.

Frasier wanted to know if Gabe had said, "If anyone molests my daughter, I will kill them."

David replied that Gabe had brought up that subject and was passionate about it. Gabe had gone on to talk about opening up a coffee shop in Silverton with Jessica. And then, according to David, Gabe had launched a verbal attack on the leaders of the LDS Church. David said, "He felt that something bad was going to happen in Utah."

Frasier looked at an investigator's report that quoted David as saying, *"Gabe Morris said that if the church leaders do not do what they were supposed to do, the people should not follow them."* Frasier asked if he had said that to an investigator.

David replied, "Not in those exact words. I recall him saying something along those lines, however."

And then according to David, Gabe started talking about another subject that irritated him very much. David said, "He was upset because his grandmother was a Jehovah's Witness and she planned to leave her house to that church. He was hoping he and his family could live there. He wanted to start fresh in Silverton. He wanted to open a coffee shop, where he could preach the gospel. And he even talked about him and Jessica opening up a bed-and-breakfast place."

And then in a real turnaround about the facts, David testified that Gabe told him that he was helping his mom by paying bills for her in Bandon. Gabe, of course, had no job and was incapable of doing such a thing, since he was the one who owed so much money. Yet, according to David, Gabe spoke of trying to sell some vehicle to help her out, and his mom and Bob Kennelly had chased the potential buyer off their property.

Frasier asked, "Did he ever tell you why he would need a car that could outrun police cars?"

David replied that Gabe had not.

Frasier next wanted to know if Gabe had mentioned anything about people who had a lot of money.

David responded, "He felt that they should share what they had."

Frasier wondered if David ever worried about his safety and the safety of his family where Gabriel Morris was concerned.

David answered, "I wasn't worried about my safety or my family's safety. Or his family. I was just concerned for him as a human being."

"When he was telling you these stories, did he seem delusional?"

"I'm not really a doctor. I can tell you he was not himself."

Ray Wetzel was next, and Fahy had him speak about Gabe's visit in late January 2010. And just like Bastian had witnessed around this time, Wetzel saw a marked change in Gabe.

Frasier only had a few questions posed to Wetzel. One was "Why did Gabe say he was up in Silverton in 2010?"

Wetzel replied, "He was up to visit his grandma. And then he said he would go back to Bandon to help his mom. He said he needed a place for his wife and daughter to stay while he went to China."

Of course, Gabe had no offers from anyone in China. It was all in his mind.

Pamela Hansen followed Wetzel to the stand and spoke of knowing Gabe since they were teenagers and that she liked him from the start. She also spoke of what she considered to be Gabe's emotional breakdown in January 2010. He had rambled on and on about dragons, pre-mortal life, the End of Days and how he was against the LDS leadership in Bandon.

When Fahy asked her what she thought should happen to Gabe now, she cried and said, "I really love Gabe." She couldn't stop crying in order to answer the question.

Frasier immediately got into the question of what problems Gabe had with the Bandon church. Pam said that he stopped going to that church in September to November 2009. She asked him why he quit going and Gabe replied that it was because of some bad things he had done. He told her of being a bodyguard or something for prostitutes in Las Vegas. He added that he stopped doing that. Pam added, "I think Jessica convinced him to go back to church."

Pam explained that Gabe had a blowup with the leaders of the Bandon church for a particular reason. She said, "Jessica had been given a position in the church for the young ladies. And they would have meetings during the middle of the week." According to Pam, Gabe was upset because he didn't think that women should be in there all alone without a man for protection. Pam said, "He brought Jessica in for a meeting, and there were no men there, so he stayed. There was another adult woman there, and she became uncomfortable about some of the things Gabe began talking about. She made a complaint to the leadership of the branch."

Pam agreed that Gabe had been called in by the leader of the branch. Then she added, "The person who made the complaint spoke to me about it. It was the situation she took issue with." Apparently, there weren't supposed to be any men present when the young women had their meetings.

Pam said, "When Gabe had his meeting about this, it was upsetting to him, because they wouldn't tell him who had made the complaint. Typically, if there is a problem like that in church, the two people are brought together and air things out. He was distressed because he felt he was being put on trial for something that was nothing. I tried to set up another meeting so that everything could be aired out. Gabe never showed."

Frasier then read from a defense investigator's report that stated Gabe was not happy about his mother living with a man without being married to him.

Pam had a little different take on this. She said, "Gabe was upset because he was working at their place and helping liquidate the antiques that were in storage. He felt put-upon, when his mother knew he didn't have a job, and still wanted money for bills. My advice to him was to just find a way to pay those bills. He was disheartened, not mad."

"Did he say that his mom was asking more than what the bills really were?"

"He just said, 'My mom is a lost cause.'"

There was one moment of levity when Frasier said, "I'd like to put some context to the story about the dragons."

Pam replied, "Good luck with that!"

Frasier continued, "In Mormon theology, there is a belief that people have an existence before coming here to live on Earth?"

Pam agreed that was so. Frasier then said, "In Mormon theology, in the pre-mortal existence, the Adversary, Satan, whatever you want to call him, is present also?"

She said yes. She agreed that in the Mormon theology, the followers of Christ helped kick Satan and his followers out of Heaven.

Then Frasier said, "There is some scriptural references to dragons being a symbol of the Devil?"

There was a long pause on Pam's part and then she answered, "I don't know."

Frasier continued, "So, what Gabriel would be

speaking about, other than the dragon part, would be consistent with theology about preexistence?"

Pam said that was correct.

Frasier followed up with a question about how Gabe reacted when Pam told him she intended to keep going to the Bandon church.

Pam replied, "That was the first time Gabe really got upset with me. He was real agitated with me as I implored him to realize these were good men."

Frasier wanted to know if Gabe told her where he was heading, when he said he was going away for a long time. Pam responded that he had not told her where he was going.

Fahy had just a few more questions for her on redirect. "Was the 'we' in the battle of Heaven, with him and God?"

Pam said, "No, when he was talking about 'we,' he was talking about him and me."

"Are you aware of times he spoke of himself as Jesus Christ or Christlike?"

"He said he was the forerunner of Christ in preparation for the Second Coming."

CHAPTER 45

It now became the province of the psychologists and psychiatrists on the stand. Fahy had Dr. Loren Mallory give all of his qualifications and the places where he had worked during his career. One of the main concerns for the defense was to refute what they knew Dr. Michael Sasser was going to present later for the prosecution.

Fahy asked Dr. Mallory what problems might have arisen by Dr. Sasser relying so heavily on the Hare test.

Mallory said, "Having a degree in psychiatry is not enough. You can't just do things by the manual. Dr. Sasser was using an older version, and I filed an addendum to his report. I believe he is not correct."

The next question was "You are aware the Dr. Sasser did not diagnose the defendant as being a psychopath?"

Mallory replied, "That's confusing to me, because the score he gave Gabriel Morris is absolutely indicative of psychopathy. I did not see any psychopathy or antisocial behavior on Gabe's part. I thought Dr. Sasser used a very structured and confrontive style. To really understand a person, it just can't be 'yes' and 'no' answers to questions. My impression was that he gave a too-structured test. Sometimes Sasser would even answer the question himself and then have Gabriel acknowledge it. I reviewed Dr. Sasser's DVD and Gabriel, in parts, tried to bring up his religious views. But the style of the interview tended to shut him down on those."

Fahy wanted to know if there had been opportunities for Dr. Sasser to explore more about what Gabe was thinking.

Mallory said yes and added, "He just went on into other closed-ended questions. There were times it was almost argumentative. I believe it takes unstructured questioning to understand Gabriel's delusions and his attitudes about others. You have to let him wind up and preach."

Fahy wondered, "When someone suffers from delusional disorder, are they that way twenty-four/seven?"

Mallory replied, "No. Sometimes it's more psychotic. Sometimes it's more delusional. Underneath, I believe, the delusional beliefs are always there, but the external aspect can wax and wane."

Fahy wanted to know what Mallory thought happened in the weeks prior to the murders.

Mallory said, "I think there is plenty of data that Gabriel was in an agitated, paranoid, psychotic state. And at the end, it's a little unclear, and I don't want to cross too many lines, because he says he has an unclear memory, but he remembers someone else being there, and someone else doing the shooting. He said his mom and her boyfriend left and then came back into the house. He did feel that Mr. Kennelly was trying to poison him and that Mr. Kennelly was dangerous to his mom. He said he took Mr. Kennelly's gun and he had a small recorder set up to capture Mr. Kennelly's conversation. He said he hid upstairs, but he saw through a doorknob hole another person go downstairs and do the shooting. That person then left, and Gabe ran out, grabbed his wife and child and they fled."

Dr. Mallory was aware of the statements Gabe had given to the Virginia investigators after being arrested. Fahy asked how Mallory could resolve the issue that Gabe told the investigators he had done the shootings, and now he was claiming he saw someone else do them.

Mallory answered, "First off, Gabriel was not okay at the interview. He was quite delusional. He went on a long spree that was very disorganized. So there are a couple of possibilities. Out of kind of a weird motive, he made sort of a confession."

Fahy said, "Let's, for discussion's sake, say that when Mr. Morris confessed to the killings, he was telling the truth. And then he comes here and begins to deny it. Is that something you have seen in research you have done?"

Mallory responded, "I think his delusional

system is kind of a way of creating a story to cover up what he had done. Something might start out as a lie, but by the time he gets into these stories, he truly believes them."

Fahy asked if Gabe was an intelligent person, and Mallory agreed that he was. Mallory also agreed that an intelligent person who was not suffering from delusions would come up with a better story than that he peeked through a keyhole and saw someone else shoot his mother and her boyfriend.

Mallory added, "It was my opinion that he was not able to appreciate the wrongfulness of what was happening nor to really control it. He believed he was in danger, and that Mr. Kennelly was poisoning him. He thought Kennelly was a danger to his mother and was carrying a gun. Mr. Morris was in a disorganized psychotic state and not in touch with reality. When you're that completely delusional, you're not in a place where you can make good judgments in understanding what you are doing is wrong. He was not able to just say 'stop' to the delusions.

"I'm a psychologist. I can't divine what really happened, but I believe his delusional, paranoid, agitated, psychotic state made him see some little thing that happened, and maybe his police training took over, because he shot like a policeman. In a dangerous situation, policemen are trained to shoot until the person is taken out."

"Would that carry over to his mother?"

"I will say to a psychological degree of certainty, something happened, he started shooting and shot until it was over. I believe it happened because of the mental illness. At the very end, he believed his mother was poisoning him. His delusions were growing bigger and getting out of control. You can't make rationality out of the irrational."

Fahy asked why Fred Eschler thought Gabe was in control of his actions not long after the shootings took place.

Mallory replied, "It probably looked like organized behavior that seemed to show he was in control of himself. But it was organized around a completely psychotic delusional-belief system. He was running from the area because he believed people were after him. He left with his family in their pajamas, with no socks on their feet, no money, no ID. Just because it was organized to a certain sense didn't mean that it was rational and in touch with reality."

In essence, it was now DA Paul Frasier's job to bring into question Dr. Mallory's diagnosis of Gabriel Morris. If Mallory was seen to be correct in Judge Stone's eyes, then, by default, Dr. Sasser's diagnosis had to be wrong.

Frasier began by pointing out all the lying Gabe had done to others when it came to why he had left the ROTC. Frasier viewed this as antisocial behavior, not delusional behavior. And this lying had started clear back in Gabe's days at BYU.

Frasier said, "Your first report was that the defendant was not competent to proceed to trial?"

"I was real concerned about it."

"Did you make any recommendations to make him competent so that we could proceed?"

Mallory answered, "Some medication and therapy. And then reevaluate him."

"Isn't it true he has not received any therapy in jail?"

Mallory said he wasn't aware of Gabe getting any therapy.

"Is it true he has not received any medication while in jail?"

Mallory replied that he wouldn't be surprised if that was the case.

Frasier then said, "Well, somewhere along the line, this guy changed, or we'd still be arguing that he was not competent to stand trial. Is that correct?"

Mallory responded, "No. I still have concerns that he might be delusional, so that [way], he could not aid and assist his counsel." And then Mallory pointed out that the "aid and assist" matter became moot when Gabe made a plea deal through his lawyers.

When Frasier wanted to know if Mallory diagnosed Gabe with any other psychological disorders, Mallory said, "I deferred on Axis II disorder. I couldn't find enough data to diagnose a personality disorder."

Frasier asked what a personality disorder was, and Mallory said, "A persistent disorder that causes problems for the individual."

Frasier then asked if Mallory thought that Gabe had a conduct disorder. When he said no, Frasier queried, "Do you recall Esther Eschler saying that before joining the Mormon Church he was using marijuana, LSD, hallucinogenic mushrooms and drinking alcohol? He had no ambitions in life. He did not work or apply himself in school. Did you take that statement into account when you considered if he had an antisocial disorder?"

Mallory said that he did, and that was inadequate to be a conduct disorder.

Frasier continued, "She said that looking back on her relationship with Gabriel Morris, she realized how selfish he was. He did what he wanted, not caring how it made her feel. She frequently paid for their dates. He often asked her to make a meal for him or lunch. If she hesitated, he made her feel guilty. He once made her say she loved him, and she wasn't ready to do so. So he made her feel guilty so that she would say it. She said of him, 'He was charming, well-liked, but very self-serving.'"

In this exchange, it was actually Dr. Mallory who asked a question. "How old was he then?"

Frasier replied, "Up to the age of twenty-two."

Mallory retorted, "Well, those are not positive behaviors, but I don't feel that it [is] strong enough evidence to diagnose an antisocial or conduct disorder."

Frasier asked, "So, when did all this delusional stuff start?"

Mallory replied, "I believe the delusions started long ago, but he could keep them under control. He could keep them inside. People saw them occasionally, but he kept them under control for a lot of years."

"So, what is the definition of a delusion?"

Mallory read from the manual, "'The presence of one or more non-bizarre delusions that persist at least one month. Delusions are erroneous beliefs that usually involve a misrepresentation of perceptions or experience.'"

"Okay, you diagnosed him with a delusional disorder with religious overtones and grandiosity. What are the religious delusions you think the defendant is having?"

Mallory said that Gabe believed he was Jesus Christ or a Christlike figure. He also believed he was a prophet and that he was receiving messages from God in a very special way. Mallory added, "I go to church. I'm a Christian, although not Latter-day Saints. But I give room for appropriate religious behavior. I do not think every religious belief is a delusion. But I believe he crossed the line very clearly."

CHAPTER 46

Frasier wanted to know how Gabe supposedly received his messages from God, and Mallory said, "It was something he shared with God daily. Sometimes he heard voices. Being a prophet or Christ-like figure was more pervasive."

"Not everyone who proclaims to be a prophet is delusional. For instance, in the Latter-day Saints, the head of the church is proclaimed to be a prophet. Does that make him delusional?"

"I don't know how to answer that. We would have to consider that in the realm of a shared and normal-belief system."

"So, when diagnosing a delusional disorder, you have to take into account the person's cultural-belief system?"

Mallory said that was true, but he added that even the Mormons who knew Gabe spoke of his bizarre, agitated and disorganized thoughts.

Frasier said, "There were Ms. Hansen's statements, and most of what he told her conformed with Mormon theology, correct?"

"I don't know much about that."

"Are you aware that the Church teaches that all members are able to receive revelations from God?"

"Sure."

Frasier stated that if Gabe was saying he was receiving inspiration from God, this was not outside the norm of someone in the Mormon Church.

Mallory responded, "It is to the extent he went. People who were in the Mormon Church, they saw it too. It went way beyond the socially acceptable norms."

Frasier came back with that many Christians thought that Mary, the mother of Jesus, had a virgin birth. He asked if that made them delusional.

Mallory responded, "Only if they became so overconcerned with that, that it was driving their lives and taking up all their time and they were pursuing it to some ridiculous and pressured degree. Then the idea would become delusional."

Frasier then asked, "So, at the time he committed these murders, what was his delusion?"

Mallory said, "He thought he was being poisoned and he thought his family was in danger. He knew Mr. Kennelly had a gun, so he took it. He was psychotic and not in touch with reality."

Frasier pointed out that Mallory had spoken of people who had witnessed Gabe in the weeks and days before the murders, but none of them had seen him on the day of the murder.

Mallory countered with the fact he had taken into account Jessica's statements. And Mallory continued, "She indicated they left the area and went up to Seattle. They then drove back through Bandon, picked up a few things and went to San Diego. Before the homicide, they came back up to Bandon because Gabe said he needed to talk to Bob Kennelly. They did not drive up directly to the house. Gabe went up the hill with a portable radio and stayed in the tree line, watching the house. Everything here sounds pretty paranoid. It sounds like an escalating mental illness."

Frasier asked why Gabe would go back to Bandon to see Bob Kennelly if the man was trying to poison him.

Mallory answered, "Because the whole plan was delusional. We're trying to make rational sense out of an irrational thing."

Frasier made a point about Gabe going into business with Kennelly to grow medical marijuana. However, instead of selling it, Gabe was smoking up all the product. Frasier then asked if Mallory was aware that Gabe owed Bob Kennelly $25,000. "The fact that Mr. Kennelly ends up dead, then the defendant wouldn't have to pay him back, would he? So there's a rational motive there, isn't there?"

"I suppose so."

"And even though the defendant said he had concerns for his mother, he had issues with her as well. He had issues over her abandoning him to the man he accused of sexually molesting him, correct?"

"Yes, I remember reading that."

"So the defendant had reasons to want his mother dead, other than the delusion, didn't he?"

"That doesn't add up to me."

"Well, there are homicides all the time where people end up dead for stupid reasons?"

"Sure. But it's a specious argument because he was delusional. If he felt abandoned, it was through the lens of mental illness."

"Do you believe the defendant when he says he was sexually abused by his dad?"

"Probably."

"Would that not create resentment if a person was abandoned in that situation?"

"Sure. But the vast majority of people who have been in that situation do not kill a person."

CHAPTER 47

Frasier attempted to show that Gabe's actions on the day of the murder had shown planning. Gabe waited up in the tree line with binoculars until he knew his mom and Bob Kennelly had left for the day. He had Jessica bring the pickup truck up the drive and hide it behind a small hill. He had Jessica and Kalea follow him into the house, and he got Kennelly's pistol and waited for Bob and Robin to return so he could ambush them. But Gabe was now saying he didn't do it. Frasier asked, "You have to decide whether he's telling you the truth to some degree, don't you?"

Mallory agreed that he didn't think there was some shadowy figure in the house who had shot Robin and Bob, but "at the time, Gabriel Morris believed it."

Frasier countered, "People who commit crimes often lie about it, but it doesn't mean they're delusional, correct?"

"Well, wait a minute. Someone who is delusional isn't truly lying. They believe it. That's their reality."

Frasier pointed out that Gabe had wanted to testify before a jury and tell them what happened until his attorneys talked him out of that. "One of the things he wanted to tell them was that there was no forensic evidence tying him to the crime. And did you know, Doctor, there is no forensic evidence tying him to the crime. If there is no DNA evidence, no fingerprints that can be used, wouldn't that be a rational thing—wanting the jury to know that?"

"Yeah. But when he talked to me, he expressed that the jury would be guided by God. And he would be able to show the jury he was a prophet. The jury would be touched by God, and there was no way that they could find him guilty."

"Didn't he want to give an explanation about why he had confessed?"

Mallory answered, "He said that if he confessed, then his wife and daughter would be allowed to leave."

"Wouldn't someone who just committed a murder want to dump a truck away from the scene so it couldn't be connected to him, as he did near the Eschlers'?"

"Yes, but such a person would probably not take their wife and daughter clad only in pajamas without any shoes on their feet. When I looked at that—the whole event—it did not seem very organized or rational."

"You keep using the word 'probably.' How sure are you of your opinion?"

Mallory replied, "I'm a trained scientist. I'm trained to not make statements beyond what I know the data to be. I'm fairly certain in my diagnosis, but I'm trained to say it in certain ways."

"For the sake of argument, let's say he is antisocial. Aren't his behaviors consistent with someone who knows he did something wrong?"

Mallory said he saw a lot of problems with that hypothesis. He said a merely antisocial person would have planned the whole thing a lot better. Such a person would have dressed for cold weather, taken an ID and money. This crime did not have the aspects of a coldly calculated plan that a psychopath might use.

Frasier pointed out that there was a television show called *America's Dumbest Criminals,* where the theme was that a lot of crimes were not planned well. Yet, those criminals were not delusional. Mallory agreed that there were a lot of "dumb crimes" that were committed.

Frasier then wondered if Gabe had said he knew that it was a lie that he'd been in the military.

Mallory replied, "When I confronted him with that, he said, 'Oh, yeah. But to cover up that I'm special in the eyes of God, I told them [the Eschlers] those spy stories. So I covered up by saying I worked for the government. No one would have believed that God had blessed me and tells me what to do.'

I do think when he's out there telling those spy stories, however, he really believes them."

Frasier then stated, "An appropriate mental defense requires that the defendant at the time of the crime was suffering from a disorder. The statute reads he could not substantially conform his conduct to the requirements of the law, and he could not substantially conform his conduct or appreciate the criminality of his actions at the time of the crime. If we don't know what was going through his mind when he pulled the trigger, how can we know to any degree of certainty that those factors have been met?"

Mallory replied, "Oh, because it was such a clear, such a severe, such a well-documented and founded belief system right up to that instance. Even though I can't take that tiny slice of time when the trigger was pulled and know what was in his head, it still looks like a clear case to me that he was not able to control or understand his behavior. I looked at my reports on murders and did a search. And I've been involved in over thirty murder cases. Almost always you can't make the case that a mental illness was building up to an event. Here that is so clear, that it's fairly remarkable how clear it is. I would say to a reasonable degree of certainty, I find it rational to say he was delusional all the way up to the point where he pulled the trigger."

Frasier pointed out that Jessica in her statements to investigators said that she did not see anything unusual about Gabe on the day of the shootings.

Mallory replied, "Yes, but she also thought she was being poisoned. So her perception at the time was intertwined with his delusional material."

Frasier asked, "So, do you believe that since she believed her husband, her perceptions of that day are not worthy of consideration?"

"No, I don't think that's fair. If I told my wife that my mother was poisoning me, she wouldn't believe me. It's not a rational thing a person would believe, even if their spouse said it. It was entering into a shared delusional system to some degree."

Frasier then said, "For the legal aspects of this case, did the defendant, when he pulled the trigger, intend to kill those people?"

Fahy objected, saying, "Your Honor, I think he misstated the definition of 'intent.'"

The judge, Fahy and Frasier all looked up the definition as defined by Oregon law, and the word "conscious" had been omitted in Frasier's statement. So Frasier restated it, using the word "conscious."

Mallory replied that he did not believe Gabe had done so in a conscious manner.

Frasier asked, "What do you think he meant when he shot those people?"

Mallory reiterated all his comments about the delusion and added, "He was cocked and ready for a terrible event to occur. I can't tell you what happened. The victim Mr. Kennelly might have just jerked the wrong way, and Mr. Morris thought he was pulling a gun on him."

Frasier let out a big sigh and said, "Do you know how many times the defendant fired that gun?"

"No, I don't. I understand it was quite a few times. But once he started, he believed it was to shoot until he took out the danger."

"When you say 'to take out the danger,' he was shooting to kill these people. That's the point, isn't it, Doctor?"

"Well, no, it's not the whole point. I'm not an attorney, and I'm not trying to quote the law here. But here's an example from a true case. Someone was a schizophrenic, hallucinating and delusional. He saw a green alien pulling out a ray gun and believed that alien was going to kill him and eat his brain. So he shot him. Did he mean to kill him? Yes. But does it mean we hold him to the intent to kill a person? I don't think he even knew who the person was that he shot."

Frasier countered that Gabe had told investigators in Virginia that he started shooting from the balcony and he went down to where the people were lying on the ground. And he didn't want his mother to suffer anymore, so he shot her in the head. Frasier asked, "Doesn't that show that he wanted his mother dead?"

Mallory replied, "Not necessarily. He said he didn't want her to suffer. And besides, in the previous three pages of that report, he went on rants that made no sense."

Frustrated with dancing around and around the issue, Frasier clapped his hands together with a loud noise and asked, "Did he act with the conscious objective to cause those people's deaths?"

Mallory answered, "I don't believe so. I believe it was a product of being cocked and ready because he was so paranoid. I surmise because he was a trained police officer, he shot to kill."

Trying a different avenue, Frasier got Mallory to tell what Gabe had said about his marijuana use and how extensive it had been. Gabe had said he used some marijuana and didn't drink very much. So Frasier read from a report about how others claimed that near the end Gabe was drinking a bottle of hard alcohol per day and smoking a fair amount of marijuana. Even Gabe's brother had testified earlier that Gabe had been drinking a bottle of alcohol per day. Frasier asked if Gabe had said otherwise to Mallory, and Mallory replied, "He minimized it."

The line of questioning now was that Gabe had been telling Mallory one thing in self-reports, while other people claimed otherwise. Frasier was trying to make a point that Gabe had just been lying about many things rather than being delusional about them.

Frasier wanted to know what Gabe had told Mallory as the reason for leaving the ROTC.

Mallory answered, "It was because his wife was

unhappy and getting depressed. So he gave it up for her to be happier."

Frasier countered, "He gave other people other reasons. He told Colonel Maher he was leaving ROTC because he had to protect his mother."

All Mallory said to this was "Okay. He didn't tell me that."

Frasier added, "The fact that he told two different stories about why he left ROTC, is it part of the delusional process, or is he someone who just can't tell the truth?"

Mallory said that he could come up with quite a few more possibilities than the ones Frasier just used. "My belief is there were issues coming up in his way of explaining it, so he came up with those reasons."

Frasier wanted to know what reason Gabe gave for leaving the sheriff's office in Idaho, and Mallory said that Gabe told him that the sheriff's office was corrupt. Gabe said he had issues when it came to getting along with some of his coworkers. So Frasier asked if Mallory knew Gabe had been turned down as a detective on the force and soon quit. Mallory replied that he did not know that. And, according to some people, Gabe said he quit because he'd gotten a job offer with a police force in Alaska. In fact, he kept changing his story and told other people that he quit because he'd hurt his shoulder on the job.

Frasier got to Gabe leaving his wife for a while and moving in with Brenda. Gabe ran up $30,000 on her credit cards and then took off for Las Vegas on his own. Frasier said that Gabe claimed to be into protecting prostitutes from their pimps down there. Then Frasier asked, "Did he tell you why he left the insurance business?"

Mallory responded that Gabe said he'd been let go for telling off-color jokes around women.

Frasier came back with the fact that American Insurance had terminated him for falsifying records. Once again, Frasier claimed that Gabe was not delusional, but rather just a liar.

Then Frasier wanted to know what Gabe had told Mallory as to his reason for moving his family out to Oregon in 2009. Mallory said it was to make a fresh start and to get back in touch with his mother. Frasier got Mallory to agree that Gabe had not told him how much debt he was in. In fact, Frasier said, "Some sources have put the figure at being around a hundred thousand dollars in debt."

Once again, to get at the crux of the matter, Frasier asked, "If a police officer was standing next to the defendant at the time of the crime, are you saying that he would have shot and killed them, anyway?"

Mallory replied, "I don't know how to answer that. I don't have any kind of information to make any kind of rational guess about that."

Frasier pressed, "If I understand your opinion, no matter what kind of circumstance was present at the time of this shooting, the defendant could not control himself, correct?"

"That is too much of a hypothetical, and my profession warns us about hypotheticals."

Frasier started to ask the same question again, in a slightly different manner, and Fahy objected, "Asked and answered."

The objection was sustained, so Frasier let it go.

CHAPTER 48

DA Frasier might have let that go, but Fahy obviously wanted to leave a different impression in the judge's mind about many things that Mallory had testified to on cross-examination.

The first thing Fahy asked: "The fact that Mr. Morris didn't go around slaughtering everybody in sight, does that mean he wasn't under a delusional disorder that would not allow him to conform his actions to the law?"

By this point, Fahy was so wound up that the judge made him slow down. In fact, Judge Stone said, "Take a deep breath," and everyone laughed.

Fahy slowed down and said, "In his Virginia transcript, Gabriel told a police officer that Bob Kennelly was making a move to pull a gun and he felt that he was under immediate threat. One of the police officers there asked, 'If a police officer walked in with them, do you think this would have happened the same way?'

And then Fahy presented the transcript:

Morris: "If a cop walked in with them?"

Coady: "Yes."

Morris: "It depends what cop walked in with them."

Coady: "Well, just hypothetically speaking, what would have happened?"

Morris: "If a cop walked in he [Kennelly] reached for a gun, and made me make the same decision, I'd be safe from all this crap, because he [the police officer] would have shot him. Thank goodness for that. Because then I could hang out with my daughter and I could have a life."

Fahy noted that Mallory had outlined the criteria for an antisocial disorder: persisting negative pattern of behavior and not understanding the rights of others. Fahy asked if Gabe fell into that category. Mallory said that he did not. And then he added, "You would have to see some pretty significant social problems. Trouble with the law and things like stealing or violent behavior." And none of that had occurred before February 8, 2010.

Fahy then asked, "If he was delusional, wouldn't he be having the same kind of problems in jail over a year-and-a-half period as he did in the beginning?"

Mallory said that was not the case because Gabe was now in a structured environment. Mallory believed that Gabe still had delusional thoughts, but the structure of jail life helped him maintain control over them.

Fahy wanted to know who had withdrawn the competency issue. Was it defense counsel or Dr. Mallory? Mallory said it was the defense. Fahy continued, "Was Mr. Morris listening to us in our explaining to him what his potential liability was in this case if he got up in front of a jury and told them this story he told of what happened? Especially in light of what he confessed in Virginia and what his wife would have said against him as a witness."

Frasier objected, saying, "Hearsay."

The objection was sustained.

Fahy tried again, and Mallory answered, "Mr. Morris's biggest problem was, he did not feel that he was at risk of being jailed for life or even facing the death penalty. He felt he didn't need to listen to defense counsel, didn't need to look at the facts, because he knew that he was right and there were no facts that would find him guilty. The jury would be touched by God and they would believe him."

Frasier had portrayed many of Gabe's thoughts on religion as not being far outside of what other Mormons believed. But now Fahy pointed out that Pamela Hansen had seen mental issues with him. Ray Wetzel thought Gabe was on drugs or hallucinating, and David Bastian had also been worried about Gabe's mental state.

"Doctor, did you see any sort of plan to murder them?"

Mallory answered, "No, it was spontaneous."

"Would it be rational for a trained police officer

to bring a wife and child to a scene where he planned to commit murder, and then rush them out immediately after the act, barefoot and in pajamas?"

"Not to me, no."

CHAPTER 49

When it was Dr. Jerry Larsen's turn on the stand, he recited all of his schooling and credentials. In fact, Dr. Larsen had even written part of a *DSM-IV* concerning alcohol and substance abuse.

One of Fahy's main objectives with Dr. Larsen, as it had been with Dr. Mallory, was to take issue with Dr. Sasser's findings about Gabe. Fahy asked if Sasser could get a full picture of Gabe if he'd only seen him for an hour and twenty minutes, as Fahy alleged that Sasser had done. Larsen said he could not.

Fahy asked if taking an adversarial role in interviewing Gabe would have been helpful.

Larsen replied, "No, it's going to end the interview very quickly. You're not going to get the information you need."

Fahy wanted to know if Larsen had been able to watch and listen to the interviews Dr. Sasser had done with Gabe. These, of course, had been videotaped.

Larsen said that he had and added, "The closed-ended questions that were used gives you data, but it did not address the thoughts and feelings and the delusional way of thinking. I thought the tone was a little confrontive."

Fahy asked about what Dr. Larsen observed when Gabe was interviewed in Virginia by police investigators. Larsen said, "I thought it was rambling, disjointed, and I thought the pouring out of all the belief systems suggested a real lack of control and a real lack of understanding on his part. Much of the things he talked about were excellent examples of delusional thinking."

Fahy wondered why Gabe's story to the investigators in Virginia was so different than the one Gabe had told Dr. Larsen about the time of the shootings. Larsen explained, "The story he gave me was that he and his wife had gone back to the house. They were waiting for his mother and her boyfriend to come home. They wanted to get some kind of understanding from them. He wanted to record the boyfriend on a recording device to convince his mother to get away from him. He was concerned about the rat poisoning, and he thought his mother was being prostituted by her boyfriend. He also thought that she was definitely in danger. He told me about the two prior wives of Mr. Kennelly, who had died.

"His wife and child went to bed. He crept out and saw a black-clad individual with a gun shoot the boyfriend and his mom. He waited for a period of time and then got his wife and child out of the house. They went downstairs past the bodies, got into the nearest vehicle and took off.

"I compared all of that to what I saw in the confession in Virginia. I asked him why the difference to what he was telling me now, as opposed to what he said to the police. In the Virginia interview, he stated, he had given the confession he did so that his wife would not be fearful about the people he believed were after him. She would then think they weren't after her, and would not have to worry about that.

"Another discussion was that if he gave a confession, his wife and child would be released, and the child wouldn't be taken away from Jessica. Neither of these stories, in my opinion, made any rational sense. He was tested out as above-average IQ. If he was attempting to come up with a believable story, he was certainly able to do that. Instead, he offered an unbelievable story, and yet he appears to believe it's true."

Fahy asked, "Is that the crux of the issue—what he believes is true?"

Larsen replied, "That's the core of the delusion, but you have to remember that a delusional disorder is a false belief that is not shared by those around you. It is non-bizarre, and besides from the delusional area, the person might be able to function pretty normally. This fits the description of Mr. Morris pretty accurately. He believed that he flew a plane in the air force, for instance. He knew some things about flying, but other information about this was not factual."

Fahy also got Larsen to talk a little about someone who was suffering from amnesia. Larsen described it as someone who was exposed to a psychological or physical trauma. Because it was so horrific, the person blocked it out of his mind. In Gabe's case, it would be the actual shooting of his mom and Bob Kennelly. Larsen said he didn't know if that was the case in this situation, but it certainly could be.

Fahy wanted to know how Gabe could have ended up shooting someone that he loved.

There was a long pause on Dr. Larsen's part, and finally he said, "In a delusional state, psychotic state, people lose control. They behave in unexpected ways. Whether he thought he was going to be harmed, we don't know because he told me he didn't know. When he said he didn't do it, I think he believes the story. It's been consistent, not just with me, but with other people as well."

Fahy asked how Gabe could have done such a violent act, but was described as a model inmate in jail.

Larsen replied, "People spoke of him as being irrational, agitated, gaunt and didn't make any sense before the crime. In that circumstance, there was no regimen. There was no control. In jail, you get up at a certain time. You eat at a certain time. You follow the rules and do what you're supposed to do. Even with a schizophrenic person, which he's not, as soon as there are controls, they get better.

I have no doubt that he's still delusional and still believes this stuff. But it's the control and his religious beliefs that are helping him to cope."

Fahy then asked, "Would it help if someone, like a lawyer, who he learns to trust, would help him gain stability?"

Larsen responded, "Absolutely. As long as they don't disagree or make light of the delusional thought."

"And don't bring up about the evidence against him?"

"That would be an example."

CHAPTER 50

Fahy noted that Dr. Sasser had diagnosed Gabe as having an antisocial personality disorder.

To this observation, Larsen said, "Antisocial disorder is a long-term maladaptive, ingrained way of behaving, or experience that deviates away from your peers. You have to be deceitful, have poor impulse controls, be reckless, irresponsible and not feel remorse. You have to have three or more of seven criteria, and Gabriel Morris did not have those. They simply weren't there. And the *DSM* states there had to be conduct disorder before the age of fifteen. And those can't be just pranks or illegal activity. It's a habitual, ongoing behavior. They have to be consistent and last for three or more months. I didn't see that in the reports from Mr. Morris or the investigative reports. Antisocial personality disorders develop over time. There are signs of it when you are a kid. Gabriel Morris does not fit the criteria for antisocial personality disorder, in my opinion."

Fahy wanted to know if it was a close call in making his diagnosis, and Dr. Larsen said, "No, this was one of those rare circumstances where there is lots and lots of corroborating reports from people literally describing a delusion."

"Was there anything you saw that indicated a planned, premeditated killing?"

"Premeditated, no. The only plan was to go and confront Mr. Kennelly and try to get his mother away from him."

"There is some testimony that he just didn't go out and start killing people at random. He was able to control himself to some degree. He seemed to know what he was doing when he went to the Eschler home right after the event. Would you expect to see nonstop, out-of-control behavior? Nonstop delusions?"

Larsen said, "By and large, a person with a delusion can engage in purposeful activities. It is not as if they're ravingly crazy."

On cross, DA Frasier started out by saying, "Just because you and Dr. Mallory have diagnosed Gabriel Morris with a delusional disorder, it does not mean he meets the legal requirements of a mental disease."

Larsen said that was true.

Frasier pointed out that Larsen also made a diagnosis of a personality disorder, which Fahy had not asked him about on direct.

Larsen said he had, and explained that a personality disorder was a long-standing maladaptive behavior that extended for years and years and adversely affected a person's functioning in daily life. Larsen also said that Gabe had bits and pieces of paranoia and narcissism. Narcissism was where a person felt entitled and that the world revolved around him. It was to see one's self as unique, and an individual would go out of his way to draw attention to himself. Larsen also explained that a personality disorder was not enough in the legal code when it came to an acquittal by a condition of mental disease or defect.

Frasier wanted to know, "So you have this Axis I delusional disorder and this Axis II personality disorder. Are they all intermixed? Where are we at here?"

Larsen said, "I think the narcissism lent itself to his difficulty with jobs and relationships." Larsen still posited that the delusional disorder was paramount when it came to Gabe.

Frasier once again brought up the fact that initially Gabe had wanted to testify in front of the jury and put forth the reasons why he wanted to do so. There wasn't any forensic evidence against him; there were no eyewitnesses to the killings; he said there was reasonable doubt.

Frasier continued, "So, isn't it true that in the course of your interviews, you've met defendants that have ignored the advice of their attorneys? They're not necessarily delusional when they tell their attorney they don't want to go along with them?"

"Some have been, but most are not."

* * *

On redirect, Fahy immediately asked Dr. Larsen if Gabe had said anything to implicate his wife in the murders.

Larsen responded, "Not necessarily implicate her, but she was convinced she was being poisoned."

"Did you read in the interviews that at no time was she scared of Mr. Morris?"

"Yes."

"And she went voluntarily with him?"

"Yes."

As far as Gabe being prescribed medication in jail, Larsen said that a person with a delusional disorder did not respond well to medication, like a schizophrenic might or someone who was bipolar. Larsen agreed that a member of the defense team could talk to Gabe in jail and calm him down, but the delusion was still there. The delusion might not be as pronounced as before, but Larsen did not believe it had disappeared.

Fahy asked if it would be rational for someone who had been a police officer to go into court and believe he could sway them with these arguments about the case at hand with the outrageous stories he had come up with.

Larsen replied, "No, it is part of the delusional system. To think you could really go into a court and convince a judge or jury to believe the delusion is in itself delusional."

Larsen was asked if he always went into court with reports to back up the defense in a case.

Larsen said no, and he noted that he looked at over one hundred cases a year and testified in about three or four per year. He added, "The vast majority of the cases I look at, even if there is some mental illness, it doesn't impact the actual event. So I never testify in those cases." Larsen stated that in this case it was clear to him that Gabriel Morris suffered from a delusional disorder and could not conform his conduct to the requirements of the law.

CHAPTER 51

As the others had done, Dr. Sasser told of his education and credentials. He testified about the competency findings and then about his style of interviewing Gabe.

When he got into that aspect of the case, Judge Stone interrupted the questioning and asked Dr. Sasser directly, "The other two witnesses critiqued your style of interviewing. Would you like to respond to that?"

Sasser said, "I don't know what their style is. If they have a passive style to sit back, kind of like a psychoanalytic thing, they're never going to get any accurate information. You have to ask questions. From a question, it should lead to other questions. In Mr. Morris's case, he would frequently give a vague, suggestive answer and then let it drop. It would be easy if you had a passive style to accept that. I tend to not do that. I want to know the next step. It is being more active in the interview process. For example, Mr. Morris told me that he left his mother's house and did lots of stuff. So I asked him what 'stuff' meant. Morris said it meant that his mother was in a bad state. Those kinds of responses were frequent on his part. It required an almost confrontive style.

"I was not able to elicit a pervasive delusional system. A person with a delusional disorder—they have a false belief and it is fixed. It doesn't go from being grandiose to persecuted. It's one fixed idea that a person can't get off of. It could be a belief that someone is breaking into their house. It's not a common condition and it's difficult to treat. It doesn't wax and wane. It's always there, but the person may not share about it if they are not specifically asked about it. But then they will, because they absolutely believe it's true.

"They don't look for a belief based upon evidence. They look for evidence based upon their belief. It may develop over time, but once it's there, it's there. There were comments by others that in the weeks before the shooting, he was acting weird, acting bizarre and not making sense when he talked. Those are not consistent with a delusional disorder. Those can be consistent with a drug-induced psychosis.

"We have a video of him admitting to the officers in Virginia what he did. Not only did he admit to the murders, he corrected the officers. They initially assumed it was a face-to-face thing, and he corrected them and said that he started shooting from the balcony. The stories about some man in black jumping out of a bedroom and shooting his mother and her boyfriend is nonsense. Was this just one more of his lies, to feed to his wife as they traveled down to San Diego? If he was delusional at all then, it was probably more to do with his marijuana use than any fixed delusional disorder. If he had a delusional disorder, he would have shared it with me."

Judge Stone asked Sasser, "You disagree that the defendant suffers from a delusional disorder?"

Sasser said that was so.

The judge then asked Sasser if it was a close call in making his diagnosis.

Sasser replied, "No, not at all. What the people who knew him said of his rambling from thought to thought, disorganized speech, that's inconsistent with a delusional disorder. It is consistent with paranoid psychosis or drug psychosis.

"People with delusional disorders don't have hallucinations. They don't hear things and they don't see things. They don't have disruption in their speech like a chronically mentally ill person does, where they jump from topic to topic without any cohesiveness. They are clear in their thinking, but their logic is backward. In a sense, they look for information to support their false idea.

"People spoke of his bizarre behavior and bizarre thoughts. A delusional disorder is almost within believability. It's things like delusional jealousy, or people moving things around in the person's house.

In light of his clear thinking now, it was more likely drug-induced bizarre behavior."

There was a break, and when it was over, Judge Stone had an admonition to people sitting in the gallery. He said, "Don't show any emotion when a witness is on the stand. I have seen individuals shaking their heads and making facial expressions. If you disagree with something the witness says, just hold it to yourself."

That done, Michael Barker did the cross-examination of Dr. Sasser. Barker asked him if delusions in a delusional disorder were always fixed and never change. Sasser replied that was so. So Barker had Sasser look up the exact wording about delusional disorders in the *DSM-IV: If auditory or visual hallucinations are present, they are not prominent.*

Barker then said, "That doesn't mean there are no hallucinations. It also says that tactile hallucinations may be prominent if they are related to the delusion. That could go into the business of smelling rat poison, could it not?"

Sasser agreed that it could. But when Barker asked if a person smelled rat poison in food, and there was none, if that was not a delusion, Sasser said it wasn't and added, "That's not a delusion. That's a hallucination. It has nothing to do with the fixed belief."

Barker then asked if Dr. Sasser had testified that delusions did not wax or wane. Sasser agreed he did say that. So Barker had him look at page 326 of the *DSM-IV*, where it stated that specialty- and persecutory-type disorders may be chronic, although waxing and waning of the preoccupation with the delusional beliefs often occur.

Sasser said that what he testified to was that the delusional belief never waxes or wanes. What Barker was now referring to was that the *preoccupation* with the delusional beliefs could wax and wane.

"Well, if the preoccupation waxes and wanes, wouldn't that give you the same effect in the person as the delusion waxing and waning?"

"No, the preoccupation is the expression of their false belief. The false belief is still there, but they are not speaking about it."

Barker said that in Dr. Sasser's report, he noted that Gabe denied being mentally ill. Then Barker stated, "Mentally ill people often take that position. You knew that he was trying to sell the idea he did not have a mental disease, did you not?"

Sasser replied in the affirmative, so Barker continued, "Since he claimed to be not mentally ill, did you expect him to come out and start describing delusional-belief systems to you?"

"I did not expect him to describe them. That's why I asked him about them."

Barker then noted that in Sasser's second interview with Gabe, Sasser had asked sixty closed-ended questions.

Sasser may have been being ironic when he answered, "I'm surprised anybody would take the time to count them."

Barker was not particularly appreciative of that answer and said, "Well, you know, if you ask a closed-ended question, you're going to get a closed-ended answer?"

Sasser replied that was not always the case. "Sometimes they lead to further questions."

Barker wanted to know if Sasser asked Gabe any questions about alleging that his father had taken him into the ocean to drown or running through the forest blindfolded and being aided by God.

Dr. Sasser said that he had not.

Barker also wanted to know if Dr. Sasser had reviewed Doug Miller's statement to police where Gabe had said he'd intentionally eaten rat poison so that he could heal himself. Sasser had not done so. When asked if that was a delusional belief, Sasser said that it wasn't necessarily one.

As far as Gabe claiming to be a dragon rider in a pre-mortal existence, Sasser said that was an example of a bizarre belief. And by definition, a delusional-belief system did not incorporate bizarre beliefs. It only incorporated things that could be true, but weren't.

Barker related, "You mentioned in testimony the possibility of a drug-induced psychosis. Is there anywhere in your report where you diagnosed him with a drug-induced psychosis?"

Dr. Sasser replied, "You need to speak up because you mumble."

Irritated, Barker shot back, "My goodness, Doctor, I'm speaking about as loudly as I can!"

Moving on, Barker asked if Dr. Sasser expected

Gabe just to come out and start telling him about his delusional disorder.

Sasser answered, "I expected to elicit answers that would support a delusional belief, if one existed."

"So, since he wasn't saying anything about a delusional disorder, you steered him in that direction?"

"Yes, I did."

"Were you aware that most of the property he and his wife had was left in the red pickup truck in the back of the house? They left the scene barefoot, and his wife and child were in pajamas. Does any of that sound like a plan to you, Doctor?"

Sasser responded, "It sounds like a situation where somebody leaves a place they don't want to be around."

Barker wanted to know if Dr. Sasser considered collateral information, and he said he did. So Barker said that there was testimony in the case where Ray Wetzel actually said the words, "He was delusional, almost hallucinating."

Sasser replied, "I don't know what he means by 'delusional.'"

Barker asked, "If you didn't read any reports about him before he was fifteen years of age, when did you think he started lying?"

Sasser said, "I can't tell you the first time someone reported him lying."

Barker continued that the first reports of Gabe lying came in about the time that Gabe quit the ROTC. And then he asked, "So in other words, you don't know if there was anything of his history of lying up to that time?"

Sasser said that was correct, and Barker got Sasser to agree that for the first eighteen months at Brigham Young University, Gabe had done well. His grades only began to slip after that time. The usually bright and amiable Gabe became withdrawn and sullen.

"Couldn't this relate to the deteriorating mental health of an individual?"

"It might."

"Don't the last few years of his life appear to be a downward spiral?"

"Yes."

"Didn't it become a consistent theme within the last couple of years of his life before the shooting, where he told people he was in black ops?"

"There were several people who reported that, yes."

"And you can't tell if those were lies or delusions?"

"No, I can't tell specifically."

DA Frasier, of course, wanted to ask more questions of Dr. Sasser on redirect. Frasier noted that Sasser had been cut off during one part of cross-examination, and asked what he was going to say.

Sasser explained, "The *DSM-IV* is not a cookbook. To go through it and list certain things is inappropriate. The *DSM-IV* is basically research material. In the clinical realm, we can use it and do use it less rigidly than they do in the research world. That's why the caveats when it is used in forensic settings. It can be misused there."

Talking about Pam Hansen's statements about dragons, Sasser called them a bizarre delusion, and that had nothing to do with a delusional disorder. Sasser continued, "If a person is suffering from bizarre delusions, things that come to mind are schizophrenia, a drug-induced psychosis or a bipolar disorder. And breathing underwater or running through the trees blindfolded weren't relevant to the time frame around the times of the murders. I was trying to get answers about the person's mental state at the time of the crime."

As far as the Eschlers went, Sasser said it wasn't a delusion. "He gave them a story to get what he wanted—a car and a gun. He admitted to me that he lied to the Eschlers to get what he wanted."

Judge Stone jumped in and said, "Clarify one thing. I want to phrase this in a way that makes sense. You said that some of Morris's testimony was that his behavior and ramblings that were taking place two or three months before the shootings—that those, in your opinion, are not consistent with a delusional disorder?"

Sasser replied, "Yes, they are not consistent with a delusional disorder. They are not inconsistent, however, with a drug-induced psychosis or schizophrenia."

"So tell me what you mean by that. I've heard

things that have happened from about Christmas, 2009, through January 2010. Your testimony is that all those things are not consistent with a delusional disorder?"

Sasser replied, "They are not. A delusional disorder is a form of mental illness where delusions may be close to okay, but when you explore it, it doesn't make sense. The person's thinking is clear, and if you talk to them, they make sense. If they try to explain to you why their ideas are true, those pieces don't fit together and make sense. People under the influence of drugs or alcohol, their thinking is disarrayed. They seem weird and they are scary to be around because of that fragmentation of their thinking."

CHAPTER 52

After all the prosecution and defense witnesses were through, Judge Stone had Gabe Morris stand. The judge asked if he wished to testify. Gabe, who had behaved himself all during trial, stood up and quietly said that he did not wish to testify. So the judge asked if that was his decision alone, and that no one had coerced him or made promises to him concerning that decision. Gabe said that was the case.

Judge Stone added, "Do you understand that you will not be able to change your mind, once the defense rests its case?"

"I do," Gabe replied.

Judge Stone had him sit back down and asked Fahy if there were any more witnesses for the defense. Fahy said there were none, but then he had a brief conversation with DA Frasier. After it was done, Fahy told the judge that they had both stipulated that all the comments Gabe made about black ops and his exploits in Las Vegas could not be corroborated by law enforcement. In other words, all of that was in Gabriel Morris's mind and he had not actually done any illegal activity in that regard.

The defense may have been done calling witnesses, but the prosecution was not. They called Laura Eschler to the stand. Laura reiterated that Gabe had dated her daughter Esther and had been very good friends with the family. Then she went over what had occurred on the evening of February 8, 2010, and basically said what her husband had already testified to. She said that Gabe had been in a hurry, but that his words were coherent.

Fahy, on cross, had no questions, but Judge Stone had one question. He wanted to know why Gabe immediately went to an area in the Eschler household and picked out some sweatshirts to wear.

Laura answered, "We always treated him like family, so he knew where they were."

It was now time for closing arguments. Paul Frasier heaved a big sigh before beginning his oration. "Many people spoke of Gabe and reported that he said this or said that. But most of the time, it was Gabriel Morris who was doing the self-reporting."

DA Frasier added that it was known that Gabe had been lying to people for a long, long time. Frasier said that all of this predated the ROTC, when the defense alleged that Gabe started becoming delusional. Frasier said that Gabe was not delusional; he was just a chronic liar.

Frasier declared that Gabe had tried to make himself the center of attention all of his life. Even Esther Eschler had commented upon how selfish he could be. Frasier said that all of Gabe's lies had nothing to do with his alleged delusional system.

As far as Jessica went, Frasier related that she was so naive she went along with whatever Gabe told her. Even when he told her that his relationship with Brenda had been platonic and not sexual, she believed him. And that was in 2008, before Gabe's supposed delusions started kicking in. Frasier stated that most things Gabe said could not be believed.

Then Frasier asked the judge to look at the crime scene photos, which he produced, one by one. Frasier said they told the real story of what happened that night. Frasier argued that the bullets came down from the balcony and went through a potted plant. Gabe had to be hiding behind that potted plant when he started firing. Frasier noted that Gabe was a trained deputy, who knew how to shoot. He wounded Bob and his mom several times; then he walked down the stairs and shot Bob in the chest. He walked over to his mom and shot her in the head.

"He is not a delusional guy who just keeps shooting from wherever. He knows what he had to do to kill them. And he had a ten-round clip. He had to reload to finish them off," the district attorney detailed.

Frasier said there were plenty of criminals who had brilliant plans, but the execution of the plans was a different story. "Was this the best plan in the world? No. But it was planned."

And Frasier said that the Eschlers' testimony had to be taken into account. They saw him less than an hour after the shootings. They both spoke of how in control of himself Gabe had been. He knew what he wanted and got it from them. And everything he got was to enable him to go on the run. By just going on the run, Frasier said, that proved that Gabe knew that what he had done was wrong.

Frasier pointed out what Gabe had told Dr. Sasser. Sasser had asked him about the Eschlers and his story about terrorists. Gabe responded, "It was just a story I could tell them and get a car and get out of there. And it worked."

Frasier concluded that on the night that Gabriel Morris killed Bob Kennelly and his mother, Robin Anstey, he was not delusional. Frasier claimed Gabe was only angry at them and his anger was fueled by excessive drinking of alcohol and marijuana use.

Peter Fahy began his closing argument by saying that he believed Judge Stone would find Gabriel Morris guilty as the shooter. That seemed to be a foregone conclusion from all of the circumstantial evidence against him. But Fahy added that Gabe totally believed that his delusions were real. Doctors Mallory and Larsen had pointed out that those types of delusions and paranoia were often directed at someone close to the delusional person. Fahy said that Gabe got to the point where he believed even his mother was poisoning him and his family. Fahy added that Gabe took his family on the run to try and escape his apocalyptic visions.

Fahy stated that Gabe had taken his family up to Silverton, Oregon, because "the chatter in his head was unbearable, and he went back to a place of stability." There in Silverton he tried to reconnect with his grandmother, his old friend Ray Wetzel and companion from his missionary days in Australia, David Bastian. All of them, however, were alarmed by the paranoid and chaotic stories he told. They worried about his physical and mental health. Wetzel had even called him delusional and wondered if Gabe was hallucinating. Gabe had hoped to bring his mom up there to Silverton, and perhaps open a bed-and-breakfast place or coffee shop. But by now, he was far beyond any rational schemes; nothing of this sort was even close to happening.

Fahy asked why, if Gabe intended to ambush Bob and Robin, he didn't do so right at the door so he could shoot them when they first came into the house. When he started firing from the balcony, he could have easily missed them. If they ran out into the darkness of night, they could have evaded him. Fahy added that descending the staircase and firing multiple times was crazy and definitely not a well-conceived plan. Gabe did not kill them with the first clip of bullets. He had to reload another clip—something he might not have had to do if he had ambushed them right at the door.

Fahy also noted that Gabe didn't even take a $300 cashable check with him, when he was in desperate need of money. Any rational person would have known that a few Walmart cards and a handful of cash were not going to get them very far. In fact, Jessica had to resort to begging for money when they were on the run.

Fahy related that there was no plan in place at all; Jessica and Kalea had to leave quickly in their pajamas, with no shoes on their feet, and Gabe was not wearing any shoes as well. They left all of their belongings in the Popes' red pickup truck and took off in Bob's pickup, which had no supplies in it. Going down the hill, Jessica said, Gabe was in such a panic, worried that the "shooter" might get them, that he nearly rolled the pickup twice and nearly skidded off the road, into the river. Fahy contended there was no shadowy gunman, except in Gabe's delusional mind.

Fahy also stated that some defendants will try to fabricate mental illness to evade having to go to prison, but Gabe never did. In fact, despite so many people saying he was mentally ill, he continued to deny it. Fahy noted that Gabe never supported an insanity defense; he merely tolerated it.

Even during his Virginia interview, Gabe tried

to disguise how mentally ill he was, according to Fahy. Fahy said that Gabe sat there stoically for four hours, and his outward appearance seemed calm. But inside he was in turmoil, and that was shown by what he said. Many of his thoughts were erratic, inconsistent and made little sense. During one time period during the interview, he went on and on, for page after page of transcripts, with no interruption.

As Fahy put it, "The paranoia came tumbling out." In fact, there was one sentence that had no breaks in it for ten lines of transcript. Everything was mixed together in one jumbled, chaotic, stressed mass on Gabe's part.

Fahy related that Gabe not only thought he was a prophet; but near the end, he had told Michael Stockford at the Bandon church, "I am Jesus Christ!" Fahy catalogued one irrational incident after another.

Fahy wanted Judge Stone to watch a DVD once again of Gabe interacting with Dr. Sasser when he was interviewed. Fahy claimed that Sasser often veered away from areas that could have been productive in showing just how delusional Gabe was.

In fact, Fahy said that the police investigators in Virginia had performed a better interview than Dr. Sasser had. Fahy said they had let Gabe talk at length and drew him out as far as his real mental state. Fahy claimed that Sasser had made up his mind early on about Gabe and only asked him questions that buttressed his premature findings. Fahy added that Sasser disregarded statements by people who knew Gabe, such as Pam Hansen, Ray Wetzel and Isabelle Hayden.

According to Fahy, Dr. Sasser had misstated what the *DSM-IV* actually said a delusional disorder was. Even Dr. Sasser's comments about the shooting seemed to help in what Fahy was arguing. Sasser had testified about the shooting, "It had made no sense." Fahy agreed with that and told Judge Stone, "Of course, it made no sense. It was delusional."

As to why the shooting happened at all, Fahy said that Gabe believed he was acting in perceived self-defense. According to Gabe, he only wanted to talk to Bob Kennelly and his mother, Robin, on the night of February 8, 2010. But Gabe had taken the precaution of arming himself with Bob's gun because he knew Bob had several guns. In fact, Gabe also knew that Bob had a concealed-weapons permit.

Fahy claimed that when Bob came into the house, Gabe perceived Bob to be reaching for a gun. Fahy said that Gabe's police training kicked in and he started firing. Gabe did what any police officer would have done. According to Fahy, he kept firing until the threat was removed. When police officers see someone pull a gun, they don't fire to wound; they fire to take out the person. Fahy related that in Gabe's delusional state, he saw Bob and Robin as threats. Only later would Gabe be so traumatized by the event that he would come up with the shadowy figure on the balcony shooting Bob and Robin. By that point, Gabe's mind could no longer accept the fact that he had killed his own mother. He had to invent in his mind someone else who had done such a thing.

As far as Frasier saying that Gabe was a known liar, and did it right up until the end, Fahy countered by stating, "He believes everything that comes out of his mouth, no matter how crazy it sounds. That's the nature of the disease. That's the nature of the delusional disorder."

CHAPTER 53

Just before he passed sentence, Judge Stone gave Frasier one last chance to speak. The district attorney began by repeating a quote from Gabe that he made to the police investigators in Virginia: "I'm not gonna sit here and try to plead my case and say that I'm innocent. No, no, I'm not gonna say that. I'm guilty of what I've done. Guilty as charged of what I've done, and much more."

Frasier stated that the case could be broken down into two main issues. The first issue was whether Gabriel Morris had been the shooter who caused the deaths of Bob Kennelly and Robin Anstey on February 8, 2010. The DA added that all of the evidence pointed to Gabe as being the killer, and he had even admitted to that in Virginia. He also told his wife he had done so, and Judy Ward as well.

The main part of this case then was whether Gabriel Morris was insane at the time of the shootings. And, of course, Frasier contended that he was not legally insane. Frasier added that he agreed that Gabe had issues in making rational decisions. Then the prosecutor said as far as the state went, they did not know what his problems were. The defense of mental illness or defect required that there be proof that was described in the statute. In other words, the defense had to prove that. It was not up to the prosecution to do so.

Frasier noted that there were three mental-health experts who had testified in the case, and not even they could agree on what issues Gabriel Morris had: Dr. Mallory believed that Gabe suffered from a delusional disorder. Dr. Larsen thought he might have a delusional disorder and possibly a personality disorder. Dr. Sasser said that Gabe did not suffer from a delusional disorder, but had behavior that was more consistent with alcohol abuse and marijuana abuse. All three doctors had said that their diagnosis was not a close call for them.

With such a wide range of opinions from the experts, Frasier stated that the court itself should not be able to find a *preponderance* of evidence of what Gabriel Morris had suffered from. And if that could not happen, then the defense had not met its burden of proof in its case, regarding the aspect of mental illness.

Frasier said there had been a lot of evidence from the defense that Gabe thought of himself as a prophet. But according to Frasier, in no way had they linked that to a motive for the killings. He hadn't shot Bob Kennelly and his mother, just because they didn't believe he was a prophet. And there was no evidence that God was telling him to kill people.

Since the doctors disagreed on whether Gabe knew right from wrong at the time of the shootings, Frasier said the evidence gave proof that he did. And the most glaring facts were what occurred directly after the shooting. Gabe riffled through Bob Kennelly's pockets because he wanted money to go on the run. He didn't take the Popes' truck, which could be linked to him, he took Bob Kennelly's truck and abandoned it in Coquille. He drove at a high rate of speed away from the house. If he didn't think he had done anything wrong, then why did he believe he had to flee?

The district attorney said that Gabe had been a police officer and he realized that investigators were going to be looking for a missing pickup truck. So he drove to the Eschlers' home and left Bob Kennelly's pickup truck there in exchange for the Eschlers' car. Gabe was mentally fit enough to ask for things he needed in a getaway. And as they drove away, he hid in the backseat, with Jessica at the wheel of the car.

The prosecutor noted that in San Diego Gabe got rid of the one piece of physical evidence that could tie him to the shootings: Bob Kennelly's handgun. In Virginia, Gabe even told the investigators about that gun: "It's not going to be found." Unfortunately for him, it was found near a place where he had been identified as robbing a convenience store with a handgun.

Frasier said that at one point in his interview in Virginia, Gabe told investigators, "I know I may have to die or go to prison for the rest of my life, but I will do that for Kalea, because she's the most important thing in my life." In other words, he knew what he had done was wrong.

As to the second part of the equation—could he conform his actions to the requirements of the law—Frasier had his answer for that as well. The DA noted that a week before the actual shootings, Gabe had taken his family away from Bob Kennelly's house. If he really believed they were all in danger of being poisoned, then they had gone beyond that danger by leaving. So there must have been some other reason that they went back. And Frasier said it was because of his anger at Bob Kennelly and his mother, Robin. Gabe didn't just burst into the house, shooting. He did surveillance on the house until they left, got Bob's gun and waited in ambush when they came home.

The district attorney used one statement after another from the Virginia interview against Gabe. And to wrap things up, Frasier said that the prosecution's position was that mental illness had nothing to do with why Bob Kennelly and Robin Anstey were murdered. Frasier declared that Gabe Morris killed them because he was angry. The attorney noted that even the judge had spoken of the killings as being an ambush.

"We feel, that given the fact that two people died, this is a situation where the maximum penalty that the court can impose should be set forth. We waived the death penalty in this case, but two people died. We feel the sentence should be life on each count, without the possibility of parole," the prosecutor declared.

CHAPTER 54

Before Judge Stone pronounced his judgment in the case, he had Gabe Morris stand and asked him if he had anything to say. Gabe had a quick consultation with his lawyers, and then he began to speak.

"I think there's a million things I could say, but I'm not sure this is the best environment in which to say them. I'm very proud of the family members and friends who came here. I think what they did was incredibly courageous. Not necessarily what they said about me, but what it said about themselves," Gabe said. Then the defendant declared that he knew that Judge Stone had a hard task before him. Gabe added that there should be "room in the world for healing."

After a short break, court resumed; and Judge Stone told all of the attorneys, "I appreciate the way both sides tried this case. It was very professional.

You both agreed about things before trial that we didn't have to fuss about." He then said he wasn't going to go back through every bit of evidence, one by one. It would take days if he did so, and he added that he'd taken copious notes as the testimony occurred.

That being taken care of, Judge Stone related, "I am absolutely convinced that the defendant, Mr. Morris, was the shooter. The story he told about some terrorist—that story is absurd."

The key now was whether Judge Stone agreed with the defense about Gabe being too mentally ill at the time of the shootings to understand what he was doing was wrong. Stone said that he'd read the Oregon statute on that factor, over and over and over again. He read it out loud now to make sure everyone knew what he was talking about: "'At the time of the criminal conduct, that the individual suffered mental disease or defect and that he lacked the substantial capacity to appreciate the criminality of his conduct, or to conform his conduct to the requirements of the law.'" Judge Stone added that the burden of proof on that rested with the defense.

The judge continued that the key language that jumped out at him was the requirements of the law for Gabriel Morris had to be in effect at the time of the shootings and not days or weeks beforehand. Stone noted that he'd listened to the testimony of one psychologist and two psychiatrists concerning whether Gabe had a delusional disorder. All three of these men were experts in their field; yet, they all disagreed to some extent with each other.

Stone noted that the defense attorneys had been very critical of Dr. Sasser's methods and opinions. However, Stone said that in his opinion, Sasser just had a different style than the others. One thing they all agreed upon was that the *DSM-IV* had to be used cautiously in a forensic setting. It wasn't a cookbook, where you could just take one ingredient and another ingredient and create a recipe.

Then the judge added something that did not bode well for the defense: "It is most significant to me, while a person may be diagnosed with having a delusional disorder, that does not mean he meets the legal definition of insanity. Even assuming in this case, that the defendant has some form of mental disease or defect, I am not satisfied from the evidence in this particular record that on the date in question the defendant lacked the capacity to understand or appreciate the criminality of his act."

He continued that it was clear to him that Gabriel Morris did many things to try and cover up the fact that he'd just killed two people. Statements that had come from Gabe and Jessica made that clear to Stone, and so did the statements of Fred and Laura Eschler. Also, the mere fact that Gabe had gone on the run, clear across the United States, was proof that he knew what he did was legally wrong.

Judge Stone said, "Mr. Morris is no dummy. He

is intelligent. He's articulate. He has training as a police officer. I think, quite frankly, his actions speak volumes. His actions were not those of a person who is delusional. The bottom line is this, did the defendant intentionally cause the death of Robert Kennelly and Robin Anstey in Coos County, Oregon, on February 8, 2010? The answer is yes. Has the insanity defense been proven by the greater weight of evidence? The answer is no."

Judge Stone then pronounced Gabe guilty of aggravated murder on Counts One and Two. There was a very short break between that point and the sentencing phase.

When the judge came back into the courtroom after only five minutes, DA Frasier said he wouldn't be calling any more witnesses in the sentencing phase. Then he added that the district attorney's office had phoned Bob Kennelly's two daughters the previous day and told them that they could speak during the sentencing phase. Neither one had responded.

Peter Fahy said he didn't need any more time as well. He added, "It would be redundant to call any further witnesses."

With that said, Judge Stone stated that he'd noted as far as mitigation or aggravating circumstances went, Gabe had robbed Bob Kennelly as he lay dead on the ground.

"He then made a series of choices, where he fled from the scene and committed at least one additional robbery. All of these facts are significant to me. They support the decision I'm going to make in this particular case," the judge stated.

Judge Stone had Gabriel Morris stand, along with his defense attorneys. Then in a clear voice, Stone pronounced, "As to Count One, the aggravated murder of Robert Kennelly, I sentence Gabriel Christian Morris to life in prison without the possibility of parole. As to Count Two, the aggravated murder of Robin Anstey, I sentence Gabriel Christian Morris to life in prison without the possibility of parole."

Judge Stone then remanded Gabe over to the Oregon prison system. By 2:50 P.M., on August 16, 2011, it was all over.

CHAPTER 55

Jessica Morris was eventually reunited with her parents and her daughter. She shunned the limelight after the case. As far as Jessica was concerned, the events that had occurred leading up to and beyond February 8, 2010, had been nothing but a nightmare.

As for Gabe, he remained as much a mystery as ever to those who had known him. Perhaps journalist Winston Ross of the *Register Guard* summed it up as well as anybody: *People who know Gabe describe him with wildly varying terms: He's a con artist; a genius; a gifted salesman; a video game junkie; a pothead; a religious fanatic; a devoted husband, father and son; affectionate; manipulative; an attention-seeker; a braggart; a man of volatile emotions, as capable of weeping as he is of screaming. To call Gabe complicated is to call Everest a big hill.*

Not even the experts could agree about Gabe Morris. On the evening of February 8, 2010, he was either so delusional that he could not control his actions, or he was just a pothead loser fueled by anger and alcohol. Whatever the circumstances, when Gabriel Morris stood on the balcony that evening, gun in hand—once he pressed down on the trigger, he destroyed his own life and the lives of so many others around him. He had indeed killed the ones he loved in more ways than one.

Don't miss Robert Scott's
next riveting real-life thriller

An e-exclusive coming from Kensington in 2014!

Keep reading for a preview excerpt . . .

CHAPTER 1

ROMEO

El Dorado Hills, California, 2009

The foothills of California's Gold Rush country sweep down from the Sierra Nevada Mountains and intersect with the great Central Valley. Perched on the edge of that meeting of hills and flatlands, El Dorado Hills is a new community compared to the other towns in the area. Placerville, "Old Hangtown," had begun along Placerville Creek when gold miners rushed into the area in 1848. In fact, gold had been discovered by James Marshall at Sutter's Mill in Coloma, only a few miles away. It was the spark that created the epic Gold Rush of 1849, when as one writer put it, *The world rushed in.*

El Dorado Hills was a developer's dream of the mid-twentieth century, with spacious lots, modern homes and small horse properties for those who wanted them and could afford them. There was even a luxurious neighborhood where people could fly their private planes onto a landing strip and park it right next to their homes. The Town Center was a collection of beautiful buildings that mirrored streets in Europe with their stone facing and wrought iron lampposts.

Nineteen-year-old Steven Colver was one of the residents of that area in 2009. Steven generally went by the name "Boston," and he liked to hang out at the Habit coffee shop in El Dorado Hills. Steven was also into the goth lifestyle. He often wore black clothes and was addicted to Japanese anime and manga.

And like many a young man in his late teens, Steven had a younger girlfriend. In Steven's case, however, the girlfriend wasn't just a year or two younger. No, she was five years younger. His girlfriend was fourteen-year-old Tylar Witt, who also lived in the area, and she, too, was into the goth scene. Over time, she began to think of Steven as her Romeo.

No two people seemed to describe Steven in the same way. To some, he was polite, quiet spoken and intelligent. To others, he was headstrong, opinionated and bombastic. But despite his love of anime with many bloody scenes depicted withn the pages, no one thought of Steven as being violent.

During the last days of spring 2009, a seven-page story that mirrored his life and that of Tylar in El Dorado County was written. It was written in one of Steven's notebooks and later either Tylar or Steven was cited as its author. Whatever the truth, the story was fiction that interweaved fact and allegory. It paralleled the actual life Steven and his girlfriend were living that year. The story was titled, "The Killer and His Raven."

The story was set in medieval times. Its protagonist was a nineteen-year-old man who met a smart, beautiful fourteen-year-old girl at a local tavern. It began with the two meeting and becoming good friends, "almost like siblings." As the young man learned more about the girl's life, he discovered that she lived with a drunken, abusive mother. He promised to protect her from her mother's wrath. As the young man and the girl spent more and more time in each other's company, they realized that they loved each other.

The young man lived in his father's home, but the girl was able to convince her mother into letting the young man move in with them. There, within the walls of the girl's house, they sealed their love by a forbidden, sexual relationship. They were deeply in love with each other; but one day, the girl's mother caught them being intimate. She immediately kicked the young man out of the house and demanded that her daughter never see him again.

The girl, however, could not keep away from

her lover, and her resentment deepened against her mother. The mother promised not to go to the authorities if the girl kept away from the young man. Secretly, the lovers met, *and their hope returned for three weeks.* But then the mother, suspicious about her daughter, vowed to go to the authorities with the girl's diary, which she had discovered. This diary detailed the lovemaking with the young man.

The story continued: *That is when their dreams shattered, that is when their hope vanished, and that is when this man, this 19-year-old man became a killer. Late one night, the mother was drunk as usual. Before she finished her last drink, the girl spiked the mother's whiskey with herbs from the forest. Herbs that would make her sleep. At around one in the morning, the girl snuck the boy into her house, leading this man, the 19-year-old man, to her mother's room. He stabbed her in her sleep, killing her, freeing themselves.*

The story continued that the lovers ran away. Knowing that they would be hunted down, they killed themselves in a suicide pact at the town's inn.

The story was fanciful, and took great liberties in some areas. Tylar Witt's mom was no alcoholic who abused her daughter. In fact, she loved Tylar and did everything for her. But in other areas, the story was hauntingly factual. Steven and Tylar's own path had been very much like what was depicted in the story.

When it was written, Tylar's mom lay dead in her

house, and no one knew about it except Steven Colver and Tylar Witt. And just like in the story, they were on the run. For the moment, only they knew how much of "The Killer and His Raven" was fact, and how much was fiction.

CHAPTER 2

JULIET

Tylar Witt may have felt she was living a happily-ever-after, fairy-tale existence with Steven Colver, her older lover, but it was soon to turn into something nightmarish that could have been written by the Brothers Grimm. Just as "The Killer and His Raven" had described its heroine, Tylar was beautiful and smart. She was also a troubled young woman who acted out against her single-parent mom. She spent hours on her MySpace page and ignored her mom whenever she could. She even cut herself on occasion and ran away a few times. One thing was very disturbing. She later claimed that she drew her own blood, because the sight of it calmed her.

Tylar wasn't some medieval peasant living in a cottage in the forest. In fact, she could have been likened more to a nobleman's daughter, ensconced as she was in an expensive home in a gated community. Tylar wanted for nothing. She had her own computer, cell phone, literally hundreds of CDs and DVDs and all sorts of electronic devices. Her mother worked hard at a local transportation agency to create a good environment for herself and her daughter. Tylar, however, only seemed to resent everything her mother did.

By the middle of June 2009, just as "The Killer and His Raven" predicted, the lovers were on the run from the law. But the modern-day Romeo and Juliet didn't go to the local inn to kill themselves—they had other plans in mind. Instead, they made their way across the Sacramento Valley to San Francisco.

And then a whirlwind of things began to happen, both for them and for law enforcement, which finally had discovered during a welfare check that Tylar's mom, forty-seven-year-old Joanne Witt, had been murdered in her own home. Detective work and sheer luck soon collided at an unexpected location—San Bruno, on the San Mateo peninsula below San Francisco, about one hundred miles away from El Dorado Hills. Also, being modern times, it didn't occur at a tavern. It happened at an AT&T store in a strip mall.

There was a "be on the lookout" (BOLO) bulletin put out by the El Dorado County Sheriff's Office (ECSO) for Steven Colver and Tylar Witt. A San Bruno policeman just happened to be going by the AT&T store when he glanced over and couldn't believe what he saw. It was a young man and a girl who matched the descriptions of the individuals wanted by ECSO. The police officer detained the couple and soon learned the individuals wanted in the BOLO were exactly the two standing in front of him.

Steven was taken to one room in the police department and Tylar to another. She sat down to an interview with Detective Mike Lensing and Detective Jeff Leikauf. These two detectives were determined to get down to the bottom of what had been transpiring over the last five days.

As fourteen-year-old Tylar Witt sat there, she began a bravura performance for someone so young. It interweaved guile, half-truths and just plain nerve, matching anything spoken by the heroine in "The Killer and His Raven."

Detective Lensing began by asking how Tylar pronounced her first name. She told him to just call her "Ty." Lensing then read Tylar her Miranda rights, and she waived them, agreeing that she would talk to both of them.

Lensing said, "Can you tell me what happened?"

Tylar said, "Thursday night?" (That was June 11.)

Lensing replied that was correct, so Tylar continued, "We just decided to go down to San Francisco. We were going to kill ourselves. It didn't work. Then we were going to try and drive somewhere, anywhere. It didn't matter. But the car got towed. So we walked. That's it."

Lensing said, "Let's go back further. What happened on Thursday? Start on that day."

Tylar responded, "I called Boston, maybe around midnight. He came to the house and I packed up some stuff in my bag. We hopped the back fence to my house and went up to the school parking lot, where he had his car."

"Let me get this straight, you called Boston?"

"Yeah. I called him throughout the day. Once in the morning, once in the afternoon and again about three more times."

"How did you contact him?"

"By cell phone."

"Was it a text message?"

"No. I called him."

Lensing asked, "Where was your mother that day?"

"She was at work. She dropped me at summer school."

"What time did she pick you up?"

"Twelve-thirty P.M. That's when summer school gets out. She took me home and returned to work. She got home again, around six-thirty P.M. She had to stay late at work. Then she and I went to Safeway and a gas station by the Purple Place. I was a little upset because we'd had a fight. We had gotten into a fight when she dropped me off the first time."

Lensing asked, "What was that fight about?"

"She wanted me to talk to a detective about something Boston supposedly had done. And I didn't want to talk to the detective, because it wasn't true, and I didn't want her pressing it. And she kept pressing it. We got into a fight. And then we went to our separate corners. We cool off and come back and talk about it later. She went back to work after that fight. I just kind of sat home."

"Did you pick up that conversation in the evening?"

"No."

Lensing asked, "Was all this in reference to a diary?"

"Yeah."

"And you refused to speak to Detective Barber?"

"Yes."

"Okay. So your mom goes back to work and she comes home at six-thirty P.M. What was the rest of your evening like?"

"I was watching a movie and playing on the computer. She had a couple of beers and she was really tired. She went upstairs and went to bed. Probably at seven-thirty. I went into her room and checked. And then I went to my room. When I checked later, she was asleep. She was rolled over on her side."

"Was she under the covers or over the covers?"

"It was dark. I really don't remember. I think she had one leg out from the covers."

"What time did you call Boston?"

"I called him at around ten. Then I called him about four times, making sure that my mom was deep enough asleep so I could get out of the house without the dog going berserk."

"What time did he arrive at the house?"

"Around midnight."

"Did he come to the front door?"

"No. He went to the back gate. He opened up the gate and he went into the backyard. He waited outside while I got my clothing. My dog knew him because he used to live in the house. He waited outside and then we hopped the fence."

Lensing wanted to know why Boston parked in the parking lot of the school behind the house, instead of parking at the front of the house.

Tylar said, "Because of the gate code. My mom can check that. It tells who's been at the gate and at what time."

"And what did you do from there?"

"We went back to his house. He took a shower and then I took a shower. We got in his car and went to sleep. We slept at the library parking lot for a couple of hours. The El Dorado Hills Library. Then we went over to Town Center. We parked in front of the Holiday Inn and stayed there and maybe dozed for thirty minutes. We decided we needed some hair dye and some food. So we got that at Safeway in El Dorado Hills. We dyed our hair at his dad's home."

"Why did you need the hair dye and food? Were you going to run away?"

"Yeah. We just bought orange juice. We also went up to the Dollar Tree and bought some Top Ramen, Cup Noodles and sunglasses."

Lensing wondered what they were going to do when they got to San Francisco.

Tylar explained, "Rent a room in a hotel and wait until Monday. We rented a room at the Holiday Inn. We just wanted to make the most of our last few days. Wait until Monday." (Author's note: Tylar

was implying that they would kill themselves then.)
"We purchased some rat poison. We consumed it,
but it didn't kill us."

"Did it make you feel sick at your stomach?"

"Not really."

"Did you reach out to anybody to tell them what
you were going to do?"

"I called my best friend, and Boston called his
best friend."

Lensing wanted to know who Tylar's best friend
was. She said, "Matthew Widman." For Boston, it
was Matthew Bogert.

Lensing asked if she had contacted any friends
on Thursday, June 11.

Tylar replied, "Um, on Friday. We met up with a lot
of our friends then. Matthew, my friend Richard—
we all went down to the Town Center and hung
out for a couple of hours. Then we went back to
Boston's house. We just hung out there, and I didn't
tell Matt this was the last time we were going to
see him, but we kind of forced him to stay with us
as a trio. Me, Matt and Boston. We're family. And
we kind of told him, 'You're not going anywhere.
You're staying here with us.' He lives kind of out in
the boonies. And we stopped near a crossroads and
hung out there for an hour and a half. Then we gave
him a hug and said good-bye. We started driving to
San Francisco."

"Did Boston give anyone his last will and testa-
ment?"

"We sent letters out. Just to our friends. And
one to my cousin. It was mostly just because Matt

(Widman) was my best friend, and I wanted him to be okay, and that I loved him like a brother. And my cousin has always been there for me. And I wanted him to know."

At that point, Detective Lensing was through beating around the bush on minor details. He said, "Okay, let's get down to the point here. Why are you here?"

Tylar responded, "Because I tried to run away."

Surprised by her answer, Lensing said, "Because you tried to run away?"

Tylar replied, "That's what I'm gonna guess."

Lensing countered, "Well, we know that's not the reason that you're here."

"What other reason is there?"

Lensing laid it on the line. "You're being arrested for murder."

Tylar exclaimed, "What! Who did I murder?"

"Okay, well, let's go back to Thursday."

Tylar insisted, "Who did I murder?"

"Your mother."

With a great deal of emotion, and what passed for surprise, Tylar said, "What? My mom's dead?"

Disgusted with her answers, Lensing said, "We don't really need to play this. We already know that your mom's dead. My partner and I have been doing this for a long time. We've done our homework. We've talked to literally everybody you know. We know lots of things. This here is questioning to give you a chance to tell your side of what's going on. As soon as we're done here, we're going to talk to Boston and get his version. Now you can help yourself. I get the feeling you're just realizing that this may be in your best interest to tell us the entire truth, and not just part of the truth."

By now, Tylar was shaking and crying.

Lensing said, "Tylar, can you pull yourself together for just a minute and talk to me about your mother?"

To this, Tylar declared, "Go away! It's not true!"

"What's not true?"

"She's not dead. She can't be dead!"

"She is dead."

Like a petulant child, Tylar exclaimed, "No, she's not!"

"Tylar, talk to me about your mother. Tell me about Thursday."

To this, Tylar replied, "I want an attorney. I want you gone! How dare you!"

Lensing replied, "You want an attorney and you want me gone? Okay. That we can do. Unfortunately, we can't talk to you again. Good luck."

By now, Tylar was sobbing and cried out, "Mommy! She just can't be dead. It's not true! She's not dead. Mommy, Mommy, Mommy! You're not dead. No, no. You're not dead! You can't be dead!"

The two detectives looked at Tylar and her hysterics and didn't believe a word of it. They were certain that Tylar knew that her mother was dead and exactly how she had died. They believed Tylar had been right there when her mother was murdered in her own bed with more than twenty knife wounds in her body. And the detectives were determined to find every shred of evidence linking Tylar and her boyfriend, Steven Colver, to this murder. They wanted to start at the beginning of the story; and in many ways, the story began on the day of Tylar's birth.